BEAN COUNTERS

'A timely exposé . . . A comprehensive yet wildly readable indictment of the "Big Four" accountancy firms.'
Sunday Times

'With forensic detail, Richard Brooks has exposed the march of the accountants from humble bean counters to a small cartel dominating modern capitalism.'
John McDonnell MP, Shadow Chancellor of the Exchequer

'Gripping. This is a must-read for anyone who seeks to expose corruption and bad behaviour.'
Margaret Hodge MP, former chair of the Public Accounts Committee

'Impeccably researched and written, this is a groundbreaking exposé of a profession that has lost the plot. Everyone in business and finance should read this.'
Ian Fraser, bestselling author of *Shredded: Inside RBS, the Bank That Broke Britain*

ABOUT THE AUTHOR

Richard Brooks is an investigative journalist for *Private Eye* magazine. He writes on a range of subjects, including financial crime, public services and taxation. His work has appeared in many other outlets, including the *Guardian* and on the BBC. He was awarded the Paul Foot Award for Investigative Journalism in 2008 and 2015 and his work was highly commended in the 2016 British Journalism awards. He lives with his family in Reading.

BEAN COUNTERS

THE TRIUMPH OF THE ACCOUNTANTS AND HOW THEY BROKE CAPITALISM

RICHARD BROOKS

Atlantic Books
London

First published in hardback and trade paperback in Great Britain in 2018
by Atlantic Books, an imprint of Atlantic Books Ltd.

This edition published in 2019

10 9 8 7 6 5 4 3 2 1

A CIP catalogue record for this book is available from the British Library.

Paperback ISBN: 978 1 78649 031 5
E-book ISBN: 978 1 78649 030 8

Printed in Denmark by Nørhaven

Atlantic Books
An imprint of Atlantic Books Ltd
Ormond House
26–27 Boswell Street
London
WC1N 3JZ

www.atlantic-books.co.uk

For Alex, Joe and Brigitte

CONTENTS

List of Figures   viii

Prologue   ix

Introduction: Meet the Bean Counters   1

Part I   **From the Tigris to Wall Street:**
A Noble Profession's Ignoble History   **19**

   1   Merchants and Mayhem   21

   2   Full Steam Ahead   42

   3   Accountancy Goes Wrong   59

   4   Trust Me, I'm a Consultant   70

   5   Free for All   84

   6   Crash!   111

Part II   **False Prophets: The Price We Pay**
for the Failure of the Bean Counters   **151**

   7   Duty Free   153

   8   Great Britain, LLP   183

   9   Crime and Very Little Punishment   211

  10   Far from Home   233

  11   Unreformed and Unrepentant   253

Conclusion: What Can Be Done?   279

Epilogue   287

Appendix: The Big Four Family Trees   295

Acknowledgements   299

Bibliography   301

Notes and References   305

Index   333

LIST OF FIGURES

1	KPMG's new club in Mayfair	x
2	The growth of the Big Four's income	9
3	The changing balance between audit and non-audit income	11
4	Medici accountant Francesco Sassetti	30
5	The 'Father of Accounting' Luca Pacioli	34
6	The twentieth-century rise of consultancy	81
7	Lead auditor on Enron, David Duncan	106
8	GlaxoSmithKline's Luxembourg tax-avoidance scheme	167
9	LuxLeaks whistleblower Antoine Deltour	175
10	PwC whistleblower Raphaël Halet	176
11	FIFA auditor Fredy Luthiger	223
12	The rise of consultancy after the financial crisis	262
13	Consultancy income v. productivity growth	263

PROLOGUE

In the summer of 2015, seven years after the financial crisis and with no end in sight to the ensuing economic stagnation for millions of citizens, I visited a new club.

Nestled among the hedge-fund managers plying their trade from some of the world's most expensive real estate on Grosvenor Street, Mayfair, No. 20 had recently been opened by accountancy firm KPMG. It was, said the firm's then UK chairman Simon Collins in the fluent corporate-speak favoured by today's top accountants, 'a West End space for people to meet, mingle and touch down'. Directors of client companies, 'who have lots of meetings, can often find it pretty lonely if they don't have a base'.[1] The cost of the fifteen-year lease on the five-storey building was undisclosed, but would have been many tens of millions of pounds. It was evidently a price worth paying to look after the right people.

Inside, No. 20 is patrolled by a small army of attractive, sharply uniformed serving staff. On one floor are dining rooms and cabinets stocked with fine wines that would cost three-figure prices in a restaurant. On another, a cocktail bar leads out onto a roof terrace. Gazing down on the refreshed executives are neo-pop-art portraits of the men whose initials form today's KPMG: Piet Klynveld (an early twentieth-century Amsterdam accountant), William Barclay Peat and James Marwick (Victorian Scottish accountants) and Reinhard Goerdeler (a German concentration-camp survivor who built his country's leading accountancy firm).

Figure 1: The cocktail bar at No. 20, KPMG's new club in Mayfair, with portraits of Piet Klynveld, William Barclay Peat, James Marwick and Reinhard Goerdeler.

KPMG's founders had made their names forging a worldwide profession charged with accounting for business. They'd been the watchdogs of capitalism who had exposed its excesses. Their twenty-first-century successors, by contrast, had been found badly wanting. They had allowed a series of US subprime mortgage companies to fuel the financial crisis from which the world was still reeling, and had offered unqualified endorsement of British bank HBOS's finances as it went to the wall. The opening of No. 20 was a revealing move during what for any other industry would have been a crisis of confidence and reputation.

'What do they say about hubris and nemesis?' pondered the unconvinced insider who had taken me into the club. There was certainly hubris at No. 20. But by shaping the world in which they operate, the accountants have ensured that they are unlikely to face their own nemesis. As the world stumbles from one crisis to the next, its economy precarious and its core financial markets inadequately reformed, it won't be the accountants who pay the price of their failure to hold capitalism to account. It will once again be the millions who lose their jobs and their livelihoods. Such is the triumph of the bean counters.

INTRODUCTION

MEET THE BEAN COUNTERS

I lower refreshed eyes to the two white pages on which my careful numbers transcribe the company balance sheet. And, smiling to myself, I remember that life, which contains these pages, some blank, others ruled or written on, with their names of textiles and sums of money, also includes the great navigators, the great saints, poets of every era, none of whom appear on any balance sheet, being the vast offspring cast out by those who decide what is and isn't valuable in this world.[1]

So reflected Bernardo Soares, the 1920s Lisbon bookkeeper who narrates Fernando Pessoa's *Book of Disquiet*, lamenting his modest craft's inability to capture the splendour of life.

It is true that accounting dwells on the business of life – transactions, assets, liabilities and profits – rather than the joy of it. But in doing so, the practice that has become a byword for tedious employment plays a central role in creating the environment in which commerce and culture can thrive.

Accounting even gave the world the written word. While the early societies of Mesopotamia could pass on their stories well enough through word of mouth, they could not rely on it for recording the activities that characterized the dawn of civilization: the sharing and trading of produce rather than its immediate consumption. 'Bean counters', who really did count beans, needed to write things down. It was the pictographic scripts representing quantities of grain, sheep and cattle stored, written on wet clay using a cut reed, that would be adapted to produce shapes representing sounds, and from there written words.

For centuries, accounting itself remained a fairly rudimentary process of enabling the powerful and the landed to keep tabs on those managing their estates. The word derives from the French *aconter*, to account for money or other assets with which one has been entrusted. But as the first part of this book explores, that narrow task has been transformed by commerce. In the process it has spawned a multi-billion-dollar industry and lifestyles for its leading practitioners that could hardly be more at odds with the image of a humble number-cruncher. The £4m-a-year, fifty-something recent UK boss of the second largest global accountancy firm, PricewaterhouseCoopers, drives the same Aston Martin model as James Bond (though, in his case, with a licence to bill). Next time you peer into a flashy car wondering if it's being driven by a film star, you're more likely to find yourself gawping at a bean counter.

Such riches come from the uniquely privileged position enjoyed by the upper end of today's accountancy establishment. Just four major global firms – Deloitte, PricewaterhouseCoopers (PwC), Ernst & Young (EY) and KPMG – audit 97% of US public companies, all the UK's top 100 corporations, and 80% of Japanese listed companies. They are the only players large enough to check the numbers for these multinational organizations, and thus enjoy effective cartel status. Not that anything as improper as price-fixing would go on. With so few major players, there's no need. 'Everyone knows what everyone else's rates are,' one of their recent former accountants told me with a smile. There are no serious rivals to undercut them: the five next-largest accountancy firms together turn over less than the smallest of the Big Four, KPMG.[2] What's more, since audits are a legal requirement almost everywhere, this is a state-guaranteed cartel. Its members then multiply their income from it threefold through consultancy practices built on the back of the captive audit market.

The largest accountancy firms effectively own a discipline that took shape alongside business in the city states of northern Italy around the time of the Renaissance. The growth of merchant trade, the arrival of Arabic mathematics and the influence of the Catholic Church (which had a few things to say on the vexed question of making money) came together to transform accounting. A system of 'double-entry bookkeeping' enabled traders to measure their performance and gauge their financial position at any given time. By recording assets and liabilities such as stocks and debts rather than simply tracking movements of goods and cash, it allowed a truer picture of an enterprise's profit to be measured. This greater insight in turn encouraged investment and partnerships with others, perhaps in foreign lands.

As the centre of world economic gravity moved north and west in the sixteenth and seventeenth centuries, the new method of accounting facilitated international trade, and then industrialization, on an ever greater scale. Some early-twentieth-century thinkers went so far as to ascribe the rise of capitalism itself to double-entry bookkeeping. When he coined the term 'Protestant work ethic' in 1904, the German philosopher Max Weber also wrote: 'The most generous presupposition for the existence of this present-day capitalism is that of rational capital accounting as the norm for all large industrial undertakings which are concerned with the provision of everyday wants.'[3] The 'capital accounting' to which he referred was in fact the double-entry bookkeeping system, which introduced the concept of 'capital' as the measure of an owner's interest in an enterprise (centuries before Karl Marx expounded his theory in *Das Kapital* in 1867). Weber's near-contemporary, Austrian-American economist Joseph Schumpeter, saw the accounting method as 'the towering monument' of what he called the 'cost–profit calculus', which itself 'powerfully propels the logic of enterprise'. Another German economist, Werner Sombart, was more categorical still.

'It is impossible to imagine capitalism without double-entry bookkeeping,' he claimed. 'They are like form and content.'[4]

None of which makes accounting an unalloyed force for good, of course. By giving an impression of probity, a nicely balanced set of figures has often been a fraudster's friend. Accounting and the information it presents, invariably controlled by proprietors rather than workers, can also be used as a tool of exploitation. Worse still, conveniently omitting the human costs of transactions and transforming them into neat ledger entries, it has been deployed for evil. History's most proficient accountants include slave traders and the administrators of the Holocaust.

The same genius of double-entry bookkeeping that so enhanced the understanding of a business's results could also be used to distort them. As one eighteenth-century English critic presciently observed, the method was 'capable of being converted into a cloak for the vilest statements that designing ingenuity can fabricate'.[5] At perhaps its lowest point, around the turn of the twenty-first century, the elite of the modern accountancy profession itself – certainly in the United States – would be less interested in ensuring business was properly accounted for than in drawing a veil over its abuses. With Arthur Andersen & Co.'s accountants waving the magic double-entry bookkeeping wand to conjure false profits and spirit away losses, Enron became the ultimate accounting trick.

THE GILDED PROFESSION

Despite the economic risks posed by misleading accounting – which would explode as the financial crisis just a few years later – the bean counters now perform their duties with relative impunity. Even before Enron, the big firms had persuaded governments that litigation against them was an existential threat. They should therefore be allowed to operate with limited liability, suable only to the extent of the modest funds their partners invested in their firms rather than all their personal wealth. Trading companies had enjoyed this concession since the nineteenth century, but it had not been accorded to professionals who had no need to attract shareholders and who didn't – indeed, shouldn't – take the same commercial risks. The unparalleled advantages of a guaranteed market with huge upside and strictly limited downside are the pillars on which the Big Four's multi-billion-dollar businesses are built. As the second part of this book examines, they use their uniquely privileged position to profit from almost every area of business and official life. And they do so without fearing serious consequences of their abuses, whether it is the exploitation of tax laws, slanted consultancy advice or overlooking financial crime.

Conscious of their extreme good fortune and desperate to protect it, the accountants then protest the harshness of their business conditions. 'The environment that we are dealing with today is challenging – whether it's the global economy, the geopolitical issues, or the stiff competition,' claimed PwC's global chairman Dennis Nally in 2015 as he revealed what was then the highest ever income for an accounting firm: $35bn. The following year the number edged up – as it did for the other three Big Four firms despite the stiff competition – to $36bn. Although they are too shy to say how much profit their worldwide income translates into, figures from countries where they are required to disclose it suggest PwC's would have been approaching $10bn – enough to put it comfortably in the top ten of the FTSE100 Index or the top twenty of the Dow Jones Industrial Average if it were a publicly traded company.[6] Among the challenges during the year, said Nally, was the 'compulsory rotation' of auditors in Europe, a new game of accountancy musical chairs in which the Big Four exchange clients every ten years or so. This is what passes for competition at the top of world accountancy. It's so 'stiff' that more than a century after they were created, and changed only by some mergers and the fall of Andersen's, the same firms still control 99% of the market. Some companies have been audited by the same firms for just as long: KPMG counts General Electric as a

106-year-old client; PwC stepped down from the Barclays audit in 2016 after a 120-year stint.

As professionals, accountants are generally trusted to self-regulate – with predictably self-indulgent outcomes. Where a degree of independent oversight does exist, such as from the regulator established in the US following Enron and the other major scandal of the time, WorldCom, powers are circumscribed. A rapidly revolving door between regulated and regulators also ensures that intervention is limited. When it comes to setting the critical rules of accounting itself – how the double-entry system works in practice and how industry and finance are audited – the Big Four are equally dominant. Their alumni control the international and national standard-setters, ensuring that the rules of the game suit the major accountancy firms and their clients.

The long reach of the bean counters extends into the heart of governments. In Britain, the Big Four's consultants counsel ministers and officials on everything from healthcare to nuclear power. Although their advice is always labelled 'independent', it invariably suits a raft of corporate clients with direct interests in it. And, unsurprisingly, most of the consultants' prescriptions – such as marketization of public services – entail yet more demand for their services in the years ahead. Mix in the routine recruitment of senior public officials through a revolving door out of government, and the Big Four have become a solvent dissolving the boundary between public and private interests. In some areas they are so influential that they have begun to undermine a model of government in which politicians act on objective advice. The accountants-turned-consultants will give a different – and more politically helpful – view of the world to the one offered by officials bearing sometimes uncomfortable truths.

There are other reasons for governments to cosset the Big Four. In the service-based economies of the UK and US that they call home, the firms have become a significant source of export earnings to counter large trade deficits. Perhaps more importantly, the disappearance of one of the four major firms – for example through the loss of its licence following a criminal conviction, as happened to Arthur Andersen & Co – presents an unacceptable threat to auditing. So, in what one former Big Four partner has admitted is a 'Faustian relationship'[7] between government and the profession, the firms escape official scrutiny even at low points such as the aftermath of the financial crisis. They are too few to fail.

The major accountancy firms also avoid the level of public scrutiny that their importance warrants. Major scandals in which they are implicated invariably come with more colourful villains for the media to spotlight. So when, for example, the Paradise Papers hit the headlines in November 2017, the big news was that racing driver Lewis Hamilton had avoided VAT on buying a private jet. The more important fact that one of the world's largest accountancy firms and a supposed watchdog of capitalism, EY, had designed the scheme for him and others, including several oligarchs, went largely unreported. Moreover, covering every area of business and public service, the Big Four firms have become the reporter's friends. They can be relied on to explain complex regulatory and economic developments as 'independent' experts and provide easy copy on difficult subjects. Back in the 1970s, one commentator reflected of the profession that 'like a skunk, it acquires immunity against attack from its repellency'.[8] This was too harsh. The accountant, even as he gets richer, remains the slightly dull-looking chap who people avoid at a social gathering until they want to know how to avoid the roadworks on the way home.

The bean counters' escape from responsibility away from home is facilitated by their legal structures. Unlike multinational corporations, which tend to be controlled by a single holding company, the Big Four operate as federations of separate partnerships in each country. While all exploit the names, branding and commercial networks of the Big Four, the arrangement allows the firms' main operations and global headquarters (HQs) to distance themselves from misdeeds elsewhere. Although the globalization of media has exposed them to slightly greater reputational harm from faraway scandal, such damage can be quickly limited with the off-the-peg PR solution of firing a few local bean counters and promising to restore trust. Most major clients can't take their business outside the Big Four in any case.

Left to prosper with minimal competition or accountability, the bean counters have become extremely comfortable. Partners in the Big Four charge their time at several hundred pounds per hour, but make their real money from selling the services of their staff (also at three-figure rates). The result is sports-star-level incomes for men and women employing no special talent and taking no personal or entrepreneurial risk. In the UK, partners' profit shares progress from around £300,000 to incomes that at the top have reached £5m a year. Figures in the US are undeclared, because the firms are registered in Delaware and don't have to publish accounts, but are thought to be similar. Average profit shares for British partners in every Big Four firm were more than £700,000 in 2015. For the lucky 700-plus at Deloitte, the figure was £822,000.[9] When I asked one of the firm's senior partners what justified these riches, he sheepishly admitted that it was 'a difficult question'. His only explanation was that 'we all put capital in, your capital is at risk and therefore there is an element of the remuneration that reflects that, but . . . I agree that the remuneration is high'.[10] The capital put in by Deloitte UK's partners in fact works out at less than £200,000 each (which itself is lent to new partners by the firm). Even if half their income could be considered due reward for their labour in accounting, consulting and managing their firms, they are still making an average annual return of 200% on their capital. This is more than ten times what shareholders in a very successful company in the real economy would expect, and can otherwise be achieved only in investment bubbles and scams.

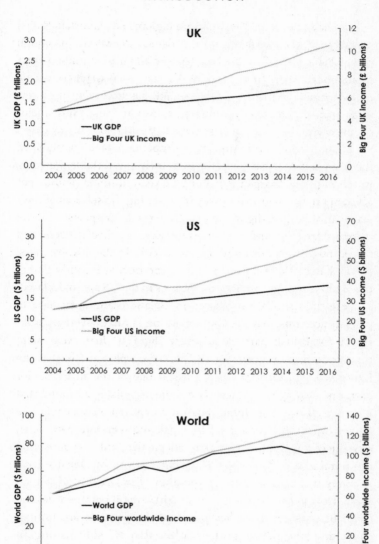

Figure 2: The growth of the Big Four accountancy firms outstrips that of the markets and world economy that they serve

But it's never enough. Targeting growth like any multinational corporation, despite their professional status, the Big Four continue to expand much faster than the world they serve. In their oldest markets, the UK and US, the firms are growing at more than twice the rate of those countries' economies. Between 2004 and 2016, their income rose by 131% in the Americas and by 123% in the UK.[11] Over the same period, by way of a crude comparison, the US economy grew in nominal terms by 51% and the UK by 49% (see Figure 2).[12] Staff numbers rose by 70% and 66% respectively. By 2016, across 150 countries, the Big Four employed 890,000 people (40,000 of them partners), which was more than the six most valuable companies in the world combined.[13]

NEW PRIORITIES

For the past decade, all the firms' real-terms global growth has come from selling more consulting services. This partly reflects a talent for turning any change into a fee-earning opportunity. Dealing with corporate governance changes after Enron and WorldCom, for example, became a consultancy industry in itself. Advising on post-crisis financial regulation has more than made up for the minor setback of 2008. KPMG starred in the ultimate 'nothing succeeds like failure' story. Although – more than any other firm – it had missed the devaluation of subprime mortgages that led to a world banking collapse, before long it was brought in by the European Central Bank for a 'major role in the asset quality review process' of most of the banks that now needed to be 'stress-tested'.[14]

With wealth come the resources and capacity to expand and adapt, too. In the digital age, cyber-security is the latest major growth area for the firms' consultants. Very little is bad news for the Big Four. The result is that, worldwide, they now make just 39% of their income from auditing and related 'assurance' services (the figure in the UK is 21%).[15] They are consultancy

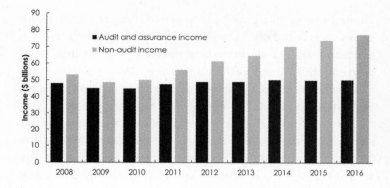

Figure 3: Post financial crisis, the share of the Big Four firms' income from non-audit services has expanded dramatically

firms with auditing sidelines, rather than the other way round (see Figure 3).[16]

The big firms' senior partners, aware of the foundations on which their fortunes are built, nevertheless insist that auditing and getting the numbers right remains their core business. 'I would trade any advisory relationship to save us from doing a bad audit,' said KPMG's UK head Simon Collins in 2015. 'Our life hangs by the thread of whether we do a good-quality audit or not.'[17] The evidence suggests otherwise. With so many inadequate audits sitting on the record alongside near-unremitting growth, it is clear that in a market with very few firms to choose from, poor performance is not a matter of life or death. Arthur Andersen folded because it was convicted for obstructing justice, not because of its connivance in fraudulent accounting.

The Big Four now style themselves as all-encompassing purveyors of 'professional services'. Their consultancy-driven slogans tell of transformation from financial watchdogs to professional jacks-of-all-trades, offering the answers on everything from complying with regulations to IT systems, mergers and acquisitions and corporate strategy. KPMG goes with 'Cutting

Through Complexity', while EY captures virtue and success with 'Building a Better Working World' (having ditched 'Quality in Everything We Do' as part of a rebrand following its implication in the 2008 collapse of Lehman Brothers). PwC leaves no room for doubt about what matters: 'Building Relationships, Creating Value'. Deloitte simply has an enigmatic dot after its name.

There is vanishingly little evidence that the world is any better for the consultancy advice that now provides almost two thirds of the firms' income. Yet all spew out reams of 'thought leadership' to create more work. A snapshot of KPMG's offerings under this banner in 2017 throws up: 'Price is not as important as you think'; 'Man, machine and strategy: don't over-hype technology'; 'Four ways incumbents can partner with disruptors'; and 'Customer centricity'.[18] EY adds insights such as 'Positioning communities of practice for success', while PwC can help big finance with 'Banking's biggest hurdle: its own strategy'.[19] The appeal of all this hot air to executives is often based on no more than fear of missing out and the comfort of believing they're keeping up with business trends. Unsurprisingly, while their companies effectively outsource strategic thinking to the Big Four and other consultancy firms, productivity flatlines in the economies they command.

The commercial imperatives behind the consultancy big sell are explicit in the firms' own targets. KPMG UK's first two 'key performance indicators', for example, are 'revenue growth' and 'improving profit margin', followed by measures of staff and customer satisfaction (which won't be won by giving them a hard time). Exposing false accounting, fraud, tax evasion and risks to economies – everything that society might want from its accountants – does not feature. Audit partners, known as 'client relationship partners', are rewarded for their wider contribution to the firm, not just sound auditing. The same senior Deloitte figure who struggled to justify the bean counters' pay packets told me how audit partners would 'be expected to win new audits [and] to actively develop relationships with management, non-executives in new [corporate] clients that we can either sell audit or advisory work to'.[20] At all the firms, audit partners are outnumbered by the non-audit partners, who are paid more directly by reference to the value of consultancy services they sell. The overall effect, one former Big Four accountant told me, is that 'the challenge has gone out of audit'.

The demise of sound accounting became a critical cause of the early-twenty-first-century financial crisis. Auditing limited companies, made mandatory in Britain around a hundred years before, was always a check on the so-called 'principal/agent problem' inherent in the corporate form of business. As Adam Smith once pointed out, 'managers of other people's money' could not be trusted to be as prudent with it as they were with their own. When late-twentieth-century bankers began gambling with eye-watering amounts of other people's money, good accounting became more important than ever. But the bean counters now had more commercial priorities and – with limited liability of their own – less fear for the consequences of failure. 'Negligence and profusion', as Smith foretold, duly ensued.[21]

After the fall of Lehman Brothers brought economies to their knees in 2008, it was apparent that Ernst & Young's audits of that bank had been all but worthless. Similar failures on the other side of the Atlantic proved that balance sheets everywhere were full of dross signed off as gold. The chairman of HBOS, arguably Britain's most dubious lender of the boom years, explained to a subsequent parliamentary enquiry: 'I met alone with the auditors – the two main partners – at least once a year, and, in our meeting, they could air anything that they found difficult. Although we had interesting discussions – they were very helpful about the business – there were never any issues raised.'[22] This insouciance typified the state auditing had reached. Subsequent investigations showed that rank-and-file auditors at KPMG *had* questioned how much the bank was setting aside for losses. But such unhelpful matters were not something for the senior partners to bother about when their firm was pocketing handsome consulting income – £45m on top of its £56m audit fees in five years – and the junior bean counters' concerns were not followed through by their superiors.[23]

Half a century earlier, economist J. K. Galbraith had ended his landmark history of the 1929 Great Crash by warning of the reluctance of 'men of business' to speak up 'if it means disturbance of orderly business and convenience in the present'. (In this, he thought, 'at least equally with communism, lies the threat to capitalism'.) Galbraith could have been prophesying accountancy a few decades later, now led by men of business rather than watchdogs of business.[24] Another American writer of the same time caught the likely cause of the bean counters' blindness to looming danger even more starkly. 'It is difficult to get a man to understand something', wrote Upton Sinclair, 'when his salary depends upon his not understanding it.'[25] Given that they were lucratively advising on the financial concoctions that would detonate the crisis, it certainly wouldn't have paid the early-twenty-first-century bean counters to understand the destructive power within them.

MEN, AND A FEW WOMEN, OF THE WORLD

The Big Four's bean counters are drawn from a pool of high educational achievers, dozens of graduates applying for each 'fast-stream' job that might eventually lead to partner status. Few arrive with much sense of vocation or a passion for rooting out financial irregularity and making capitalism safe. They are motivated by good income prospects even for moderate performers, plus maybe a vague interest in the world of business. Many want to keep their options open, noticing the prevalence of qualified accountants at the top of the corporate world; one quarter of chief executives of the FTSE100 largest UK companies are chartered accountants.[26]

When it comes to integrity and honesty, there is nothing unusual about this breed. They have a similar range of susceptibility to social, psychological and financial pressures to any other group. It would be tempting to infer from tales like the senior KPMG audit partner caught in a Californian car park in 2013 trading inside information for a Rolex watch and thousands of dollars in cash that accountancy is a dishonest profession.[27] But such blatant corruption is exceptional. The real problem is that the profession's unique privileges and conflicts distil ordinary human foibles into less criminal but equally corrosive practice.

A newly qualified accountant in a major firm will generally slip into a career of what one academic has called 'technocratism', applying standards lawfully but to the advantage of clients, not breaking the rules but not making a stand for truth and objectivity either.[28] Progression to the partner ranks requires 'fitting in' above all else. This partly explains why, although for decades half of their graduate recruits have been women, fewer than 20% of their partners are – leading to fairly homogenous cultures that are not conducive to sound accounting.[29] The highest reaches of the Big Four, meanwhile, are reserved for those with a flair for selling services and keeping clients happy. With serious financial incentives to get there, the major firms end up run by the more materially rather than ethically motivated bean counters. In the UK in 2017, none of the senior partners (equivalent to company chief executives) of the big firms had built their careers in what should be the firms' core business of auditing. Worldwide, two of the Big Four were led by men who were not even qualified accountants.[30]

The core accountancy task of auditing can seem dull next to sexier alternatives, and many a bean counter yearns for excitement that the traditional role doesn't offer. As long ago as 1969, Monty Python captured this frustration in a sketch featuring Michael Palin as an accountant and John Cleese as his careers adviser. 'Our experts describe you as an appallingly dull fellow, unimaginative, timid, lacking in initiative, spineless, easily dominated, no sense of humour, tedious company and irredeemably drab and awful,' Cleese tells Palin. 'And whereas in most professions these would be considerable drawbacks, in chartered accountancy they're a positive boon.' Palin's character, alas, wants to become a lion tamer. In 2016, EY's 'managing partner commercial', Martin Cook, was not being so satirical when he welcomed his firm's sponsorship of London's Tate art gallery because it was 'an extremely cool brand to be associated with'.[31]

The dangers of a bean counter's head being turned have been obvious ever since a fifteenth-century Medici accountant was seduced by the Renaissance art scene and stopped questioning what was appearing on the bank's ledgers. They were in evidence again when a PwC partner fouled up the 2017 Oscar presentation because he was tweeting photos of the best actress rather than concentrating on the envelopes. The bean counter's quest for something more exciting can be seen running through modern scandals like Enron and some of the racy early-twenty-first-century bank accounting. The same ex-Big Four accountant who bemoaned the lack of challenge in auditing told me that if there was a single thing that would improve his profession, it would be to 'make it boring again'.

Instead, the Big Four have adopted the techniques of the most ardent twenty-first-century profit-seekers, schmoozing corporate and government leaders and joining bankers and captains of industry as sponsors of prestigious sports and cultural events. EY's British head Steve Varley claimed of his firm's Tate deal: 'we think we can take advantage of this not just in the UK but around the world as well'.[32] At the same time, like any shrewd modern multinational, the Big Four uniformly trumpet their social value. The highest-earning firm in 2016, Deloitte, boasts of 1.3m employee hours given to good causes, with £75m cash donated. This largesse allows the accountants to tell heart-warming stories about causes ranging from mental health to child literacy (and indeed to make some real contribution). But the publicity value exceeds the real value. Deloitte's donations equate to about half a day per employee and 0.2% of its income, or around 0.5% of profit. That's the money lost to public services from just a handful of tax-avoidance schemes. Any comparison with the economic costs of poor auditing would yield an even harsher comparison.

Where once they were outsiders scrutinizing the commercial world, the Big Four are now insiders burrowing ever deeper into it. All mimic the famous alumni system of the last century's pre-eminent management consultancy, McKinsey, ensuring that when their own consultants and bean counters move on, they stay close to the old firm and bring it more work. The threat of an already too-close relationship with business becoming even more intimate is ignored. EY's 'global brand and external communications leader' recently waxed biblical on the point: 'You think about the right hand of greatness; actually the alumni could be the right hand of our greatness.'[33]

The top bean counter's self-image is no longer a modest one. 'Whether serving as a steward of the proper functioning of global financial markets in the role of auditor, or solving client or societal challenges, we ask our professionals to think big about the impact they make through their work at Deloitte,' say the firm's leaders in their 'Global Impact Report'.[34] The appreciation of the profound importance of their core auditing role does not, alas, translate into a sharp focus on the task. EY worldwide boss, Mark Weinberger, personifies how the top bean counters see their place in the world. He co-chairs a Russian investment committee with prime minister and Putin placeman Dmitry Medvedev; does something similar in Shanghai; sat on Donald Trump's strategy forum until it disbanded in 2017 when the US president went fully toxic by appeasing neo-Nazis; and revels in the status of 'Global Agenda Trustee' for the World Economic Forum. The latter is the annual convention of political and business leaders in Davos that *Financial Times* columnist Edward Luce calls a 'gathering of the world's wealthiest recyclers of conventional wisdom', something that a 'steward of the proper functioning of global financial markets' should be challenging, not recycling.[35] All the other Big Four firms also send platoons of senior partners to the Swiss mountain resort to get 'connected with global stakeholders', as Deloitte puts it. The pinnacle of modern accountancy stands confidently among the peaks of political and financial power.

The price of seats at all the top tables is a calamitous failure to account. In decades to come, without drastic reform, it will only become more expensive. If the supposed watchdogs overlook new threats, the fallout could be as cataclysmic as the last financial crisis threatened to be. As legendary American investor Charlie Munger put it: 'widespread corrupt accounting will eventually create bad long-term consequences as a sort of obverse effect from the virtue-based boost double-entry bookkeeping gave to the heyday of Venice'.[36] Yet such is their ambition and lack of self-awareness that the same bean counters who were found wanting last time round are already looking to take accounting into new and dangerous realms.

Global efforts to combat climate change and the impact of industry and government on the environment, for example, require scrutiny and auditing that could well transform accountancy in a way not seen since the Industrial Revolution. Already accountants and standard-setters are working on 'integrated reporting' methods to cover such matters, with the Big Four pre-eminently powerful. The international chairmen of Deloitte, EY and PwC, plus KPMG's audit boss – who between them serve every one of the world's largest fossil-fuel companies – all sit on the International Integrated Reporting Council.[37] New forms of accounting will fall to the same accountancy establishment that has already proved unable and unwilling to hold powerful financial interests to account. It will become another business line, with the same corrupting incentives and conflicts of interest but with potentially more devastating results.

Bean counting is too important to be left to today's bean counters.

PART I

FROM THE TIGRIS
TO WALL STREET

A Noble Profession's
Ignoble History

1

MERCHANTS AND MAYHEM

THE BIRTH OF MODERN ACCOUNTING AND THE SEEDS OF ITS CORRUPTION

Leonardo Fibonacci is now almost exclusively associated with his eponymous sequence in which each number is the sum of the previous two (1, 1, 2, 3, 5, 8 and so on). But the son of a wealthy twelfth-century merchant from Pisa did more than define a numerical progression; he also helped to transform the world of commerce and thus the course of Western civilization.

Fibonacci was schooled among Arab mathematicians in one of the city-state's trading enclaves on the North African coast and travelled extensively around Egypt, Byzantium and southern Europe. There he studied not just the classical Greek disciplines, such as geometry, that his European contemporaries learned. He also mastered the Arabic number system that had already revolutionized mathematics, science and astronomy.

When the 32-year-old Fibonacci published his great treatise *Liber Abaci* (*The Book of Calculation*) in 1202, the Arabic method that we use today, with its 'place value' system for units, tens, etc., wasn't entirely unknown in Europe. But it was his *Liber* that brought it into the *abbaco* schools of Venice, Florence and Pisa as they churned out successive generations of merchants. It was both textbook and business manual, covering geometry and algebra (an Arabic term for completion or balance), alongside techniques for such matters as allocating money among business partners. A chapter explaining principles that have been boring schoolchildren ever since, 'On the Addition and Subtraction of Numbers with Fractions', was followed directly by one on 'Finding the Value of Merchandise by the Principal Method'.[1] Crucially, wrote one accounting historian, Fibonacci 'demonstrated the superiority of Arabic numbers by presenting accounts in which Roman numerals in the text were contrasted with Arabic figures in columns on the right'.[2] Just as science and maths would become more practicable using the Arabic numbering method rather than the cumbersome Roman one (try subtracting VDI from MMCDXLIX or dividing CDLXXV by XIX),[3] so would accounting. From counting stock and cash to more complex tasks like computing investment returns, the new numbers were eminently superior.

The era of measurement ushered in by Fibonacci transformed medieval northern Italy. It laid the foundations, sometimes literally, for Renaissance art and architecture. But nowhere were the new methods to prove more revolutionary than in commerce, where they made possible an ingenious new way of accounting called double-entry bookkeeping.[4] As economist Werner Sombart would later write of the method's origins: 'Double-entry bookkeeping was born out of the same spirits as the systems of Galileo and Newton, as the theories of modern physics and chemistry'; it 'discloses to us the cosmos of the economic world'.[5]

First used by Florentine merchants at the end of the thirteenth century, the system allows not just for the recording of a transaction; it simultaneously registers its financial consequences and thus automatically keeps a tab on the things that matter: sales and purchases, debtors and creditors, and so on. The state of an enterprise – its profits, its assets, its debts and much else – can be readily judged. The golden rule of double-entry bookkeeping is that every transaction is recorded by debiting one account, or ledger, and crediting another. That's the 'double-entry'. When, for example, a business sells something for cash, its bookkeeper records a sale through a credit to the 'sales account' and an increase in its cash through a debit to the 'cash account'. (Somewhat counter-intuitively, assets of the business are recorded as debit balances and liabilities as credits.) If the sale is made not for cash but for settlement later on, there will be a credit to the sales and a debit to the account of the particular debtor (someone who owes the business money, derived from the Latin for 'to owe', *debere*). When the customer pays the bill, his account is credited – netting it to zero – and the cash account debited. Again, matching credit and debit entries. The sums of debits and credits are thus always identical and, in the absence of errors, the books 'balance'. And while the process is now highly automated, the rules remain essentially unaltered many hundreds of years after they were devised. When the publisher of this book, for example, sells a copy to a bookshop, the publisher's entries will be to credit its sales ledger and debit an account in the name of the bookshop (which would become its debtor). When the bookshop pays the bill, the publisher's entries are to credit the 'bookshop account' – reducing it to zero – and debit the 'cash at bank' account, reflecting the publisher's increased bank balance.

When the accounts are reckoned at any particular point, such as the end of a year, the sales and expenses ledgers would be closed with balancing entries in a profit-and-loss account. So if sales were worth 100 florins in the year, there would be credits in the sales account totalling this amount. It would be closed for the year by a debit of 100 and a corresponding credit in the profit-and-loss account. If in the same year there were purchases costing 60 florins – debits in the purchases account totalling this amount – it would be closed with a credit of 60 and a corresponding debit in the profit-and-loss account of 60. The profit-and-loss account would then have a credit balance of 40 florins. As a final step, this account would be closed with a debit to the profit-and-loss account of 40 and a corresponding credit would be made to the proprietor's 'capital' account. This is effectively what the business owes him and is therefore a liability in the balance sheet. The balance sheet then 'balances' because there would have been an identical increase in the business's net assets. In the example here, if all sales and purchases had been for cash, there would be 40 florins more cash in the business at the end of the year.

Double-entry bookkeeping represented a huge advance on previous accounting methods. Without a handle on matters like an enterprise's assets and liabilities, it was impossible to divide the spoils of a business among partners or shareholders rationally, to gauge the credit-worthiness and viability of a business or to decide how much employees can be paid. All such assessments are fundamental to investment and trading and thus to a functioning market economy. Some consider the Roman period to have been a commercial flop for this reason. In the words of one scholar, 'the Romans' failure to develop double-entry accounting served as a structural flaw which deprived them of the impetus for economic rationalism and profit-seeking behavior'.[6]

There was more of a demand for reliable accounting in late-medieval and early-Renaissance northern Italy. The mercantile ethos of the city-states was at odds with the Church's distaste, bordering on hostility, for the business of making money. New patterns of society and improved agricultural productivity had increased wealth and expanded commercial opportunities. But with these came exploitation, turning the Church's attention to sins associated with money. The Third Lateran Council in Venice in 1179, for example, determined that 'usurers' who lent money at interest should be excommunicated. In this climate, any merchant concerned for his reputation, not to mention his afterlife, was at pains to show the worthiness of his commercial success. Accounting presented the possibility of doing so, superficially at least. Double-entry bookkeeping in particular resonated with the tradition in Christianity and more ancient belief systems of balancing rights and wrongs.

The new accounting method was of special interest to those plying the morally dubious trade of financing the merchants. Their activities really amounted to moneylending for profit but were structured to evade the Church's strictures. Under 'bills of exchange', these merchant bankers would advance money to a trader in his home city. Then, once he had sold his merchandise abroad, he would repay the debt to the banker's agent in the foreign land in local currency. The exchange rates would be set to give the banker a profit. A Florentine merchant might borrow 100 florins, worth say £40, at home and be required to repay £45 in London three months later. What was in substance interest had been transformed into something that wasn't. But still a cloud of suspicion as dark as a priest's cassock hung over the activity, and the least the financiers could do was account properly.

One man with more need than most for accounting's commercial and exculpatory qualities was fourteenth-century merchant Francesco di Marco Datini, a Tuscan who made a fortune from bills of exchange and dealing in everything from cloth to weapons. Rigorous accounting was essential both commercially and, perhaps even more importantly, to assuage Datini's conscience. As his biographer noted, he 'was preoccupied by the thought that his very skill in making profit was sin'.[7] From around 1380, Datini operated a full double-entry bookkeeping system. The main account books, the *libri grande* that consolidated the contemporaneous notes of his transactions into double-entry accounts, explain his diligence. Each carried one of two headings: 'In the Name of the Holy Trinity and of all the Saints and Angels of Paradise', or sometimes simply 'In the Name of God and Profit'.[8]

For the merchants and their bankers seeking wealth and piety, double-entry bookkeeping offered security and a certain salvation. But, one family was to discover, only if it was done properly.

RENAISSANCE MEN

In 1397, Giovanni di Bicci de Medici, a 37-year-old banker, returned from Rome to his home town of Florence and established a bank that would survive for just short of one hundred years.

Maintaining a branch in Rome to take deposits from the Vatican, the Medici Bank offered the full suite of early-Renaissance banking services and quickly became one of the leading *banchi grossi* of Italy. It lent extensively using bills of exchange, took interests in trading ventures and handled the savings of the leaders of the Catholic Church (cleverly evading the ban on usury by turning interest into *discrezione*, or optional payments that – it just so happened – would invariably be paid). It sent tithes, taxes and indulgences across Europe to Rome. And as much to earn public acceptance as anything else, it diversified into trading, notably in the woollen industry operating from the Cotswolds in England. 'To deal in exchange and in merchandise with the help of God and good fortune', ran the mission statement.

The key to the Medici rise was to combine scale and attention to detail, whether at home in Florence or in branches that by the middle of the fifteenth century stretched from London to Venice. In Giovanni's son Cosimo, the architect of the bank's achievements from his succession in 1420 until his death in 1464, the Medici had the right leader. As well as being a control freak who had spies in every corner of Florence, Cosimo understood the value of good accounting.

He needed to. Banking depended on assiduously applied double-entry bookkeeping. Bills of exchange, the bread-and-butter of the business, paid slim margins. A default on one could wipe out the gains on many times the number that were honoured. Keeping close tabs on borrowers, spreading risk and not over-exposing the bank to more suspect customers was therefore critical. Distant branches were partnerships between a Medici Bank holding company and local managers in a federated structure that would work only if the results of the branches were fairly shared. The profits needed to be properly measured.

Double-entry bookkeeping met these specifications ideally. It wasn't merely a means of accounting for the Medici business. It was central to actually doing it. In his book *The Reckoning – Financial Accountability and the Making and Breaking of Nations*, historian Jacob Soll goes so far as to say: 'The Great Masters of the Medici Bank used accounting to create a financial machine that allowed them to dominate their age, both culturally and politically, like no family before them.'[9]

This was the achievement of Cosimo and his trusted general manager and chief accountant from 1435, Giovanni Benci, who had begun his career as an office boy at the Rome branch twenty-five years earlier. He had risen through the Geneva branch to become Cosimo's most trusted adviser, earning the nickname *ministro*, or minister. In the words of leading Medici historian Raymond de Roover: 'It was during the years of Benci's management that the Medici Bank witnessed its greatest expansion and reached the peak of its earning capacity.' Crucially, Benci was 'thoroughly familiar with double-entry bookkeeping'.[10] Under his searching accounting regime, Medici branches were required to close their ledgers and balance their accounts every year. The books would then be sent to Florence for the annual 'audit' (a word originating in the more feudal traditions of landowners 'listening' to managers read out their estate accounts). The ledgers were statements of great detail, with balance sheets identifying the amounts owed by each customer, or debtor, and thus containing hundreds of items that the accountants back in Florence could check. Their chief concerns were, firstly, to identify debts that might go bad – perhaps because the debtors were already behind with payments – and, secondly, to spot indulgent lending to the wrong customers. Defaults had done for a number of fourteenth-century Florentine financial powerhouses,[11] and Cosimo was not going to let the Medici go the same way. The double-entry system allowed his auditors to pick out doubtful debts and track their history through the branch's records. If they weren't happy, they would summon the branch manager to Florence for a grilling from Cosimo and Benci. The result was controlled success in a manner that later bankers would have done well to emulate.

DEATH OF AN ACCOUNTANT

Cosimo had, however, become over-dependent on Giovanni Benci. When the accountant died in 1455, he was not replaced for three years. During this period it emerged that Benci had been the sole signatory on the Medici Bank holding company's partnership agreements with all its local managers. The contracts now lapsed and the holding-company structure was torn up. Instead, individual members of the Medici family – not all of them entirely reliable – would become partners in local branches with their managers. Effective control of the Medici empire from Florence died with the accountant who knew how to exercise it.[12]

Cosimo had already become distracted by the wonders of the Renaissance and the fashionable Neoplatonist, humanist philosophy that prized a good life in the present over a ticket to the afterlife. This may have been enlightening, but it also eased the moral requirement for sound accounting and proved disastrous for the banking business. As did the transition to the next Medici generation. Five years after Cosimo's death in 1464, leadership of the richest bank in the world passed to his 20-year-old grandson Lorenzo. He was the brightest of the new breed but had been educated by clerics and philosophers and was destined to devote his intellectual energy to poetry. Accounting, it would be fair to say, was not his thing.

'Il Magnifico', as Lorenzo would become known, duly left the task of controlling the bank to a useless lieutenant called Francesco Sassetti. He *was* an accountant, who had risen through the ranks in Avignon and Geneva before returning to Florence. Cosimo had made him Benci's successor as general manager in 1458, and now, ten years later as sole director, his ascent was complete. But Sassetti had also become diverted by the wealth and wonders of the Renaissance. His main preoccupation was building a chapel bearing his name, replete with frescoes featuring him alongside the Medici luminaries among whom a once humble bean counter yearned to belong. It stands as a monument to the dangers of a bean counter's head being turned.[13]

It wasn't a good time for a banking group to have an absent boss and no serious accountant. From the mid 1450s, the economic climate had also begun to turn against the Medici business model. A shortage of gold pushed the value of the florin steadily upwards against other currencies. The Medici Bank tended to take deposits, and thus have to repay depositors, in florins, since this was the currency used by the Church hierarchy and wealthier merchants. It was owed money, however, in a mixture of relatively weakening currencies. The combination eroded its margins significantly. At the same time, after being milked of profits to fund Cosimo's and later Lorenzo's extravagance, its branches were highly leveraged. The effect of any losses on the Medici would be magnified, just as in the twenty-first-century banking crisis. But to the extent that it could still be considered one bank, it remained the largest in Europe and as a matter of pride rarely refused deposits. Nor would it reduce the generous *discrezione* interest rates it paid on them. Most of its branches were consequently on the lookout for ever higher returns from lending this money out. This in turn meant loans to the warring kings, princes and dukes of Europe. Unfortunately, their appetite for funds was matched only by the likelihood that they wouldn't repay them. The result was toxic lending, Renaissance-style.

Figure 4: Errant accountant Francesco Sassetti (second right) alongside Lorenzo 'Il Magnifico' Medici (second left)[14]

The London branch's excessive loans to Edward IV to fund his War of the Roses, indulging him in return for wool export licences, duly bankrupted it in 1478. More than 50,000 florins – tens of millions of pounds today – had to be written off. Greater losses followed at the branch in Bruges, a city then ruled by the Duke of Burgundy. His nickname, Charles the Bold, might have given a prudent bank manager pause for thought. Instead, he was lent 6,000 groats, or twice the branch's entire capital, to fund his squabbles with Louis XI of France.[15] Good money was thrown after bad, and by the time the branch was liquidated in 1478, it had lost 100,000 florins.[16] Both disasters could have been averted if financial control had remained as strong as in Cosimo's heyday. Audits of any substance would have registered the parlous state of these and other branches' finances much earlier, and prevented the growth of bad debts over many years. But Sassetti had more or less abdicated his responsibilities, subcontracting scrutiny back to the branch managers. While they marked their own homework, he fretted over how his chapel was coming along.

Gone were the days when branch managers feared the missive from Florence summoning them to account to Giovanni Benci in person for their books. Nowhere were the consequences of this laxity starker than in the Lyons branch. Lending extravagantly to the region's spice and silk traders, plus Charles the Bold's enemy Louis XI, the branch boasted returns of between 70 and 105% for most of the 1460s. This was treble what was considered good elsewhere and would surely have raised a sober auditor's eyebrow. A glance at the books would then have exposed the reason for the spectacular success: the absence of any recognition of bad, or even doubtful, debts among the bank's diverse clientele. Financing at the time worked on charging effective 'interest' rates running into double figures to compensate for significant levels of default. Ignoring the latter therefore grossly inflated returns. This in turn enabled partners to extract handsome if undue rewards, further depleting the branch's capital in a manner that would be repeated more than five hundred years later through the payment of dividends and enormous bankers' bonuses out of similarly illusory profits.

Just as money had bought the Medici power, so financial failure brought political defeat. Lorenzo responded to the demise of the Medici Bank by plundering municipal funds (bank mismanagement then, as now, hitting the public in the pocket). In 1494, an enraged Florentine mob invaded the great Medici Palace and set fire to most of its records. The bank that had been built on books and accounts disappeared in the smoke from burning them. The fall of the Medici proved that the power of sound accounting is balanced by the dangers of poor accounting. It gave an early warning that when the bean counters are distracted, become too close to power and neglect their core responsibilities, disaster follows.

It was therefore timely that, in the same year that bad accounting claimed its most famous victim in Florence, not so far away somebody was preparing to tell the world just how it should be done.

BY THE BOOK

As immortalizing epithets go, 'Father of Accounting' wouldn't be the most sought after by history's great figures. But it's the one destined to be borne forever by Luca Bartolomeo de Pacioli, a mathematician from the market town of Sansepolcro, near Florence, who was educated in the methods pioneered by Fibonacci two hundred and fifty years earlier.

By the time the middle-aged Pacioli arrived in Venice in 1494 with a manuscript containing what is still the blueprint for accounting, he had already scaled the heights of Renaissance mathematics as a professor at Perugia University. He'd also taken vows as a Franciscan friar. More importantly for the future of accounting, while tutoring a wealthy Venetian fur merchant's children, Pacioli had doubled up as an agent for his boss's maritime business and studied at the Scuola di Rialto in the city's commercial district. There, in the hub of European commerce, he had taken the opportunity to learn what had become known as the 'Venetian' style of accounting: double-entry bookkeeping.

At the age of 49, Pacioli was ready to publish the magnum opus he had been working on for twenty years. *Summa de arithmetica, geometria, proportioni et proportionalita* brought together for the first time the fundamentals of all branches of mathematics and its most important applications. It came in five volumes: arithmetic and algebra; their use in trade; bookkeeping; money and exchange; and geometry. The elevated status of bookkeeping as a discipline was clear from its prominence in the *Summa* (encyclopedia) as a whole volume, titled *Particularis de computis et scripturis* or *Details of Computing and Recording*. Written in the vernacular Italian rather than Latin, it was launched into the ideal business-book market. The merchants of Venice, grappling with the numerical complexities of trade, exchange, credit and investment partnerships, provided an eager customer base. (The book also brought Pacioli a fame that prompted Leonardo da Vinci to summon him to Milan, where he would teach the painter the rules of perspective that framed such masterpieces as *The Last Supper.*)

The *Particularis* volume on bookkeeping is part handbook, part manifesto for a way of doing business. In its constant appeal to personal discipline and improvement, it bears some resemblance to the self-help guides for aspiring executives that fly off the shelves in airport bookshops today. After setting out detailed instructions for the preliminary stage of accounting – drawing up an inventory – Pacioli hits his readers with the first of several bracing lectures. 'God promised the crown to the watchful ones,' he reminds them in a chapter headed 'Very Useful Admonition and Good Advice to the Good Merchant'. Conscientiousness is essential, too, 'for he who lies on feathers or under covers will never amount to anything', he adds, quoting Virgil's rebuke to slackers in Dante's *Inferno.*

Religion and moralizing pervade Pacioli's manual. He recommends marking each accounting book, before any entry, with 'that glorious sign from which every enemy of the spiritual flees and before which all the infernal spirits justly tremble – that is, the holy cross'. An effective double-entry bookkeeping system then starts with the memorandum book, or scrapbook, in which every transaction is immediately recorded comprehensively. He gives the example of having 'bought from Mr Filippo d'Rufoni of Brescia several pieces of cloth – for instance, 20 white bresciani at 12 ducats a piece'. In recording such a transaction, the trader should 'state here whether the transaction was made through a broker and whether it was made in cash entirely or part only in cash and part on time [i.e., credit]'. These details would form the raw information for the accounts and their accuracy was therefore

Figure 5: The 'Father of Accounting' Luca Pacioli, with mathematics at one hand and bookkeeping at the other[17]

paramount. Pacioli then patiently takes his readers through the mechanics of completing the various ledgers required for a full set of accounts and how to close them when the time comes. Which should be often. 'It is always good to close the ledger each year, especially if you are in partnership with others,' he writes. 'The proverb says: frequent accounting makes for long friendships.'

After following Pacioli's guide, a merchant would enjoy the happy ending of seeing the enterprise's profit revealed. Unless there was a loss. But 'from [this] state of affairs', says Pacioli, 'may God keep everyone who really lives as a good Christian'. That losing money was thought so ungodly at the same time as profits were viewed suspiciously gives an idea of the moral quandary in which commerce was caught. Not much had been resolved in the thousand years since St Jerome had said: 'A merchant can seldom if ever please God.'

ORIGINAL ACCOUNTING SIN

Pacioli's piety slips in one telling passage of the *Particularis*, the spirit of which has echoed through the centuries. It is necessary to understand a bit more bookkeeping to appreciate why. Suppose a trader buys some clothes for 10 ducats in cash. If he hasn't sold the clothes by the end of the year, his balance sheet will show stock increased by 10 ducats and cash reduced by the same amount. He hasn't lost anything. But what if the stock becomes damaged? Or the clothes go out of fashion in Venice that year? They might now be worth just 6 ducats. When he closes his book, he needs to reflect the change in value of the stock. In this case, he would do so by crediting the stock account by 4 and correspondingly debiting the profit-and-loss account by 4 (the debit and credit always matching). His profit would take a 4-ducat hit.

A trader's returns thus vary with how he assesses his stock, making Pacioli's view on the matter remarkable. 'Make the prices rather higher than lower,' he advises when valuing, by way of example, silver items in the inventory. 'For instance, if it seems to you that they are worth 20, you put down 24, so that you can make a larger profit.' This invitation to cook the books was a major departure from the notion of accounting as a truthful practice. The Father of Accounting was not just confirming that accounting is an act of judgement. He was advocating exercising this judgement dishonestly.

Accounts produced using the double-entry method were never unimpeachable. Indeed, by purporting to present a complete picture of a business with debits and credits in perfect balance, they brought the new danger of misplaced trust. The Medici Bank's overvaluation of its customer loans – which in a banking business are similar to stock-in-trade and similarly inflate profits if not marked down when impaired – was a case in point. So would be the subprime lending debacle a few centuries later. Yet, despite its susceptibility to abuse, double-entry bookkeeping as expounded by Pacioli would prove its worth. Over the coming centuries, businesses that accounted well generally prospered; those that did not failed. In the words of the Father of Accounting: 'If you are not a good bookkeeper in your business you will go groping like a blind man and may meet great losses.' Those remain some of the truest words of the past five hundred years of financial history.

IMPERIAL MEASUREMENTS

Double-entry bookkeeping received an enthusiastic welcome in new commercial centres as the trading world began to look west. In Antwerp, then capital of the Spanish Empire's Netherlands province and the world's busiest port, a merchant who had spent years trading in Venice, Jan Ympyn Christoffels, wrote *Nieuwe Instructie* (1543), largely derived from Pacioli's *Particularis*. Accounting schools appeared across the Netherlands as the value of the 'Italian system' became apparent, and it wasn't long before England was embracing accounting innovation. In the country that would produce Newton and Halley and the Royal Societies, measurement was becoming fashionable, and accounting acquired a corresponding cache. When the East India Company changed from operating as a series of discrete ventures – each wound up at the end of a voyage – to a continuous business with long-term shareholders from 1657, it immediately adopted double-entry bookkeeping.[18]

In this era, however, balanced accounting was again also used as a moral varnish. Where it had once covered mercantilism in the face of Church doctrine, now it put a veneer on colonialism and slave trading. In her 2007 history *Saltwater Slavery*, Stephanie Smallwood describes how slave traders' ledgers showing stocks of gunpowder, tobacco, gold and other commodities would be debited and credited while corresponding double entries were made in ledgers for another commodity: people. The Royal African Company's books show the movement of hundreds of men, women and children from the 'account of chain slaves' to another account when the ship carrying them left the Cape Coast Castle in west Africa. The profit-and-loss account would be credited when it arrived at its destination. 'Through their graphic simplicity and economy,' wrote Smallwood, 'invoices and ledgers effaced the personal histories that fuelled the slave trade.'[19] Another historian captured how the great accounting innovation had been co-opted into evil: 'Like the closet, the conventions of double-entry bookkeeping were intended to manage or contain the excess.'[20]

Accounting was central not just to the rise of the seventeenth century's new trading monopolies but also to that of the emerging financial giants. Like those in Renaissance Italy, northern European bankers understood what the double-entry method offered their business. When the English government addressed the economic fallout of wars against the French by creating a central bank in 1694 – converting existing government debts into shares in the Bank of England – the words at the head of its opening ledger hinted at accounting's importance: '*Laus Deo*', or 'Praise be to God'. Beneath were the columns of debtors and creditors that would form the pillars of what is now the world's longest-surviving central bank. 'No accounts in the world are more exactly kept, no place in the world has so much business done, with so much ease,' wrote novelist Daniel Defoe in the 1720s of the bank's books (then on public view).[21] So crucial was accounting that when the anti-Catholic Gordon Riots erupted in London in 1780, the bank put preserving its ledgers from looters above protecting the vaults containing hard currency. According to one historian, this sense of priorities showed 'that the fundamental capital of the Bank lay in its mastery of the algebra of double-entry bookkeeping contained within these material objects'.[22]

The northern European accounting story had some calamities of its own, however. With symbolic balance, as in Florence all those years ago, the economic achievements of sound bookkeeping were followed by the equal destructiveness of false accounting.

GOING SOUTH

However successful it became in the long run, the Bank of England was no instant remedy for the country's economic woes. Thanks to further expensive conflict in the form of the War of the Spanish Succession, in the early years of the eighteenth century, national debt ballooned once again. The costs of servicing it were burning through more than half the government's income, and Europe had hardly reached a peaceful enough state for the country to disarm, as spending cuts would have demanded. It was time for another cunning plan from the brains behind the creation of the Bank of England.

Facing government debt redemptions that his Treasury couldn't afford, in 1711 Queen Anne's Chancellor Robert Harley repeated the trick of exchanging government bonds for stakes in a new company. This time the government's creditors would become shareholders in 'The Governor and Company of the merchants of Great Britain, trading to the South Seas and other parts of America, and for the encouragement of fishing'. Better known as the South Sea Company, it was granted monopoly rights over trading with Spanish South America. But with Britain and Spain still at war and piracy in its golden age, the Atlantic Ocean was profitable only for the likes of Blackbeard and Henry Morgan. The South Sea Company was destined not to turn a real profit. It would, however, report some accounting ones.

In 1719, with precious little to show for their early efforts, the South Sea Company directors set about buying up *all* remaining government commitments (around £30m). The idea was to give a share nominally worth £100 in the company in exchange for every £100 worth of government annuity or debt. But with hype and speculation about the company's prospects swirling around the coffee shops (the Spanish had relinquished their trading rights, according to one false rumour, probably emanating from the company itself), each £100 share was soon changing hands at £114. So somebody trading in £1,000 worth of annuities would accept nine shares instead of ten and still consider himself £26 in pocket. The South Sea Company, having sold nine shares for more than £1,000, would be free to sell another one – for the market price of £114. This, decided entrepreneurial company chairman Sir John Blunt and his chief accountant John Grigsby, amounted to *profit* rather than capital raised from shareholders. It was an important distinction, because common law allowed companies to pay dividends only out of profits. The company duly paid dividends to existing shareholders, convincing would-be investors that they were onto a winner. More money flowed in and the price spiralled.

By June 1720, a £100 share was changing hands for £1,000.[23]

The wheeze illustrated the power of accounting. A company could look like it was making money when it was really pouring it down the drain. By misrepresenting the capital it raised as income, a commercial basket case could be made to appear profitable. Double-entry bookkeeping could be manipulated to transform the image, if not the reality, of a company's financial position. The episode was a landmark in the accounting story, and one that was destined to be repeated through the centuries. Much the same technique, claiming profits from an artificially pumped-up share price in order to boost it yet further, would be used 280 years later by Enron.

When the bubble burst in September 1720, it became obvious that the nation's finances had been hijacked by breathtaking fraud, underpinned by false accounting. Prime minister Robert Walpole – who had initially called the scheme an 'evil of first rate magnitude' before investing and then getting out at the top of the market – kept the 'too big to fail' South Sea Company afloat with the first government bailout. Meanwhile, a committee of MPs began investigating the affair. Thanks to investigations by 'master accomptant and writer' Charles Snell, who could stake a claim to being the first independent auditor, they discovered that fraudulent accounting had both fuelled the vertiginous 1720 rise in the South Sea Company's share price and concealed unprecedented levels of corruption in launching the 1719 government debt swap scheme in the first place. The Chancellor of the Exchequer no less, John Aislabie, had received a handsome bribe to promote it. Through secret books, he and a couple of hundred other parliamentarians had been allocated free 'notional' stock that they cashed in when the company was set up.

The chief accountant responsible, Grigsby, had also been a director of the company and had aspired to more than keeping the books. Issuing stock (real or not) and conniving in scams and manipulations with fellow directors had been more to his liking. In the process, he'd achieved a status far above that of an ordinary bean counter. One author reported that 'at the Company's governor's birthday gala he was helped out of his coach by the Duke of Marlborough'.[24] Like Sassetti's at the Medici Bank, Grigsby's head had been turned away from the books and ledgers towards more remunerative and glamorous possibilities.

The bursting of the South Sea Bubble induced a British recession deeper than any until that following the 2008 financial crash.[25] The affair had even farther-reaching consequences for business. So-called joint stock companies, which brought together investors as 'shareholders' and had sprung up in imitation of the South Sea Company, were banned. This, however, meant that a critical lesson for the long term was missed. Companies, especially monopolistic ones, will always be prone to abuse and corruption. The real message of the South Sea Bubble was the paramount importance of professional and, above all, independent accounting to expose and prevent such things. It would take a revolution to bring home this truth.

2

FULL STEAM AHEAD

THE INDUSTRIAL AGE CREATES
A NEW PROFESSION

The South Sea debacle made the value of sound accounting painfully clear. Accounting academies sprang up across Britain, particularly in the Scottish cities, to bring what one of its champions called the 'happy invention' of double-entry bookkeeping to a new generation of businessmen. The Italian method, said Ayrshire maths master John Mair, was 'very fit for improving the minds of youth, exercising their wit and invention, and disposing them to a close and accurate way of thinking'.[1]

Protestant Britain proved to be another conducive moral climate. Double-entry bookkeeping's emphasis on observance and scientific method chimed in particular with Noncomformists. By precisely measuring a business's affairs, it complemented the diaries and personal accounts in which Quakers, Presbyterians and other dissenters routinely kept a balance of their sins and good deeds. Although less troubled by religious qualms over making profits, businessmen still had to conduct their affairs correctly. 'See'est thou a man diligent in his business?' the Proverbs asked. 'He shall stand before kings.' Double-entry bookkeeping was central to that diligence.

Many British industrial pioneers were avid bookkeepers. James Watt, whose steam engine propelled the Industrial Revolution, owed his commercial success to accounting as well as engineering. The Clydeside Presbyterian kept double-entry books charting the progress of his early enterprises, partly to justify the funding provided to him by his shipowning father. By the time Watt and his partner Matthew Boulton were making steam engines in Birmingham in the 1790s, it wasn't just the invention of a separate condenser that was giving them the edge over less sophisticated rivals. So was accurate and innovative accounting. With not much of a market to determine prices for their engines, the pair used their accounting records for 'job costing' to determine what price would generate sufficient profit on each engine sold. The same principles went for the engines they leased to the tin miners of Cornwall and others. Detailed cost calculations demonstrated how Watt's machine would produce savings that would be shared between lessor and lessee, allowing the miners to prosper and Watt to invest in further improvements.[2] Accounting turned innovation into real industrial progress.

Double-entry bookkeeping became key to commercial success on any scale. Although Josiah Wedgwood's tea sets and dinner plates were all the rage in Regency England, for some time he struggled to turn a profit or to understand why he was doing a roaring trade while watching debts mount up. It was only in the early 1770s, when Wedgwood, himself a radical Dissenter, closely examined his accounting system and teased out the constituent costs, that he fully understood his own business. Some expenses 'move like clockwork and are much the same whether the quantity of goods made be large or small', he noted.[3] Interrogating the data, he could see how the costs of his equipment, through depreciation, plus the labour of his workers and administrative and selling expenses each affected profitability. His biographer called Wedgwood's analysis 'an exercise in self-taught cost-accounting, one of the earliest documents of its kind in the history of manufacturing'.[4] When a credit crisis hit Britain in 1772 and prices collapsed, Wedgwood was able to adapt by trimming the right costs. Without thorough accounting, the business might well not have survived.

Industrial business was radically different to merchant trading. With so many moving financial as well as physical parts, the information provided by accounting became invaluable. The 'cost accounting' that the likes of Wedgwood and Watt pioneered got inside business in a way that nothing had before, showing the owners of the new industry how they were making profit. In doing so, it became simultaneously a tool for advancement and exploitation. It helped generate greater returns and thus investment, but it also laid bare, for example, the financial appeal of child labour. It was the next phase of the Industrial Revolution, however, drawing in public investment, that really brought home the power of accounting and the need for it to be done professionally.

DE-RAILED

'Railway mania' hit Britain in the 1840s, thanks not just to George Stephenson's 1829 'Rocket' but also in large part to the repeal of the 1720 Bubble Act a few years before. Companies could now be incorporated through a private Act of Parliament rather than a royal charter. By 1847, a couple of hundred of railway companies were vying to add a planned 20,000 miles of track to the existing 6,000, making lavish promises to would-be investors. Since there were few conditions on entering this hot new market and those seeking to capitalize were not always among the nineteenth century's most upstanding figures, this was to present accounting with its biggest test to date.

The ultimate railway fraudster was George Hudson, a businessman and sometime Tory MP from York. The 'Railway King', as he became known, chaired several railway companies in the north and east of England. Before meeting ignominy in 1849, he controlled around 1,450 miles, or almost 25%, of the railways. Like John Blunt at the South Sea Company in the previous century, Hudson fed his ambitions by demonstrating to potential investors that he could pay the dividends they were after. And just like the South Sea Company, his companies didn't really have the requisite profits, so he too used false accounting to create them. His favourite trick was the old South Sea one of treating premiums raised on issuing shares in his companies as profits from which dividends could be paid (which in turn meant he could demand greater premiums for later share issues). He also manipulated his companies' profits by using them to buy and sell shares in each other, selectively accounting for what were in reality equal gains and losses.

The Railway King's downfall came when the president of the Board of Trade, and future prime minister, William Gladstone, tried to bring some order to the manic and dangerous industry. Along with a host of safety measures, his Railway Regulation Act of 1844 required the companies to open their accounts for inspection. A committee of investigation into just one of Hudson's companies, the York & North Midland Railway, concluded that he had 'lost his better judgement and moral rectitude' while 'the Account books of the Company were entrusted to a person utterly incompetent for the task'.[5] Hudson's various wheezes had enabled his companies to pay 'improper dividends' worth around £50m at today's prices (but of greater significance in economic terms). He had also been running personal rackets – such as selling steel to companies he chaired at over the odds – that exacerbated the need to inflate profits artificially. Thanks to the committee of investigation and the Glaswegian accountant it brought in to expose these scams,[6] the Railway King would be bankrupted and eventually see the inside of a debtors' jail cell.

The building of the railways, and Gladstone's opening up of them to audit, was a formative stage in the creation of the modern chartered accountancy profession. Partly this was because of its sheer size. Over the second half of the nineteenth century, the value of railway company stocks and shares rose fivefold to be worth around two thirds of the country's gross domestic product. They accounted for well over half the value of the stock market.[7] As well as uncovering rampant abuse on behalf of investors, the accountants set about addressing new questions thrown up by this and other industries, such as how to account for tracks or machinery: were they investments or expenses? Such issues had acquired added significance with the permanent reintroduction of income tax in 1842 and its application to business profits. The bean counters were making themselves increasingly indispensable.

The man who gave his name to the world's largest accountancy firm today made it by exposing malpractice in the railway companies. William Welch Deloitte was the grandson of an aristocrat who had fled revolutionary France, learning his craft in the City of London's bankruptcy court before setting up on his own in 1845 at the age of 27. Four years later, he was called in by concerned shareholders in the Great Western Railway. There he uncovered accounting that was shoddy even by the standards of the day, forcing the amateur auditors and four of the company's directors to resign. The young bean counter was immediately given the task of periodically auditing the company's books, making him the first independent ongoing professional auditor of a major company.

Deloitte became the scourge of the railway companies' untrustworthy proprietors. A few years later, he detailed how Leopold Redpath, a record keeper for the Great Northern Railway company, had stolen £150,000 (around £15m today) from under the noses of its amateurish in-house auditors. While the 'King's Cross Fraudster' had been embezzling this fortune, the abject bean counters had informed shareholders: 'Gentlemen. The accounts and books in every department continue to be so satisfactorily kept, that we have simply to express our entire approval of them, and to present them to you for the information of the shareholders, with our usual certificate of correctness.'[8] One hundred and fifty years later, a similar assurance would be given by the firm bearing Deloitte's name to the Royal Bank of Scotland's shareholders just before its £45bn bailout by the British taxpayer. Old William might well have spun in his grave once or twice.

THE PROFESSIONALS

Exposing railway finances to investigation wasn't Gladstone's only favour to the burgeoning business of accounting. His other major piece of legislation in 1844, the Joint Stock Companies Act, also gave it a boost. The idea was to enable everyday businesses to operate as legal companies, raising funds by selling shares to investors. But the corporate veil afforded by 'Gladstone's Act' came at the price of greater accountability. In return for being allowed to incorporate a company with a handful of signatures (as opposed to an Act of Parliament), directors would have to report to shareholders with audited balance sheets giving a 'full and fair' view of the company's affairs.

Gladstone couldn't, however, legislate for the inept amateur auditors of the day to understand what they were looking at. So all too often, in the words of one leading accountant at the time, these early audits were 'a complete farce'.[9] Yet, with the explosion in the numbers of companies and investors putting savings at risk – and plenty of corporate horror stories around to scare them – the reassurance of a good audit was at a premium. If a trusted auditor certified a company's accounts to be 'full and fair', it would be much better positioned in the competition for investment. It was to address this demand that the small accounting practices already established in the commercial centres of Scotland and England grew into something far more substantial. Soon the scale and importance of professional accountancy was such that, in the mid 1850s, Queen Victoria granted royal charters to the Edinburgh Society of Accountants and the Glasgow Institute of Accountants and Actuaries.[10] The early establishment of professional institutions in Scotland reflected the depth of accounting expertise and the esteem in which the craft had been held north of the border for a century. The profession's first luminaries, however, saw greater opportunities elsewhere. In pursuing them, they would create the firms that still dominate accountancy today.

Among them was William Barclay Peat, a landowner's son from Fife, who headed to London as a 17-year-old in 1870 to join the office of an accountancy firm that itself had relocated from Aberdeen. Within seven years he was running the firm, renamed W. B. Peat & Co. Another Glaswegian, James Marwick, was sent in 1891 to Melbourne by investors worried about money at risk in an Australian banking crisis. He set off home via North America but didn't make it back. Instead, spotting the potential in a United States booming on the back of rail, steel and oil, he set up a new firm in New York. There the six-foot-six Glaswegian – described by a biographer as 'a big man in every way, his personality, his stature, and his role as a mover and shaker'[11] – established his reputation by identifying the overvaluation of securities at a mortgage finance company. A couple of years later, he bumped into an old school friend from Glasgow, Roger Mitchell. Marwick needed a partner to stay in New York while he travelled, and Mitchell rightly saw a brighter future in accounting for Gilded Age America than in his family's weaving business. In 1897, Marwick & Mitchell was formed.

Fourteen years later, on one of his transatlantic trips, Marwick sat at the same captain's table as William Peat. Before long, Peat, Marwick, Mitchell & Co. was among the major players in the US accountancy profession. Late-twentieth-century mergers would turn this firm into the KPMG that paid millions of dollars to settle class actions for covering up overvalued mortgages on the books of subprime lenders Countrywide Financial and New Century in the run-up to the 2008 financial crash – which was pretty much the reverse of how James Marwick had made his name a hundred years before.

England's leading bean counters, meanwhile, were to be found in its capital and its ports. In Bristol, Samuel Lowell Price quit the family pottery business and joined a local firm of accountants before setting up on his own in 1849. As size became more important for accountancy firms, mirroring the industry that demanded its services, Price teamed up in 1865 with an in-demand bankruptcy expert, William Hopkins Holyland. He in turn persuaded Price to take on Edwin Waterhouse, the son of a Liverpudlian mill-owning Quaker. Like William Deloitte, Waterhouse would make his – and his firm's – reputation in the railways. When Holyland left a few years later, the firm became Price Waterhouse & Co. It retained the name until its 1998 merger with Coopers & Lybrand (which itself goes back to a firm set up in London in the 1850s by William and Arthur Cooper), when it became PricewaterhouseCoopers. By depriving him of his capital letter, late-twentieth-century branding fashions didn't quite do justice to Edwin's contribution. (See Appendix I for the current Big Four firms' family trees.)

In 1880, England's disparate accounting institutes came together and acquired their own royal charter, 26 years after the Scots had done so. It promised 'the existence of a class of persons well qualified to be employed in the responsible and difficult duties often devolving on Public Accountants'. Across the United Kingdom chartered accountancy was now elevated to somewhere approaching the status of other professions, with demanding training and examinations for its practitioners. In its first thirty years, at its new home in the City of London, the Institute of Chartered Accountants in England and Wales would count as president the men whose names still stand at the top of the profession: William Deloitte, Edwin Waterhouse, William Peat and both of the Cooper brothers.

BUST AND BOOM

Nineteenth-century *laissez-faire* economic policy certainly gave these professional accountants (and plenty of unprofessional ones) much to do. A new 1856 Act promoted by the 'father of the modern company', Liberal MP Robert Lowe, enabled companies to be formed with 'limited liability'. Shareholders in such companies could lose only the amount they had invested and not be held liable by suppliers, customers or anybody else for any more. In the same reforming spirit that extended the democratic franchise in the nineteenth century, the new type of company would open up business to men who weren't already wealthy. (Liberal philosopher John Stuart Mill was a keen supporter for this reason.) Nothing, said Lowe, should 'throw the slightest obstacle in the way of limited companies being formed'. This in turn meant that the audit requirement that Gladstone had imposed on companies was dropped. As Lowe told the Commons, 'the best course would be to leave these matters to the agreements and provisions of the parties interested' – which meant the directors and shareholders.[12]

Even with auditing returned to voluntary status, limited companies proved another boon for the accountants. Almost 25,000 were incorporated within six years of Lowe's Act, multiplying the number of investors, customers and suppliers wanting to know that their money was safe or, all too often, looking to get some of it back when companies failed.[13] History would arguably vindicate limited liability status for corporate business, but the thousands of new companies that went bust after 1856 also showed that the concession encouraged more speculative and sometimes fraudulent enterprise. Limited liability clearly made sound accounting even more essential. And the unemployed workers, bankrupted suppliers and fleeced customers left behind by corporate bankruptcy proved that 'the parties interested' in a company went far beyond its directors and shareholders. Within a few years, more legislation on bankruptcies and liquidations carved out further official roles for professional accountants. With around half of companies becoming insolvent within ten years of incorporation, these provided so much business for the bean counters that the 1862 Companies Act creating them became known as 'the accountant's friend'.

In the second half of the nineteenth century, however, the growing number of independent banks exposed to this less than stable business environment brought home the importance of getting the accounting right in the first place, rather than just picking up the pieces afterwards. In 1866, Overend & Gurney bank failed when investors took fright following suspicions of some dubious investments it had not valued properly, leaving a trail of destruction in its wake (plus fees of £71,000, or £8m at today's prices, for the accountants who cleared up). When another bank went under, this time the City of Glasgow Bank in 1878 – with falsified accounts concealing losses on American railroads and Australasian land– it was clear that something had to change. Hundreds of ensuing company bankruptcies and wrecked livelihoods showed how systemically important banks had become. The lesson, not destined to be perfectly remembered, was that they had to be properly accounted for. Up stepped the chartered accountants, volunteering to audit the banks *independently*. Whereas auditing was voluntary for other companies, under the 1879 Banking Act, it became a condition of holding a banking licence. The accountants had secured for themselves a central role in safeguarding financial and economic stability.

Not much that happened in the world of business *wasn't* good for the accountants. The rapid expansion of international trade thanks to innovations like transatlantic telegraph cables and improvements in ship construction drove cross-border investment and further boosted demand for good accounting from investors looking to protect their interests in remote businesses. Between

1880 and 1900, the number of chartered accountants in England and Wales almost trebled to 2,700, with armies of junior bean counters assisting them.[14] These men (the first woman joined their ranks in 1920) continued, however, to be heavily occupied by company insolvencies, some brought on by regular economic slumps, others by the fraud and abuse that remained routine. The gap between the promise of limited liability companies and the reality had become a national scandal, satirized in Gilbert and Sullivan's 1893 opera *Utopia, Limited*. 'They . . . trade with all who trust 'em,' sang the aptly named company promoter Mr Goldbury, 'Quite irrespective of their capital / It's shady but it's sanctified by custom.' When Liberal peer Lord Davey established a parliamentary committee to examine the situation a couple of years later, among his main suggestions was compulsory audits for *all* companies.

This was another victory for the accountants. For decades they had been pointing out, in the words of one writer of the time, that fraud and malpractice would 'not have continued if the certificate of a qualified auditor had been required'.[15] Duly legislated for in a 1900 Companies Act, auditors henceforth had to certify that accounts showed a 'true and correct view of the state of the company's affairs as shown by the books of the company'. Within a decade, auditing accounts overtook dealing with insolvency as the major role of a now established accountancy profession. And with British capital finding outlets in the world's new economic powerhouse, it was also an increasingly international one.

GO WEST

By the time the big accountancy firms began venturing across the Atlantic towards the end of the nineteenth century, oil, steel and the railroads had already turned the United States into the world's largest economy. What was missing was an accountancy profession capable of taming it.

It wasn't that accounting itself was un-American. Far from it. The nation's Founding Fathers had themselves been avid bean counters. As a pre-Independence Postmaster General in the mid 1750s, Benjamin Franklin had instituted double-entry bookkeeping across the early American postal system. George Washington had kept a copy of Scottish accounting academic John Mair's tome, *Book-keeping Methodiz'd*, at his Virginia plantation and maintained scrupulous double-entry accounts of his Revolutionary War spending.[16] Later, oil magnate J. D. Rockefeller would put his business success down to his training in accounting and applying it assiduously to his early ventures. But American business still had a shorter history of using double-entry bookkeeping, no real academic tradition in the subject and consequently less professional accountancy. It was only around the turn of the twentieth century, fifty years later than in Britain, that a status comparable to a chartered accountant's appeared in the US in the form of the 'certified public accountant'.

By this stage, some prudent accounting was badly needed stateside. Expansion of the railroad network, the driving force of American industrial growth, came with even fewer financial safeguards than there had been in Britain. As 240,000 miles of railroad were built in sixty years or so up to 1910, hundreds of the companies behind them went bankrupt (700 in the last twenty-five years of the nineteenth century).[17] One reason was that investors in US companies at the time preferred bonds for their fixed returns. But this meant companies became more highly geared and vulnerable to economic vicissitudes. In just two years after an 1873 financial crisis there were around 18,000 corporate bankruptcies.

When they began establishing themselves in the US in the 1890s, Britain's bean counters were thus entering a very different commercial world. First to make the move was Price Waterhouse.

After a number of assignments from the UK for a London company promoter putting his British investors into the New York beer business, Edwin Waterhouse remarked that 'an American connection was springing up'. Although he was initially reluctant to set up a permanent outpost of the firm in the US, the volume of work – mostly checking target companies' numbers – eventually persuaded him otherwise.[18]

In 1890, Price Waterhouse dispatched 30-year-old Lewis Davies Jones, one of a budding new breed of ambitious chartered accountants, to set up an agency on New York's Broadway. Within a couple of years, he was generating 10% of the firm's revenue from financial investigations prior to corporate deals. Soon an equally able colleague, Edinburgh accountant John Caesar, was running a Chicago office. The pair began lobbying London for powers to recruit locally and advertise their services, noting that 'generally quite a different view is taken of professional advertising or circularizing [in the US] to that held in England'. This most un-British request was sternly rebuffed. Jones and Caesar would have to play by 'London rules' and 'wait patiently and trust in getting known by degrees for doing good work and for not charging exorbitantly'.[19] The pair threatened to shut up shop, forcing a rethink from London. Now they could take on work not just as agents of the London firm but also on their own account, allowing them to expand while protecting Price Waterhouse against the consequences of anything they might do in their own name. The arrangement foreshadowed the federated structure of the international accountancy profession. It also meant that Price Waterhouse was well positioned when the largest bean counting contract so far came along.

John Pierpont Morgan was the most powerful of a collection of bankers who controlled Wall Street. Through his J. P. Morgan bank, he transformed mergers and acquisitions from a private affair among corporate barons into the more public business of stock promotion. Morgan funded the creation of General Electric out of the businesses of Thomas Edison and his competitors, making it one of the original stocks on the New York exchange in 1896. But his biggest deal came in 1901, when he created the United States Steel Corporation, responsible for two thirds of US production and sold on the stock exchange that year for $1.4bn (over $100bn today but in economic terms akin to a Google or Apple worth several times that). The largest chunk came from Andrew Carnegie's empire, but another important element was the American Steel and Wire Company, itself a consolidation of dozens of companies orchestrated by J. P. Morgan three years earlier. In this, Morgan had employed the well-regarded Jones and Caesar for the vital task of investigating the target companies. With this understanding of disparate parts of the new United States Steel, Jones and Caesar's parent organization, Price Waterhouse, became the natural choice for the job of auditor. It proved to be the springboard to the firm's dominance of American accountancy within a couple of decades. Audit and investigatory work servicing the exponential growth of the New York Stock Exchange flooded in.

Price Waterhouse used its pre-eminence to shape accounting to fit the new world. From 1901, its US arm was led by an accounting intellectual named Arthur Dickinson, the holder of a mathematics degree from Cambridge who had taken first place in the Institute's exams. Under him, Price Waterhouse led the way in accounting innovation. It produced the first 'consolidated' accounts, aggregating the results and balance sheets of the hundreds of individual companies within the United States Steel group in a way that set the template for large corporate reporting as it remains today.

British and American accounting firms nevertheless retained very different styles. Reflecting the economic and social history of the countries, British accountants tended to act in the interests of investors, their US counterparts more in those of the companies and their directors. Where the Brits viewed the main job as assessing the soundness of a company's affairs in order to protect investors over the long term, the Americans saw their role more as diagnosing problems, offering solutions and not getting in the way of the pressing business of making money. On one occasion, when Jones and Caesar insisted that a brewery should account for the cost of its depreciating plant, a Chicago newspaper complained that 'the whole charge was an invention of these tiresome English Accountants, got up to rob the poor ordinary shareholder of his . . . dividend'.[20]

Charles Waldo Haskins – co-founder of the largest US firm at the end of the nineteenth century, Haskins & Sells – considered an accountant to be the 'consulting physician of commerce and finance'. He was as serious a thinker on his subject as Dickinson, but with an emphasis on business improvement as opposed to accountability. In Haskins' view, it was essential that an accountant 'understands the anatomy and physiology of business . . . [and] diagnoses abnormal conditions and suggests approved remedies'.[21] It was this approach that prevailed when the bean counters began to debate the profession internationally. The 1904 World Congress of Accountants in St Louis (a hot ticket if ever there was one) brought together leaders of the profession including Haskins, Marwick, Mitchell, William Lybrand (of what became Coopers & Lybrand) and Arthur Young (of what became Ernst & Young). They agreed that an accountant's 'wide experience and varied practice peculiarly fit him as a business adviser and enable him to assist the financier, the merchant and the manufacturer in the development of the country'.[22] The bean counter was to serve industry, not just account for it.

In the face of corporate failures, runs on banks and economic slumps, the need for sound accounting certainly hadn't gone away, though. A 1902 congressional commission, which led to President Theodore Roosevelt's crusade against the abuse of corporate power, condemned the industrial behemoths for 'deceiving investors and the public, either through suppression of material facts or by making misleading statements'. They should publish annually audited accounts 'under oath to be subject to government regulation'.[23] But with corporate law a matter for individual states, this was no more than an aspiration. New York, Delaware and others were competing for company incorporations with lax regulations and weren't going to bring in new ones. It would take the collapse of the world economy to persuade Congress that sound accounting was perhaps a matter of federal importance.

CRASH

Although American accountancy gave no great protection to the country's shareholders, there is little evidence that this was a direct cause of the Great Crash of 1929. Some critics, notably Harvard economics professor William Z. Ripley, did complain of the poor state of corporate accounting during the 1920s. The practices deployed were 'enigmatic', and corporate reports were consequently 'obfuscated and darkened over with fuliginous matter'.[24] Yet unlike many other bubbles before and since, this one was largely blown in stocks – such as General Motors – that appeared not to be hiding too much or to be inflating profits.

The aftermath did, however, show that quite a lot of fraud and false accounting had gone unnoticed. When the 'Match King', Ivar Kreuger, killed himself in his Paris hotel room in 1932, it emerged that the man who had controlled two thirds of the world match market had also been running a huge investment scam. Price Waterhouse would later find previously hidden losses of hundreds of millions of dollars. As economist J. K. Galbraith remarked in his history of the crash twenty-five years later: 'One of the uses of depressions is the exposure of what auditors fail to find.'[25]

Persuaded that investors needed to know more about their companies, in 1933 President Franklin D. Roosevelt's new administration brought in the 'Truth in Securities' legislation.[26] It borrowed heavily from the recent 1929 English Companies Act, which demanded regular balance sheets and profit-and-loss accounts for shareholders. 'What is deemed necessary for sound financing in conservative England ought not to be unnecessary for the more feverish pace which American finance has developed,' concluded a congressional report.[27] Companies issuing stocks and bonds would have to publish independently audited accounts, giving the accountancy profession a statutory role. The world's largest economy would officially rely on its accountants for the integrity of business.

When a Senate committee met to debate the laws, one exchange between Democrat Alben Barkley and Haskins & Sells partner Arthur Carter caught the essence of the new order:

Senator Barkley: You audit the controller [now a company's chief financial officer]?

Arthur Carter: Yes, the public accountant audits the controller's account.

Senator Barkley: Who audits you?

Arthur Carter: Our conscience.

The bean counters had taken on an onerous duty. A great deal hung on how well they were to discharge it.

3

ACCOUNTANCY GOES WRONG

AS TWENTIETH-CENTURY BUSINESS BOOMS, ITS WATCHDOGS LOOK THE WRONG WAY

Just as the Industrial Revolution had posed the challenge of reporting on new forms of business, the economic boom that followed the Second World War presented the accountancy profession with the task of accounting for the corporate finance deals that were now transforming the commercial world.

In the United States, mergers and acquisitions between companies with assets of more than $10m rose from fewer than ten per year in 1950 to more than 2,000 at the height of the so-called 'Go-Go' years in 1968.[1] This was the age of the diversified 'conglomerate', in which the largest 200 came to own more than 60% of the country's corporate assets. ITT Corporation, set up as a telecoms company in 1920, had by the end of the 1960s bought up 300 other companies, including the hotel chain Sheraton, bread-maker Continental Baking, timber company Rayonier and Avis Rent-a-Car.

The theory went that one company would buy another (which following a 1950 anti-trust law had to be in a different sector), impose superior management, cost accounting and reorganization, and then reap the rewards. It was a seductive picture painted by accountants who had taken over the job of advising on investment decisions from the banks. The same post-Great Crash legislation that had split investment and commercial banks, the 1933 Glass–Steagall Act, had also barred them from advising on deals from which they would earn banking fees. But with the accountancy firms also responsible for auditing the companies and standing to earn more fees advising on the many accounting issues thrown up by mergers, the result was simply to create another, arguably more harmful, conflict of interest. For the increasingly commercial twentieth-century bean counter it was, of course, good business. In fact, a critical rule change some years earlier ensured it was *very* good business.

BLACK'S MARK

The accidental architect of the post-war mergers and acquisitions boom was William M. Black, an accountant who played a central role in the Second World War Lend-Lease assistance programme for Britain before going on to lead Peat, Marwick, Mitchell & Co.'s US arm. It was, however, shortly before this that he made his enduring contribution to corporate accounting.

In 1941, Black was auditing chemicals company Celanese when it proposed merging with its rival in the synthetics business, the Celluloid Corporation. Both were successful companies and the merger was expected to have what are now called 'synergies', i.e., commercial benefits. Yet the effect of traditional accounting methods on the combined group's profits would be to suppress them, making it unattractive to the stock market. This was because Celanese would have to pay more for Celluloid than its assets – such as its debts, stocks, plant and technology rights like patents – were worth in isolation. There was nothing unusual about that in an acquisition. But the extra cost, which double-entry bookkeeping dictated would be treated as acquiring an intangible asset known as 'goodwill', would have to be written off over the following years. Predicted future profits would be reduced.

Black reasoned that this would not give a fair picture of the combined enterprise. So he formulated a new method of accounting for such a merger, which he called 'pooling-of-interest' accounting. If one company bought another with assets of, say, $60m and liabilities of $40m – i.e., net assets of £20m – but paid $50m for the acquisition, it would be paying $30m for goodwill. Under traditional accounting it would then have to write this off in its subsequent accounts, reducing or even eliminating later profits. But under Black's proposed system, the combined business would be accounted for as if it started from scratch, its balance sheet merely showing the buying company's and the acquired company's combined real assets and liabilities. Its subsequent profits, which were what the stock market was interested in, would not be hit.

Black's idea was treated with suspicion by the Securities and Exchange Commission. But it had delegated the task of drawing up rules and guidelines to the accountants' own professional body, now called the American Institute of Certified Public Accountants. Black's method was duly allowed under certain conditions, chiefly that the merging companies should be of similar size and in the same business. On the face of it, this wasn't a bad compromise. In fact, it set the scene for the *de facto* self-regulation of accountancy to chalk up its first major scandal.

When takeovers peaked in 1968, the pooling-of-interests method was used in 60% of deals, even though the conditions in which Black had thought it suitable, it would later emerge, were met in just 5% of them. This was largely because a 1950 anti-cartel law had all but outlawed mergers of the sort for which the concession was actually intended.[2] But deals had been structured with the help of advisory accountants who claimed that they had jumped through the right regulatory hoops. The generous accounting method could be found behind ITT's bewildering array of acquisitions, and those of the man the *Wall Street Journal* called the 'Conglomerate King', Royal Little, whose Textron group now stretched from upholstery to helicopter manufacturing. The chief accountant of the Securities and Exchange Commission (SEC) remarked impotently that accounting concepts were shaping US industry, while a retired Bill Black ruefully observed that his method had been 'trampled on'.[3]

The fact that more than half of mergers and acquisitions were inappropriately accounted for so that huge fee-generating deals could go ahead showed that by the end of the 1960s the accountancy profession was no longer the upright one of James Marwick and Arthur Dickinson. The tone of the major accountancy firms was changing markedly. At the height of the stock market frenzy in the late sixties, one of the profession's leading figures lamented that 'competition to obtain a client for the lowest fee or to obtain or retain a client at the expense of technical standards is debilitating'.[4] Price Waterhouse's senior US partner throughout the decade, Herman Bevis, condemned the 'aggressiveness on the part of some firms to bring themselves and their services to the attention of the business public'. Accountancy, he argued, should be 'a profession, not a competitive industry'. Bevis was taking aim at Arthur Andersen & Co., which under a driven leader named Leonard Spacek had became more mercenary and acquisitive by the year. One Price Waterhouse partner had already objected to the Andersen man calling on his long-standing and highly valued client, United Steel, seeking to sell an array of services. 'I'll visit anywhere I'm asked to visit,' replied Spacek. 'Yes,' said the PW man, 'but do you have to send eight partners?'[5]

Andersen's aggressiveness certainly generated growth. Between 1950 and 1970, its US income rose from $8m to $100m. But then none of the major firms, despite varying degrees of scepticism and conservatism within their ranks, entirely rejected the commercialism of corporate America's 'Go-Go' era. In 1968, *Fortune* magazine estimated that between 1960 and 1968 the Big Eight had more than doubled their revenues in the United States to between $57m for the smallest, Arthur Young & Co., and $125m for the largest, Peat, Marwick, Mitchell & Co.[6] The sixties had been party time even for accountants. But when the music stopped and the lights came on, things suddenly didn't look so great.

DIRTY DEALS

Misleading accounting often passes unnoticed in the good times. If a company overvalues some assets or debts to inflate its profits one year, for example, the loss when they're sold or valued at a lower figure later on will be buried in other profits. But in the not-so-good times, the fiddles are exposed. As Warren Buffett famously put it, 'When the tide goes out, you discover who's been swimming naked.'

In late 1960s America, the waters did indeed recede. Spending on the Vietnam War and tax cuts under the Lyndon B. Johnson administration ratcheted up inflation and killed economic growth. The conglomerates created on the back of indulgent accounting were especially vulnerable, as the debts they had taken on to do their over-optimistic deals became more onerous. One of the first to go, in 1966, was an investment company called Westec. Its share price had risen thirty-fold after a string of acquisitions accounted for under the pooling-of-interest method (or 'dirty pooling', as one critic called it). When Westec's chairman and president started to manipulate the market to hold up the unrealistic share price, the regulators stepped in and discovered large-scale false accounting and theft.[7] The men ended up behind bars, while the audit firm that certified the misleading accounts at the same time as advising on the company's acquisition, Ernst & Ernst, was suspended from taking on audit clients for six months. (The regulators would overturn the ban on appeal, starting a now fifty-year-long pattern of protecting an over-concentrated audit profession from serious punishment.)

A raft of cases showed that, while acting as advisers for their audit clients, the accountants were becoming less suspicious of what they were up to – and sometimes downright complicit in their manipulations.[8] When the Penn Central Transport Company became the largest bankruptcy in US history in 1970, telling details emerged about the relationship between the company and its auditor, Peat, Marwick, Mitchell & Co. Diligent junior bean counters from the firm had consistently challenged dubious techniques to conceal the parlous state of the company's finances, such as lending money to subsidiary companies so they could pay what looked like real dividends to Penn. But then the company's chairman Stuart Saunders and his counterpart at Peat Marwick, Walter Hanson, lunched somewhere agreeable and the auditors' objections to the ruses were withdrawn. Perhaps Saunders reminded Hanson that his company had paid Peat Marwick $5m in fees, much for advising rather than auditing it, over the previous decade.[9] An SEC examination of the scandal said a great deal about the anatomy of a modern auditing failure, in which commercial priorities at the top overrode objective accountancy thinking. Penn's wheezes had been 'presented to the auditors with a variety of sophisticated justifications', and the auditors had 'viewed these justifications too narrowly and did not consider whether [they] were applicable in the circumstances'.[10] A later Senate banking committee was blunter: 'Peat, Marwick, Mitchell & Co. played a substantial role in these successful attempts to misinform the investing public.'

At least public accountants were facing a degree of professional accountability, if still at a level below other professionals. The opportunities for those who had paid the price for their failings to get some sort of redress were also opening up. Changes in 1966 to laws governing class-action lawsuits – partly prompted by the Civil Rights Movement – allowed one shareholder in a company to bring an action on behalf of many others. There was no shortage of aggrieved investors either, many of whom had exchanged stock in one Go-Go-era company for what turned out to be a worthless ragbag of shares and debentures in the company buying it out. As the litigation floodgates opened, the number of American lawsuits naming public accountants as defendants rose from 71 in 1970 to 200 by 1972.[11]

The bean counters' response was a now familiar one: a new committee to set supposedly better standards but no admission of the error of their ways.[12] Coopers & Lybrand reacted to the conviction of a couple of its auditors for signing off accounts they had been told concealed fraud by claiming that the risks for professional auditing were 'virtually intolerable'.[13] The now familiar bleat about an 'expectations gap' between what the public asked of auditors and what they could do grew louder. One prominent critic gave the obvious riposte to this: 'The first object of an audit is to say that the accounts can be relied on . . . it is absurd to say that they are alright subject of course to the possibility that undetected fraud may have made them all wrong.'[14] What some have called the 'golden years' of accounting was in fact a period when the American accountancy profession, fattened on fees, became hopelessly out of condition. One Price Waterhouse partner later recalled that the profession had become 'so spoiled that we didn't really have the muscles that we needed to cope with the 1970s'.[15]

GENTLEMEN ACCOUNTANTS

Three and a half thousand miles away, Britain experienced its own 1960s mergers-and-acquisition boom, kicked off by a young chartered accountant named Jim Slater. His skills in reading companies' books told him how much hidden value there was in stagnant companies often run but no longer owned by the old industrial families. They just needed to be broken up, stripped down and sold off. Where Slater led, a gang of infamous corporate raiders including the likes of James Goldsmith and Roland 'Tiny' Rowland followed, egged on by a Labour government that saw takeovers as the way to shake up moribund industries. It was a cut-throat business, and one in which – just as in the US – company balance sheets, profit statements and earnings forecasts moved centre stage. It said something about the British accountancy profession that it emerged from the period with its reputation far less tarnished than its American counterpart's.

Not that there weren't shortcomings and disputes. When Associated Electrical Industries defended itself in 1967 against a hostile takeover bid by one of prime minister Harold Wilson's favourite industrial champions, the General Electric Company (GEC), it forecast annual profits of £10m for that year and demanded a correspondingly high price. After GEC took the company over, its bean counters calculated that there should really have been a loss of £4.5m. Soon afterwards, a failed 1969 merger exposed dubious accounting at printing company Pergamon, owned by a Labour MP and businessman named Robert Maxwell. One professor was moved to write to *The Times* that the accountants were 'a pretty ineffective and inefficient lot'. But that was the very British limit to the outcry.

The UK's chartered accountants escaped the scandals and the opprobrium heaped on the certified public accountants of America largely because, even if they occasionally dozed off, they got it horrendously wrong less often. The British system, underpinned by the 1948 Companies Act requirement for accounts to present a 'true and fair view' to shareholders, was based on similarly prudent principles in law going back a century. Conservative judgement was implicit. Accounting standards in the US, by contrast, had been framed to restore confidence in financial markets after the Great Crash. Instead of broad principles demanding 'fair' accounts came a system of specific accounting rules for every part of a company's financial statements on which investors would rely.

In place of judgement, there was a rulebook. And rules could be gamed.[16]

This enabled American auditors to turbo-charge the Go-Go era with misleading pooling-of-interest accounting, overstating the value of merged companies at the behest of their biggest fee-paying clients. 'In practice you could see there were some poolings that probably should not have been poolings, but they met what was then considered to be the letter of the law,' recalled one Price Waterhouse partner many years later.[17] (Strictly, they almost certainly did *not* meet the letter of the law, but they could be 'considered' by fee-hungry advisory accountants to do so.) Britain's accountants, on the other hand, resisted what they called 'merger accounting' in favour of the more traditional but less flattering alternative; in most cases, it gave a truer and fairer view.[18]

British bean counters also had the confidence, deriving from their heritage and status, to resist clients' unreasonable wishes. Chartered accountants had formed professional institutions in the same era as the country's lawyers. Many of their roles, such as administering wills and bankruptcies, were enshrined in statute. In America, where the profession was about fifty years less mature, such matters were the province of the legal profession. Tax was important too. The British accountants who approved figures of profit to be taxed had a quasi-statutory role and a public importance that grew as the tax became the government's most important source of revenue in the first half of the twentieth century. The United States' far younger income tax ran on its own laws, largely independent of accounting profits, and was thus a matter primarily for the lawyers.

Company shareholders also valued accountants more in Britain. Even after a post-war transfer of corporate control from the old families to institutional shareholders like pension funds, the owners of companies still wanted to know their money was in good hands. In 1966, *The Economist* commented that British shareholders were 'probably the biggest factor working in the auditor's favour'.[19] In the US, where stocks were more actively traded and 25 million private citizens were looking at share prices with their morning coffee, shorter horizons meant less of an audience for uncomfortable accounting truths.

Status translated into influence and a certain amount of power in Britain. Ever since Sir William Peat had become auditor of the Privy Purse (the royal finances) in the Edwardian era, the top bean counters had enjoyed a place in the establishment. (Peat's great-grandson Sir Michael Peat combined his partnership in KPMG with the role in the 1990s, while another ex-KPMG partner currently holds the position.[20]) At the end of the sixties, thirteen members of the House of Lords and nine members of the Commons were chartered accountants. Under prime minister Harold Wilson, the Chief Secretary to the Treasury (the Cabinet minister who holds the public purse strings) was one. By contrast, there were no certified public accountants among the US Congress's 535 members.[21]

Britain's top bean counters were accordingly listened to at the highest corporate level. A landmark 1969 comparison of the professions either side of the Atlantic by New York accounting professor Lee J. Seidler found: 'In Britain, most important client contacts made by partners of the accountancy firms were directly with the chairman of the board.' In the US, they 'were almost always conducted with treasurers or controllers' a rung or two down the ladder. Accountancy in Britain was a gentleman's profession, increasingly drawing graduate recruits from the better universities. In the States, Ivy League high-fliers headed straight into the white-shoe law firms and investment banks while the accountancy firms picked up the slightly lower achievers. [22] The most senior British accountants were men to be reckoned with and company executives generally knew better than to argue with them. 'Auditors were treated with more respect in that the auditor was the sole arbitrator of what was true and fair,' recalled an accountant who became finance director at ICI, one of the country's largest companies at the time. 'There was no negotiation because you had to get it right without fear or favour. In my day, the auditor was a semi-god.'[23]

Advisory and consulting services for clients were also less developed in Britain, so accountants weren't as conflicted as the corporate servants across the Atlantic. In one study Seidler presented finance professionals with a scenario in which 'there was a substantial disagreement on accounting between a large firm of accountants and the management of a company'. They were asked in what circumstances 'might the client influence the auditor to accept its view?' British stockbrokers and stock exchange officials unanimously thought none. Their Wall Street counterparts overwhelmingly replied that US auditors would accede to a client's wishes. 'Accountants are so tied to the corporations whose financial statements they audit', was one typical response, 'that they are unable to bite the hand that feeds them.'[24] And this was at a time when even American accountants were merely on the appetizer. The main consultancy course was yet to come.

4

TRUST ME, I'M A CONSULTANT

THE BEAN COUNTERS BRANCH OUT

What is now a $250bn-a-year global consultancy industry was born out of accounting.[1]

It had been clear since eighteenth-century potter Josiah Wedgwood saved his business by understanding the numbers as well as he did England's taste in tableware that accounting was a powerful tool for business improvement. The practical experience of industrialists like Wedgwood became a recognized discipline of 'cost accounting' thanks to the work of academics like Aberdeen philosophy professor Robert Hamilton. 'When a person is engaged in several branches of manufacture,' he explained in his 1788 *Introduction to Merchandise*, 'he should keep his books in such a manner as to exhibit the gain or loss on each.'[2] The great English mathematician Charles Babbage extended the principle to different stages of production, famously breaking down the manufacture of pins into seven steps to arrive at the time and labour costs of 'making each part of a single pin, in millionths of a penny'.[3]

The insights of Hamilton and Babbage were seized on in the United States. The giant corporations spanning the country towards the end of the nineteenth century as a result of the railroads changed the nature of American business. The modern company might source raw materials in one part of the country, manufacture something from them elsewhere and sell its wares in yet another place. No longer could the industrial pioneers run such companies themselves, especially following the mergers-and-acquisitions frenzy that saw 1,800 major companies become just 157 in the ten years from 1895. These sprawling concerns had to be managed by other people both for practical reasons and because the likes of Rockefeller, Carnegie and Ford were, said one business historian, 'the conquerors of capitalism, not its administrators'. [4] Those who could tell the new managers of corporate America what made up their profits, and therefore how they could be increased, were useful people to know.

The technicians who took the theories of cost accounting and scaled them up for the new age were led by a mechanical engineer from the steel heartland of Philadelphia called Frederick Winslow Taylor. He refashioned industrial methods using 'scientific management': detailed classifications of cost, time, materials and output. 'Taylorism' would be credited with innovations such as the production-line system, with each worker performing a small part repetitively. Its brutal efficiency was satirized by Charlie Chaplin in *Modern Times*, but it enabled Henry Ford's workers to make a Model T in a couple of hours, compared to half a day beforehand.

Frederick Taylor's own business card read: 'Consulting Engineer – Systemizing Shop Management and Manufacturing Costs a Speciality' (more informative if a little more wordy than today's slogans, like Accenture's 'High performance. Delivered.'). While scores of other firms were set up to satisfy the demand for Taylor's transformational principles, the best qualified to offer the new cost-accounting consultancy services were the large US accountancy firms like Ernst & Ernst and Arthur Young & Co. The latter's efforts, for example, helped the British government work out how much it should be paying for the Enfield rifles that armed its troops in the First World War. But the firm that found the most consultancy success was the one that hit on the winning commercial formula of blending it with its core accountancy business.

KING ARTHUR

If Renaissance Italy was the cradle of double-entry bookkeeping and Lowland Scotland nurtured the accountancy profession, then Illinois can stake a decent claim for setting it on the path to becoming the 'professional services' business that it is today.

When two ambitious Price Waterhouse-trained Chicago accountants bought the Audit Company of Illinois in 1913, they set out to do more than just audit the companies proliferating in the hub of industrial America. Arthur Edward Andersen, the red-haired son of Norwegian immigrants, and Clarence M. DeLany also promised 'investigations for special purposes, such as to determine the advisability of investment in a new enterprise or the extension of an old business' and 'the designing and installing of new systems of financial and cost accounting'.[5] According to the firm's official history, Andersen thought that 'the most important service that a public accountant could render to his client began, rather than ended, with the issuing of the certified financial statements'. It was the accountant's job to 'look behind' the figures.[6]

By the time DeLany left the firm five years later, Arthur Andersen & Co. was forging a distinct identity as both an accountancy and a consultancy operation. It was built on two solid foundation stones. One was the work ethic of a proprietor who had been orphaned at 16 and laboured in mailrooms while studying accounting at night to become, at 23, Illinois's youngest certified public accountant. The other was his ramrod-straight personality. Imposing the Norwegian mantra 'think straight, talk straight' that he had been brought up on, Andersen insisted that his firm's auditing could never be compromised by the lure of consultancy fees from the same client. When the president of a railroad company threatened him with the loss of business after he insisted certain maintenance expenses be set against the company's profits before he signed off a report to shareholders, the youthful red-haired accountant stood his ground. 'There's not enough money in the City of Chicago to make me change that report,' he famously (or maybe apocryphally) told the businessman. The sinking of a steam freighter on Lake Michigan prompted an equally firm response. The incident had occurred just after the period for which its owner was reporting, and Andersen thought accounts on which shareholders and bankers would rely really ought to mention the catastrophe (as what would be known to today's accountants as a 'post-balance-sheet event'). The company relented.

The firms of British origin still doubted whether an accountant could ever advise a client and remain an impartial auditor. Nobody felt these qualms more than Price Waterhouse's George May. Arriving in the US from Devon in 1897, he rose through the firm's ranks, succeeding Arthur Dickinson as its leader in 1911 and becoming American accountancy's leading public figure. May created the first accounting standards in 1918, formulated the idea of 'generally accepted accounting principles' that remain a cornerstone of accounting today, and would later be instrumental in persuading Congress to force listed companies to be audited in the wake of the Great Crash. As well as being a visionary accountant, he was a shrewd judge of human nature. As one writer put it, he 'understood that accountants were no less susceptible to temptation than anybody else'.[7] He and his staff steadfastly avoided all potential conflicts of interest, eschewing consultancy work and refusing to socialize with clients.

Where May saw danger, so did Arthur Andersen. But the latter believed strong values could overcome them. 'To preserve the integrity of his reports, the accountant must insist upon absolute independence of judgment and action,' lectured Andersen. This would be achieved by vigorously enforcing 'certain standards of conduct'.[8] The 'Andersen way', as the required conduct was known, put integrity and public service above all else, at the price of losing clients if necessary. Under a 'one firm' ethos, all partners were expected to adhere to the same values and working methods. It may appear ironic that the firm that collapsed in 2002 through its conflicts of interest and misconduct in the Enron affair should once have had such standards. But it was this ultimately naïve ethos that justified the entrenchment of incompatible roles within a single organization. If everyone could have been as upstanding as Andersen, all would have been well. And for a time it more or less was. Future generations of accountants in different economic times were not, however, going to live up to his exacting standards. It was thus Arthur Andersen's virtue, as much as his late-twentieth-century successors' vices, that would bring down the firm bearing his name.

FIRM FOUNDATIONS

Although its name has come almost to define management consultancy, McKinsey & Co. owes its place in business history to accountancy. And through its shaping of the consultancy business that is now the major accountancy firms' main preoccupation, it has in turn played a key role in the bean counting story.

James McKinsey, born four years after Arthur Andersen in Missouri in 1889, was another bright working-class Midwesterner who achieved remarkable success through hard work and accountancy. After formative war service in the US Army's haphazard ordnance department, McKinsey took an accounting degree and found a job with a local firm. He also started to write extensively on subjects that showed the development of his thinking on the role of accounting in business. His most important work, a 1922 page-turner called *Budgetary Control*, paved the way for the system of estimating expenditures and then monitoring variances from them that is still used by companies and public bodies for financial planning today.

When McKinsey struck out on his own in 1926, at the same time as becoming professor of business policy at the University of Chicago, his description of his new firm showed how he would use accounting. James O. McKinsey & Co. would be 'accountants and management engineers'. Significantly for the future of consulting, however, he didn't target factory-floor operations, in the way Frederick Taylor had; rather he advised companies on structuring and running their entire business, from the top down. His insights were worth paying for. Anti-trust laws against corporate collusion prohibited corporations sharing information, so the advice of a firm that was also privy to competitors' methods was highly valuable. Like Arthur Andersen across town, McKinsey & Co. defied the depression and even prospered from it. As companies struggled to survive, the firm was there with its 'General Survey Outline', a formulaic business review covering finances, organization and market information that set a trend for consultancy 'products' that companies still snaffle up today.

James McKinsey's successor in the late 1930s, Marvin Bower, was a lawyer rather than an accountant and an early graduate of the Harvard Business School. He found accounting a distraction from the intellectually superior task of consulting, and dropped it. McKinsey & Co. were no longer 'accountants and management engineers' but slicker 'management consultants'. Bower evangelized about the new discipline's transformational powers (and in the process inflicted on the world the painful management-book genre, his gems including *Unleashing the Department Store*).

As companies grew and merged post-war, the demand for consultants who could talk convincingly about organization and strategy expanded correspondingly. Alongside its advice on corporate structuring – which, then as now, generally involved carving companies up into separate divisions – McKinsey developed many of the services that the big accountancy firms would later take into the multinationals' boardrooms. A popular one emerged in the early 1950s when one bright McKinsey spark discovered that workers' pay was rising faster than management's (partly because by now the unions had redressed some of the iniquities imposed by cost accounting and scientific management). Before long an executive pay consulting service was born, with bosses rewarded handsomely under schemes carrying the McKinsey stamp of approval. Since the advice would generally be to pay executives slightly more than their competitors – who wants below-par bosses? – the still spiralling gap between executive and employee wages was inevitable.

McKinsey also led the way in consulting for governments, an area that the accountancy firms now dominate. In 1951, the firm was brought in by new president Eisenhower to reorganize the White House and identify the key positions through which he could control the federal government. Over the following years, the firm won scores of government contracts, notably in the defence and security sectors, creating what one historian called the 'contractor state'. When the National Aeronautics and Space Administration (NASA) was formed in the late 1950s to run America's space programme, McKinsey designed an operating model that relied heavily on contracting out tasks to companies for which the firm also worked. Encouraging the government to bring in private operators on the one hand and advising those same operators on the other, foreshadowed the fee-generating game that the big accountancy firms would come to play in the later era of privatization and outsourcing.[9]

By 1967, the former accountancy firm was working for 19 of the largest 25 US industrial companies. McKinsey had turned consultancy from problem-solving into a permanent presence at the elbow of the world's most powerful businessmen. When the major accountancy firms later expanded their narrower consultancy offerings into the services the firm had pioneered – to hugely lucrative effect – they would owe a large debt of thanks to the bean counter James McKinsey.

BRISK BUSINESS

Arthur Andersen & Co. led the accountancy pack into the post-war consultancy business. Its founder's death in 1947 served, if anything, to sharpen the firm's commercial focus. Its partners wrote to staff that 'the firm will continue to operate aggressively and will adhere to the same policies of integrity, high level of service and opportunity'.[10] Its new leader was Leonard Spacek, the son of an Iowan mechanic with origins as humble as his predecessor's and standards even more exacting. His approach was typified in a 1954 memo in which he instructed staff not to lean back on chairs, read newspapers or gossip in the office. In the corridors, he commanded, they must 'walk briskly'.[11] More importantly, Spacek believed that his 'Arthur Androids' – as staff were known to the firm's detractors – could be trusted not to compromise the core task of auditing for commercial benefit. With the conviction of Arthur Andersen himself, he would combine accountancy with the next consultancy revolution.

Spacek's most influential appointment came soon after the Second World War, when he hired a veteran named Joseph Glickauf from the US Navy's Bureau of Supplies and Accounts. It might not sound like the proving ground for a significant figure in business history, but it was there that Glickauf had seen the transformational potential of computing then being pioneered in the military.[12] Soon afterwards, as an Arthur Andersen consultant, Glickauf heard about a 'universal automatic computer', or UNIVAC, being developed on similar lines at the University of Pennsylvania. He immediately set off for Philadelphia to study what is now recognized as the first commercial computer. When he got back to the office, he didn't undersell what he had seen. It represented 'a new technological era as different from the one which we have just passed through as the industrial era differs from the agricultural age', he told the firm's partners. The pitch persuaded his bosses to invest in a new administrative services division through which to sell the technology, with Glickauf in charge.

His breakthrough wasn't long in coming. When General Electric sought his advice at a new plant in Kentucky, Glickauf adapted the UNIVAC to its particular needs, taking the company's business processes such as running the payroll to new levels of efficiency.[13] Spacek saw the future of consulting. It clearly lay in selling expensive systems to the firm's own audit clients. Even some Andersen partners were wary, given the obvious conflicts of interest. But Spacek was untroubled. As long as the firm simply *advised* the client and didn't make decisions on its behalf, any conflict was negligible. The legendary Andersen ethics and independence of judgement could handle it.

Within a couple of years, Glickauf's operation hit a turnover of $1.8m. Although still a small proportion of the firm's $40m or so business, this was a major growth area. It was also one for which a firm that was auditing a company and perhaps advising on accounting practices – with all the insight that gave into the client's operations – was ideally positioned to offer. The point was not lost on Price Waterhouse's new senior partner John Inglis. Since George May's retirement in the early 1940s, the firm had been dipping its toe in the consultancy waters through a 'management advisory services group'. But even with the new technological possibilities, it remained – true to May's traditions – cautious. Its auditors feared that botched consulting work could cost them long-standing clients and were suspicious of the encroachment of the machines. When eventually Price Waterhouse did move into 'systems consulting' in the mid 1950s, Inglis forced his consultants to commit to 'conservative and ethical promotion methods' – in contrast, he meant, to the buccaneering ways of Arthur Andersen & Co.[14]

Other firms responded a bit more enthusiastically. Around the same time, Peat, Marwick, Mitchell & Co. poached a McKinsey man to run a consulting division that began selling advice on everything from data processing to marketing and even executive recruitment. The big accountancy firms were all now players in the consultancy game and realized that this would be an important area for the income growth they were increasingly looking for. Even Price Waterhouse's reticent management team reported in 1966 that 'the future of management consulting belongs to the accounting firms because of our continuing, close, confidential relationship with our clients'.[15] By 1970, Arthur Andersen was earning 14% of its income from consultancy. After restructuring its business into 'client service teams' to maximize consultancy sales opportunities, by the end of the 1970s the share had risen to 23%. The other firms didn't publish figures but appeared to be growing at a similar pace. The hand that was ever more generously feeding the accountants, as the academic Seidler had put it, was that of consultancy.

The accounting scandals of the sixties and seventies – exemplified by the Westec and Penn Central Transport cases, where the auditors had also been the companies' advisers – illustrated the dangers. And the risks had only intensified since then. Under pressure from the US Federal Trade Commission, in 1973 the profession had lifted a self-imposed ban on competing for audits on price. This in turn prompted the firms to 'low-ball', i.e., underprice, bids to win or retain audit work. The lost revenue could be made up by using audit contracts as a 'foot in the door' to sell more profitable consultancy services. Forty or so years earlier, when Congress had made auditing compulsory in the wake of the

Great Crash, a leading accountant had answered the question of who would audit the auditor with the response 'our conscience'. To anybody who cared to look at what had happened since, this was clearly no longer good enough. One latter-day congressman dared to say so.

LET SLEEPING WATCHDOGS LIE

A 1976 Congressional report on *The Accounting Establishment*, commissioned by Democrat senator Lee Metcalf, was damning of the state the accountancy profession had reached. 'It appears that the Big Eight firms are more concerned with serving the interests of corporate managements who select them and authorize their fees', wrote his staff, 'than with protecting the interests of the public, for whose benefit Congress established the position of independent auditor.'[16] Metcalf's answer was simple. Auditors should not provide consulting services to clients, except where they were merely advising on accounting itself.

Oblivious to their recent record, the bean counters took this as a great affront. Their professional body commissioned a rival report from former Securities and Exchange Commission chairman Manny Cohen. He gave the bean counters what they wanted: some essential minor criticisms but, far more importantly, the conclusion that providing other services to an audit client didn't impair independence. The report allowed the SEC to fudge the issue. It rejected the ban proposed by Metcalf in favour of a requirement merely to disclose consultancy fees from audit clients (which would be rescinded four years later under the new Ronald Reagan administration). Even with its reputation at such a low ebb and with the consequences of failure growing more serious, the profession was making the rules of its own game.

With this reprieve, the major accountancy firms accelerated their transformation. Between 1977 and 1984, the proportion of their income accounted for by consultancy – excluding tax advice – roughly doubled to between 11% in the case of Price Waterhouse and 28% for Arthur Andersen & Co. In 1983, Andersen overtook McKinsey as the largest consultancy firm by income (to which the McKinseyites disdainfully responded that they were 'the marines to Andersen's army'). Two years later, Andersen hit another landmark. Its army of consultants was earning 30% of the firm's fees, which, taken with 21% of revenues from tax advisory work, meant that America's largest accountancy firm by income was now more of a consulting than an accounting business. (The same threshold would be crossed by all the then Big Six firms in the early 1990s, as the trend continued throughout that decade – see Figure 6.)[17]

Like the lapels on their suits, the horizons of the 1980s accountants were widening dramatically. As well as tried and tested areas like tax, payroll and investment appraisal, there was now the more stimulating business of advising on management and industrial practices that looked sluggish next to those of a resurgent

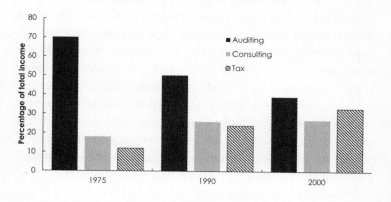

Figure 6: Over the last quarter of the twentieth century, the Big Eight, Six and then Five ceased to be primarily auditing firms

Japan. Corporate finance, once the preserve of investment banks, was also opening up as a rich new seam. But most important was the IT systems consulting business, as accelerating technological development turned the promise of earlier decades into hard cash. All the big firms scaled up to compete with the likes of IBM and Electronic Data Systems. In 1984, Price Waterhouse, once the most reluctant player in the consultancy game, set up its own technology centre in Palo Alto in Silicon Valley. By 1986, the firm of Arthur Dickinson and George May no longer called itself an accountancy practice. It was a 'full-service business advisory firm', promoting more consultants than auditors to its partnership ranks.[18] The following year, five of the top ten management consultancies in the US were Big Eight accountancy firms.[19]

Even the most conservative audit partners had to adapt to the new world, or they were out. Deloitte's senior US partner from 1985, wrote one historian of the business, 'awarded the biggest bonuses and highest salaries to those who proved themselves capable of graduating from being [an] "auditors' auditor" to being business advisers'.[20] For 'mediocre performers' there would be a 'pink slip', i.e., redundancy notice, waiting in the pigeonhole. That year Peat Marwick was revealed to be firing partners who failed to meet targets for selling consultancy services. Meanwhile, wrote US accounting author Mark Stevens, 'some of the best minds have been pushed into the bowels of the organization because they cannot charm the clients into the fold, [and] the quality and accuracy of the firms' [audit] opinions has to suffer'.[21] A former partner in Big Eight firm Touche Ross[22] described how the effect was 'to change the balance of the professional mindset – moving farther from an audit mentality and toward a consulting mentality'.[23]

More than just creating conflicts of interest with the core task of auditing, consultancy corroded accountancy culture. 'For generations, members of these huge influential practices considered themselves professionals who happened to be in business,' wrote Stevens. 'But beginning in the 1980s this view flip-flopped: increasingly, they saw themselves as businessmen who happened to be professionals.'[24] As they did so, the world economy was embarking on its greatest phase of liberalization for at least a century. It needed its financial watchdogs alert, not distractedly chewing on juicier consultancy bones.

5

FREE FOR ALL

THE BEAN COUNTERS EXPLOIT
A NEW ECONOMIC AGE AND
CONNIVE IN FALSE ACCOUNTING

Chicago, the city that did so much to shape American accountancy, also gave the world an economic model that presented the profession with both its sternest test and its biggest commercial opportunity. The bean counters' special genius was to cash in prolifically on the latter even as they badly flunked the former.

With the election of Margaret Thatcher in the UK and Ronald Reagan in the US, early 1980s Anglo-Saxon capitalism was in the grip of 'Chicago School' economics. First came the tough medicine of monetarism, restricting the money supply to cure the inflation of the post-oil-crisis 1970s in line with the theories of economists such as Milton Friedman at the University of Chicago. Then came the equally transformative prescription of deregulating the banking system and freeing cross-border finance from the old shackles of exchange controls. Whatever else this course of treatment achieved, the financialized world economy it created would become a theme park for false accounting, tax avoidance and regulation-dodging, with the bean counters marshalling their customers from one ride to another.

That the profession wasn't going to be up to accounting for this new world was clear from its first major challenge. America's savings-and-loan mutuals, otherwise known as 'thrifts', were supposed to be as safe as the houses they funded. They lent savers' deposits to mortgage borrowers with a federal government guarantee, bringing property ownership to the masses. But when interest rates moved as high as 15% to defeat the inflation of the late 1970s, the survival of institutions whose income came from fixed-rate long-term mortgages set well below those levels was threatened. Salvation for this part of the American dream was to come in the form of textbook Chicago School deregulation.

Out went restrictions on borrowing and investing, enabling the thrifts to gear up to unprecedented levels, lend to customers on riskier terms and invest in everything from equities to high-yield, high-risk 'junk bonds'. There followed an orgy of theft and fraud, epitomized by events at Lincoln Savings and Loan in California. Soon after construction tycoon Charles Keating bought the once conservative company in 1983, the manipulations began. First he fiddled the accounting for the $50m he had paid for the business, allocating too little of the cost to a portfolio of loans that, when quickly sold, produced an artificial profit. When ill-judged bets on junk bonds put further holes in Lincoln's finances, Keating filled them with more elaborate frauds. Large tracts of land were bought and then sold for inflated prices to companies run by cronies and funded by Lincoln itself, generating more artificial profits and debts that would never be recovered.

When Securities and Exchange Commission inspectors eventually got hold of Lincoln's books, they unearthed remarkable complicity from two of the big audit firms. Arthur Andersen had assisted in the deceit by backdating documents, before resigning in 1986 without acknowledging any problems. Its successor, Arthur Young, went even further in the cover-up. Lead audit partner Jack Atchison lobbied hard to keep the regulator at bay. 'Lincoln's strategies have thus far proved successful', he wrote to a group of senators, 'and have turned an association headed for failure into a strong and viable financial entity.' A year later, after signing off the 1987 audit, Atchison took a top job with a Keating-owned construction firm on a salary of $930,000 – far higher than any bean counter could dream of at the time.[1]

Atchison's successor, a woman named Janice Vincent, did speak out. The following year she disputed Lincoln's treatment of a deal with British corporate raider James Goldsmith, refusing to admit that a swap of financial assets had immediately generated a $55m gain. 'Lady, you've just lost a job,' Keating told her. Arthur Young did now resign from the audit, but Vincent's stand made a couple of important points. It showed that, however skewed the major accountancy firms' priorities had become, there were still people of integrity and courage within them. And in disrupting the masculine dynamic of serious accounting failures, in which alpha-male executives usually prevailed over beta-male bean counters, it showed that a few more women at the top of the big firms might be a good idea. Although they were now being recruited into the profession in equal numbers to men, the legacy of older traditions meant that in 1989 just 4% of the Big Eight firms' partners were female.[2]

When the Securities and Exchange Commission finally got to grips with the Savings and Loan debacle, it accused Charles Keating and his acolytes of stealing around $1bn. The businessman went to jail, but the defrauded investors and creditors knew that he couldn't have done it without the bean counters. 'Since when does the outside accountant – the public watchdog – become a proponent of the client's affairs?' asked one lawyer.[3] The accountants were forced to make record payouts to investors. Arthur Andersen settled for $23m, and Ernst & Young (as Arthur Young had become by merging with Ernst & Whinney in 1989) forked out $63m.[4]

Lincoln Savings and Loan was just one of more than a thousand thrifts that failed as they threw good money after bad under the bean counters' less than watchful gaze. In the words of a regulator who testified at the subsequent congressional hearings, 'any thrift in America could obtain a clean audit opinion despite being grossly insolvent'.[5] So widespread was Arthur Young's negligence that Ernst & Young eventually handed over $400m to settle multiple claims from regulators covering a decade of failure. Deloitte and KPMG had to cough up $500m between them. Government investigators examined a sample of cases and in more than half of them found 'inadequate audit work'. The bean counters, said one congressman, had been 'derelict in their duty'.

FRAUDULENT SLIP

The same dereliction was spreading far beyond the towns and cities of America. Post-war global business expansion brought a wave of mergers among the big firms as they sought to service the sprawling multinationals. Existing co-operation between Coopers Brothers of the UK and Lybrand, Ross Bros & Montgomery of the US had turned into a full-scale merger as early as 1957, producing the transatlantic Coopers & Lybrand. Further consolidations at the end of the 1970s gave all the big firms a presence in every major economy. When British-based Whinney, Smith & Whinney merged with the US's Ernst & Ernst to become Ernst & Whinney in 1979, a 'Big Eight' elite multinational firms controlled world accountancy. The process homogenized accountancy culture. In the age of free markets it was, unsurprisingly, the traditions of the US profession that gained the upper hand. The British arms of the firms, which had once shied away from consultancy, began to expand these services with an aggressiveness resembling the American approach. The consequences, mirroring those seen across the Atlantic for a couple of decades, were evident when the era's most infamous financial crook fell from his yacht and drowned in the ocean.

Official warnings had already been sounded over printing mogul Robert Maxwell in 1971, when British government inspectors examining the takeover of his Pergamon printing company had called him 'a person who cannot be relied upon to exercise proper stewardship of a publicly quoted company'.[6] When he died twenty years later and his whole business empire collapsed, the fraud that many suspected was exposed. Maxwell's companies had been propped up by a series of artificial transactions and more than £400m had been looted from pension funds belonging to workers at the *Daily Mirror* newspaper. Its auditors, Coopers & Lybrand, had not noticed. Or, more likely, had not wanted to notice.

Reflecting priorities now prevailing on both sides of the Atlantic, Coopers & Lybrand had earned many times its audit fees from advising Maxwell on corporate finance deals through the 1980s, culminating in a public flotation based on fraudulent figures. Just how far the firm would go in compromising standards was clear from one memo that the lead audit partner, Peter Walsh, wrote to his staff at the time: 'The first requirement is to continue to be at the beck and call of RM [Robert Maxwell], his sons and his staff,' he instructed them, 'appear when wanted and provide whatever is requested.'[7] Although the senior Coopers partners on the case would admit 59 serious errors of judgement, eight years after Maxwell's death they were merely censured, fined a few thousand pounds and allowed to carry on.

The absence of serious consequences even for catastrophically bad auditing (not to mention the time taken to administer a slap on the wrist) reflected the British profession's gentlemanly traditions of self-regulation and indulgent discipline. This might have been relatively harmless in more innocent times, but was now dangerously inadequate. A more aggressive breed of accountant at the top of the big firms by the 1980s, targeting revenue almost as ruthlessly as their US colleagues, took full advantage. Maxwell wasn't the only corpulent fraudster to cash in.

So too did Peter Clowes, who claimed improbable returns for his investment company while cruising on his yacht, flying in and out of the country on a collection of personal jets and luxuriating in a chateau in France. If ever a business warranted the sceptical eye of a good bean counter it was his Barlow Clowes operation. But when a rival planning to take over the company in the mid 1980s appointed Big Eight firm Touche Ross to check out the numbers, that wasn't what it got. Instead, the firm swallowed spurious assurances about money being held in unaudited offshore funds and a non-existent sale of software to a Jersey affiliate. One smaller firm of accountants had turned down the job because it was refused access to the offshore funds, but Touche was not to let such quibbles keep it from the big payday. It approved the numbers and the takeover went ahead. Then the truth emerged. Barlow Clowes was a Ponzi scheme that had been channelling investors' money into outlandish investments, not the safe government bonds it had claimed. When it imploded in 1988, around 18,000 investors lost their money.

Seven years later, a disciplinary panel found that the 'professional efficiency, conduct and competence' of the Touche partner whose work had been relied on by the buying company's shareholders 'fell below the standards that should be displayed by, and may properly be expected of, a chartered accountant'. As a result, the information given to the shareholders 'did not give a true and fair view of the profits record and liabilities of the relevant Barlow Clowes entities'.[8] Touche protested that, just like the investors, it had been duped by Clowes (who ended up with a ten-year prison sentence). But it was clear that it had failed the auditor's defining task of seeking and presenting anything like a 'true and fair view'.

The accountant who came in for this withering censure – plus an official reprimand reflecting the 'seriousness of [the disciplinary panel's] criticisms' – was John Connolly, a senior partner in Touche's north of England practice. Just four years later, he took charge of the UK arm of Deloitte & Touche (as his firm had become after its 1989 merger with Deloitte, Haskins & Sells). The bullish bean counter, described in one profile as 'frequently wrong but never in doubt', would go on to power Deloitte up the ranks of the big firms. He would unhesitatingly buy up Arthur Andersen's UK practice when it collapsed in 2002 and tell one interviewer: 'Our ambition is to be the most successful firm, which will mean we grow more quickly than our competitors.'[9] For a major British accountancy firm, 'success' now meant not excellent accounting, but higher fees. The partners who elected him their leader did so because he would boost their bottom line. Five years later, average partner income was £621,000, up from £419,000 the previous year (the first for which the firm published figures). The nobler traditions of the profession, it seemed, came a poor second to such riches.

The absence of any official intervention in Connolly's appointment spoke volumes about the self-regulatory comfort zone in which accountancy operated. It is hard to imagine that the Bank of England would have allowed a banker whose 'conduct and competence' had recently been found wanting to take the top job at one of the main banks. Some commentators have suggested that a less prominent bean counter might have been struck off in similar circumstances.[10] Others would accept that it is possible to learn from such an episode and, suitably chastened, work to restore a reputation. But to be put in charge so soon of a firm that audited a large slice of the FTSE100 and was therefore an important economic player was by any measure forgiving, especially in a profession for which financial probity should have been (and once was) the essence. The decision would have far-reaching consequences – not least when Deloitte went on to pick up the audit contract for Britain's second biggest bank, the Royal Bank of Scotland, just a year after Connolly's elevation.

REFORM CLUB

Dramatically higher levels of debt and financial complexity in the age of financial liberalization meant that the bean counters' shortcomings now posed threats not just to those unfortunate enough to invest in or work for charlatans like Keating, Maxwell and Clowes. They presented more serious economic dangers as well. Along with complicity in the savings-and-loans scandal, deficient auditing also played a big part in the downfall of British bank Johnson Matthey in 1984 – necessitating a Bank of England rescue – and allowed the shadiest financiers of them all, Bank of Credit and Commerce International, to loot and launder with abandon throughout the decade. The bean counters' failings were becoming a systemic problem, exacerbated by changes in the profession itself. The same commercialization of accountancy that had brought about the conflicts of interest, the low-balling and the substandard auditing led to yet more consolidation in the already over-concentrated profession. By the time Deloitte & Touche and Ernst & Young were created in 1989, there were only the 'Big Six' firms auditing large companies. The loss of just one of these would cause serious disruption to the all-important markets, giving the bean counters leverage over governments. They would use it to seek what they really wanted: an almost complete escape from responsibility for their mistakes.

As the world cried out for better auditing, the accountants began a concerted campaign to limit their liabilities in the event of more corporate disasters. Very quickly US state legislatures, first in Texas in 1991, succumbed to the same threat that had produced weak company regulation over a century. To keep the accountancy (and law) firms from setting up elsewhere, they were persuaded, they would have to offer concessions. Within four years, half of US states had introduced 'limited liability partnerships', capping each partner's liability for failings anywhere in the firm at what he or she had put into the business.[11] For the bean counters it meant that their considerable private wealth was safe, no matter what their colleagues got up to. This was just what the major firms wanted, and in the mid 1990s they duly re-formed as LLPs in the secretive low-tax state of Delaware.

Accountants weren't supposed to be taking risk; they were there to provide protection against it. But risk-taking was what they were being encouraged to do. Accountants in limited liability partnerships had little incentive to question what fellow partners were up to. They would have an interest in colleagues ratcheting up fee generation for the partnership pot. History had shown what havoc limited liability could wreak, while the more recent conversion of most investment banks into publicly traded companies with limited liability and stock market investors of their own to impress – such as Lehman Brothers in the US in 1982 and Baring Brothers in the UK in 1985 – was turning them into nakedly profit-seeking operations.[12] Similarly limited liability for the watchdogs was asking for trouble.

Further diminishing the bean counters' accountability, in 1995 Congress took an axe to investors' rights to sue companies. In response to heavy lobbying from the Big Six firms, it exempted the accountants from class actions of the sort that had hit them following their conglomerate-era failures in the 1970s. Instead of being on the hook for all the losses of a corporate collapse, they could be sued only for a proportionate share judged to be their fault.[13] The effects of this would become clear over future years, when the most egregious auditing behind multi-billion-dollar audit collapses incurred compensation bills only in the tens of millions of dollars. Over in the UK, the bean counters had scored a comparable win in 1990 when House of Lords judges decided that most parties affected by corporate failures could not sue negligent auditors. Only the company (or, if it went bust, its liquidators) could do so. Shareholders investing on false prospectuses or workers losing their jobs thanks to poor accounting were deemed too 'remote'.[14] Even many accountants privately thought this gave them too easy a ride.[15]

Not content with this protection, Britain's top accountants were enviously eyeing the overall limited liability status enjoyed by their American sister partnerships. They moaned that litigation was costing them 8% of their revenues (which turned out to be as exaggerated as some of the 1980s corporate profits they had signed off), and fretted that a big cock-up could wipe them out.[16] In fact, existing limitations on their liability now made this vanishingly unlikely.

A detailed review by the Law Commission found no case for limited liability partnerships. Nor could the early 1990s Conservative government see one, given the accountants' recent win in the House of Lords. None of the serious scandals of the 1980s had penalized the big firms that much, never mind threatened their survival, anyway. Even the governing council of the Institute of Chartered Accountants in England and Wales opposed efforts by its own members from the Big Six partnerships to limit their liabilities. They were guilty, it said, of 'special pleading on behalf of the big firms' that 'put sectional self-interest above public interest'.[17] But the pleading clearly wasn't working. It was time for something a little more devious.

MIND THE RAMP

The manner in which the major British accountancy firms did become limited liability partnerships is a particularly shabby episode in accountancy history. A new Companies Act in 1989 had in fact already allowed accountants to operate as limited liability *companies*, but this came at the price of the partnership status that the firms supposedly valued for its 'cultural' importance. In fact, the bean counters were more wedded to it for the tax advantages that came with being self-employed partners rather than company directors subject to pay-as-you-earn tax and National Insurance levies.

If Westminster wouldn't listen to their pleas for the best of both worlds, there was a government just off the French coast that certainly would. The States of Jersey, as the island's parliament is known, exists largely to create laws demanded by the financial services on which the Crown Dependency bases its economy. So when Price Waterhouse and Ernst & Young arrived with ready-prepared LLP legislation in their attaché cases, they received a warm reception. Led by a senator who also worked for the law firm that was helping the accountants, the island's lawmakers pushed aside less pressing commitments and fast-tracked the new bill. One of the minority of local politicians who was not a fully paid-up member of the island's political-financial establishment, Senator Stuart Syvret, said the bill 'reeked of sleaze'. Back on the mainland, accounting professor Prem Sikka and Labour MP Austin Mitchell led a campaign against the law and tried to persuade the UK's Privy Council – the arcane body of senior politicians who advise the monarch and effectively rubber-stamp the British tax havens' laws – to reject the statute. They had no joy, beyond the satisfaction of being called 'enemies of the state' in St Helier. In November 1996, the bean counters duly got their Jersey LLP law.[18]

They wouldn't actually use it, but then the manoeuvre had never really been about Jersey. It was an attempt to blackmail the British government into giving the bean counters what they wanted. Sure enough, the big firms immediately threatened to set up offshore if a similar British law were not enacted. The mainland press belatedly cottoned on. The Jersey law was 'a cosh with which to threaten the [UK] government if it fails to come up with a workable LLP law', noted the *Financial Times*.[19] It was actually more of a comedy sponge cosh that wouldn't have worked in practice anyway. If the accountancy firms had become Jersey LLPs, they would still have been taxable and suable in the UK, where they were bound to remain physically. But, ever more reliant on the country's service sector, successive governments wouldn't contemplate a scrap with the Big Six (or Five, following the Price Waterhouse and Coopers & Lybrand merger of 1998). They caved in. Citing the LLP developments in the US and Jersey, Tory business secretary Ian Lang said his government was 'determined to maintain a competitive and up-to-date legal framework'.[20] Accountancy, like everything else in the age of deregulation, was to be competed for. In 1998, a draft bill creating LLPs was published by Labour's business secretary Peter Mandelson. A few months later, after being forced to resign for failing to declare a large loan from a colleague, he found advisory work with Ernst & Young – or, as it would soon be known, Ernst & Young LLP.

When a 1999 parliamentary committee looked at the history of the legislation, the chairman called it 'an accountants' ramp'.[21] Within three years of the law entering the statute book, all the major firms had converted to LLP status. Their partners, now averaging nearly £500,000 a year in profit shares, could keep their favourable tax position and relax confident in the knowledge that no matter how badly their firms messed up, their personal fortunes – unlike everybody else's – were safe.

The world's major accountancy firms had shaken off the shackles of responsibility, just as global capitalism entered a particularly potent phase.

THE NUMBERS GAME

By the late 1990s, Western capitalism was triumphant. The Cold War had been won, free markets ruled supreme and a real economic surge was accompanied by dizzying hopes for internet technology. From 1995, the Dow Jones rose almost unremittingly to more than double in value over five years. But all was not quite as it seemed.

The markets that drove share prices valued consistent growth in profits, preferably every quarter. And, through share options and other schemes often designed by the accountancy firms, executives were now highly incentivized to deliver what markets wanted. There were two ways to achieve this. One was through permanent improvement: innovating, increasing sales and producing more efficiently. This was difficult, in both established industries and emerging ones. The other, easier, way was to fiddle the numbers using the implements of deception found within the double-entry-bookkeeping toolbox.

Arthur Levitt, a stock market veteran who chaired the Securities and Exchange Commission from 1993, watched the circus from a ringside seat. 'Too many corporate managers, auditors and analysts are participants in a game of nods and winks,' he told a New York audience in his famous September 1998 'Numbers Game' speech. 'In the zeal to satisfy consensus earnings estimates and project a smooth earnings path, wishful thinking may be winning the day over faithful representation . . . Managing may be giving way to manipulation; integrity may be losing out to illusion.'[22] Levitt outlined the more common accounting scams. 'Merger magic' deceptions, along the lines of the old pooling-of-interests profit-boosting techniques, were particularly popular for acquisitions of 'new economy' companies with barely any income but sky-high valuations. Other companies were restructuring and creating excessive reserves for future expenditure. Wall Street ignored the cost of doing so as one-off 'exceptional' items but didn't object later when the costs didn't turn out so large and the reduction in the reserves boosted profits. Smaller so-called 'cookie jar' reserves for other readily manipulated matters such as customer refunds could be used to shift income from one year to another, smoothing out profit growth. More brazenly, fictitious sales could be created with the magic of double-entry bookkeeping.

When household-appliance maker Sunbeam collapsed in 2001, it emerged that it had been selling stock to retail stores months in advance of their need for it, with an agreement to take it back if not needed. No cash changed hands and Sunbeam generally ended up not delivering the stock, but it counted the sales as income. In November 1997, as the American winter set in, the company reported record sales of barbecues. Four years later, it was bankrupt.[23]

Such gaming could have been stopped by conscientious auditing, in Sunbeam's case by Arthur Andersen & Co. The firm eventually had to pay $110m to the company's liquidators, although even this was a small fraction of investors' losses. The absence of effective accounting created a vicious circle in which companies came under pressure to fiddle results in order to keep up with both their competitors' exaggerated numbers and their own from previous periods. The upshot was that between 1997 and 2000, Levitt wrote in his memoirs, '700 [publicly listed] companies would belatedly find flaws in past financial statements and restate their earnings' (compared to a historic record of around 25 a year).[24] Far from learning from the savings-and-loans scandals of a decade earlier, the accountancy firms appeared to have made audit failure all part of the service.

They were no longer really accountancy firms, though, either by inclination or income. All of the Big Five were now earning more from advisory services than they were from auditing.[25] (They weren't always doing so honestly, either. PwC, Ernst & Young and KPMG would all eventually pay substantial fines for overcharging clients during the 1990s through ruses such as billing for travelling expenses without deducting large rebates they had received. PWC also paid a seven-figure sum to settle without admission of guilt allegations of paying kickbacks to government officials on technology contracts.)[26] Checking the numbers was merely a first step in bagging other work. 'Some firms even paid their auditors on how many non-audit services they sold to their clients,' Levitt would recall, echoing criticisms made more than a decade before. 'Consulting contracts were turning accounting firms into extensions of management – even cheerleaders at times,' he thought.[27] The executives had rich incentives for rigging the numbers. Stock market analysts who were routinely talking up their own books, sometimes criminally, stood ready to believe them. But the bean counters should have been prepared, Levitt had pointedly told their professional body in late 1996, 'to splash a bucket of cold water on overly exuberant ideas about performance'.[28] Instead, fatally conflicted, they colluded in the numbers game.

Levitt spent his years at the SEC trying to ban auditors from providing other services to clients. He did force a short-lived tactical retreat. Between 2000 and 2002, all of the top firms apart from Deloitte sold their management-consulting arms, which were focused largely on selling a new generation of IT systems. But when it came to changing the rules to prevent conflicts of interest, he was up against a Congress more schmoozed and funded by the accountants than ever before. Between 1990 and 2000, the big firms made political donations of $53m. A quarter of this came in 2000 as Levitt's efforts intensified. In that year's presidential campaign, all of the Big Five featured in the top twenty donors to George W. Bush.[29] 'And boy did those donations get results,' lamented Levitt.[30] Against this wall of money and influence, when he retired in 2001 Levitt had achieved little more than reinstating the woefully inadequate requirement for companies to disclose what they paid their auditors for consultancy services.

'American markets enjoy the confidence of the world,' Levitt had said in his 1998 Numbers Game speech. 'How many half-truths, and how much accounting sleight-of-hand, will it take to tarnish that faith?'[31] In fact, more financial chicanery than even accountancy's foremost critic could have imagined was already going on in Texas. It was about to do more than tarnish the faith. It was going to trash it.

HOUSTON HAS AN ACCOUNTING PROBLEM

Plenty of bosses order in fizz to celebrate a commercial success. But when a company's executives start popping champagne corks over a change in accounting method, it's time to worry. That's one lesson from the greatest accounting crime of the modern era, more commonly known by the name of the company where it all happened: Enron.

The man buying the bubbly in Houston in January 1992 was Jeff Skilling, Enron's 38-year-old chief operating officer. The Harvard Business School graduate – who claimed to have told his selection board there that he was 'fucking smart' – had been recruited eighteen months before by the company's chief executive, Kenneth Lay. His task was to complete the transformation of an oil and gas distribution company into a trading business exploiting newly deregulated energy markets. Having already been immersed in the plan as a partner in Enron's consultant, McKinsey, his big idea now was to create a gas bank within the company that would buy and sell contracts for oil and gas deliveries from producers. But they were reluctant to sell at fixed long-term rates and miss out on price increases, so Enron was faced with buying at volatile current, or 'spot', prices and selling at fixed, long-term ones. To mitigate the risks from this mismatch, it would then enter 'hedging' transactions on the new gas futures market.

Able to present the gas bank as a financial trader rather than an old-fashioned fuel distributor, Skilling persuaded the Securities and Exchange Commission to allow Enron to account for its contracts in the way banks did for their trading books. This 'mark-to-market' accounting had become favoured by regulators as a supposed corrective to the savings-and-loans scandal, supposedly to impose the discipline of market values on balance sheets. But it was another tool of deception. As soon as a contract was struck – for example to supply gas for anything up to twenty years – the value of the contract was recorded as income. So if Enron judged that a deal would generate $500m income and cost $400m to fulfil, the contract would instantly generate a profit of $100m. If it didn't work out that way and ended up costing, say, $500m to fulfil, a compensating $100m loss would appear – but, happily, only some years down the line.

As Luca Pacioli had observed when discussing merchants' inventories five hundred years earlier ('if it seems to you that [stocks] are worth 20, you put down 24, so that you can make a larger profit'), the question of valuation was subjective. This was especially so when there was no active, or 'liquid', market against which to gauge assets like long-term contracts. The new accounting method thus gave Enron plenty of scope for manipulation. In a jaw-dropping spoof video he made soon after the change, a wide-eyed Skilling tells colleagues: 'We're going to move from mark-to-market accounting to something I call HFV – hypothetical-future-value – accounting. If we do that, we can add a kazillion dollars to the bottom line.'[32] The joke would turn out to be ruinously close to the truth.

While accounting could conjure make-believe returns on gas trading, *real* profits in the hard-scrabble energy business weren't easy to come by. It was trickier still for a firm to make more every quarter than it had made – or rather reported – in the one before. But this is what Enron assured the markets it would deliver on its way to the 15% annual growth that chief executive Lay promised them. So fixated on the company's stock price were he and Skilling that the figure was posted daily in the office lifts. Nobody was in any doubt about Enron's priority to 'make the numbers'. And for a remarkably long time, it did so. Throughout the 1990s, the company's profits rose as smoothly as one of its Falcon 900 corporate jets on a windless day. Between 1995 and the end of 2000, while the rest of the market roughly doubled, the Enron share price quadrupled.

It was, of course, an illusion. It was also one that became harder to sustain every quarter. Enron was using mark-to-market accounting to steal profit from the future, which meant that in the next period even more had to be stolen from the subsequent one. Ever more new deals had to be signed to create the required growth in 'profit'. And as if this wasn't demanding enough, Wall Street also needed to see some cash to back up the supposed returns. But the absence of real income meant borrowing to get it, and the markets valued companies with less borrowing.

How did Enron reconcile the apparently irreconcilable? How did it record profit while actually losing money? How did it borrow without reporting more debt? How did it show cash coming in without actually earning it? How, as chroniclers of the Enron saga Bethany McLean and Peter Elkind put it in *The Smartest Guys in the Room*, was the company 'defying the laws of financial gravity'?[33]

TRICKS AND TREATS

When Enron's chief financial officer Andrew Fastow gives talks on business ethics these days, he holds up his old prison identity card in one hand. With the other he brandishes an award for services to off-balance-sheet financing from *CFO* magazine. That, in a nutshell, is how Enron defied financial gravity before crashing to earth late in 2001.

Fastow was Skilling's first major appointment back in 1990. At the age of 28, the ambitious economics graduate had already spent a few years at Chicago's Continental Bank. There he'd picked up useful experience in the burgeoning business of 'securitization', a technique pioneered for banks in the 1980s Wall Street trading rooms that involved packaging up loans and selling them, using the proceeds to reduce the bank's own borrowings. Usually taking debt off the books in this way would be legitimate, but it could also be used to paint a misleading picture of a company's finances by purporting to rid it of debts when not really doing so. Even at Continental Fastow had been pushing at the limits. But he'd been constrained by his superiors at the conservative bank, where one former colleague later questioned whether 'he ever had a moral compass'.[34]

By the mid 1990s, Enron had already made a series of disastrous investments around the world, from Vietnam to Teesside in the north-east of England. It was also haemorrhaging cash on everything from inflated traders' commissions to executives' strip-bar bills. Mark-to-market trickery, much of it involving a $4bn contract to supply gas to a New York power plant for twenty years that could be conveniently revalued when necessary, enabled these losses to become market-pleasing profits. But this could achieve only so much; it couldn't hide Enron's ballooning debt, or generate the cash that analysts also wanted to see. Fastow had brighter ideas for these conundrums.

A series of off-balance-sheet structures with names like Whitewing and Osprey, which borrowed and then invested in Enron stock, allowed the company to repay some borrowings and appeared to turn the debt that the markets were wary of into the share capital they preferred. Other ruses created cash flow like a rabbit out of a hat. One particularly brazen scheme, Project Nahanni, involved setting up a special entity to buy $500m of US Treasury bonds, selling them and passing the money to Enron to give the impression of real business cash flow. The flattering results should not have survived a diligent accountant's scrutiny.

At this point it might be asked where the auditors were. The answer was that they were in the building. That was the problem. About one hundred Arthur Andersen & Co. accountants and consultants were permanently housed in the Enron Tower in

Houston, sucking up tens of millions of dollars in fees advising on how to organize the transactions to get the desired accounting – and then auditing it. The dual role could never produce sound accounting, but that wasn't what Andersen was about. In 1989, even Andersen's fabled fee-seeking had been turbo-charged by an acrimonious split between the management-consulting and accounting sides of the business. The latter was now desperately trying to compensate for lost revenue with more consulting income of its own. Its leaders would go to toe-curling lengths to drive home the priorities. At that year's partner conference, lead US audit partner Richard Measelle had arrived on stage to the strains of 'Eye of the Tiger' with . . . a live tiger. Hitting financial targets would, he informed colleagues, 'require the eyes of a tiger'. The man running the firm in the late 1990s, Steve Samek, gave a speech accompanied by a violinist and instructed his audit partners to act as 'maestros' in pursuit of a '2×' strategy of bringing in twice as much from non-audit services, such as IT consulting and tax, as they earned from the audit.[35]

For the ambitious 1990s android buying into this mission, the Enron Tower was the place to be. 'It was like these very bright geeks at Andersen suddenly got invited to this really cool, macho frat party,' recalled one Andersen veteran. 'They were out of control, and they didn't even know it because it was so cool to associate yourself with the top, with the guys who run a multi-billion-dollar company.'[36] Many moved through a well-oiled revolving door into Enron jobs laden with stock options and other perks. But it was at the top that the relationship was particularly close.

As Fastow turned up the financial-engineering dial, Andersen chose as its new lead audit partner for Enron 35-year-old David Duncan, described in profiles as impeccably polite and non-confrontational. A later court case heard he was a 'client-pleaser'.[37] He had become a partner only two years earlier, but was thought the right man for this major account because he was friendly with Enron's chief accounting officer (and former Andersen auditor) Rick Causey. What would once have been a disqualification for such a role was now a standout advantage. Duncan duly gave Enron's financial shenanigans their regular rubber stamps and Andersen banked its ever-rising fees, reaching $25m for auditing and $27m for consulting in 2000. The firm even became Enron's internal as well as its external auditor, effectively marking its own homework. Unsurprisingly, Causey and Duncan found they were getting on better than ever. They holidayed together, took trips to the Masters tournament at Augusta and co-ran their own golf days where colleagues could simultaneously raise money for charity and celebrate Enron's rocketing share price.

The intimacy suited Enron. In response to SEC chairman Arthur Levitt's proposal to separate auditing and consulting, Kenneth Lay told him with as much sincerity as he could muster: 'Enron has successfully used its independent audit firm's expertise and professional skepticism to help improve the overall control environment.'[38] In truth, although it would be exposed a few months too late for Levitt, the relationship allowed Andy Fastow to get away with financial murder.

OFF BALANCE

Concerned by the number of financial time-bombs he had buried beneath the headline numbers using one-off schemes to hide debt and generate cash, by the late 1990s Fastow needed some major off-balance-sheet structures as more permanent hiding places and magic money boxes. The first was LJM, a Cayman Islands set-up bearing the initials of his wife and two sons. To be able to claim the arrangement was independent of Enron and thus 'off the books', Fastow needed to fund just 3% of it from outside Enron. He and some chosen colleagues could provide this, while the rest of the money came from a few friendly banks. At the same time, Fastow would be in control of LJM (and take fat fees from it). As it would be transacting with Enron, of which he was chief financial officer, this presented the mother of all conflicts of interest to go with the sham of independence.

This extreme scheming had raised eyebrows in one corner of Arthur Andersen & Co. While the firm's Houston operation was the apogee of the fee-driven transformation of a traditional accountancy firm, another part of it could still claim to be upholding its founder's steadfast values. This was the Professional Standards Group, a Chicago-based centre of accounting excellence that advised on how to account for the most difficult transactions. One member of the group had looked at the LJM proposal and asked: 'Why would any director in his or her right mind ever approve such a scheme?' Even the client-pleasing Enron audit partner David Duncan had initially said 'the whole thing is a bad idea'.[39] But with Skilling egging him on, Fastow had pushed ahead and the amenable bean counter had acquiesced. LJM was soon taking swathes of Enron's riskier business off the company's books. It inspired a host of further ruses, given the predatory name 'Raptors', to magic away dubious investments while holding onto those that seemed safe. The LJM vehicles generated $2bn in cash flow in 1999 alone, while the Raptors were estimated to have artificially spared Enron $1bn in losses, half of that in 2000 when its reported profits were $979m. And these were just the two main strands of a huge web of creative accounting, stretching to more than 3,000 'special purpose entities', on which the reported results depended.

A new lead accountant at Andersen's Professional Standards Group dealing with Enron was less biddable than Duncan. Carl Bass was an expert old-school bean counter who had worked as an audit manager on the company in Houston before joining the technical unit in 1999. He had no trouble seeing see what

Figure 7: Arthur Andersen & Co.'s lead audit partner on Enron, David Duncan, appearing before a Congressional committee, 24 January 2002

Enron was up to. One of the deceptions Bass objected to involved a venture between Enron's new broadband services division and the Blockbuster film-rental group to provide 'on demand' video across the US. Neither the technology nor the demand existed and it was clearly worthless. Nevertheless, to milk some essential accounting profit from it, Fastow sold the hypothetical future profit stream for an inflated sum to another off-balance-sheet structure. This had obtained the funds for the purchase from a bank that was given a secret assurance that it would get its money back within months. 'Project Braveheart', as it was known, was really a loan and should have been accounted for as such. But it allowed Enron to book an entirely fictitious $58m profit. When Bass complained about the accounting, he was, as often, overruled.[40]

Andersen veterans describe ignoring the revered Professional Services Group as once being 'unthinkable'.[41] By the turn of the twenty-first century, however, the sales culture at Arthur Andersen & Co. had comprehensively defeated the notion of sound accounting. The awkward Bass was removed from Enron work at the company's instigation. A handwritten note from Duncan would later reveal why: 'Client sees need to remove Carl.' In court some time later, Duncan explained how Bass had complained about his removal. 'I told him I would make an appeal to [Enron's chief accounting officer] and see if there were some movement there,' he said. There wasn't. Bass was off the case. By this stage, internal memos would later reveal, Arthur Andersen & Co. was anticipating fees from Enron reaching $100m a year. Such a piper could call any tune it wanted. It could demand not just the individual auditors it wanted but also their approval for as much false accounting as it needed.

In the summer of 2001, after the collapse of the broadband division, an outspoken Enron accountant named Sherron Watkins was redeployed to Fastow's immediate team. With the benefit of her own Arthur Andersen experience a decade before and her understanding of several Enron projects, she realized the deceptions being practised at the centre of the company and the losses being improperly concealed. Watkins pointed out the emperor's nakedness, direct to chief executive Kenneth Lay. It was clear that many of the obscure structures would have to be wound up, and the losses reported to the stock market. When this dented the third quarter's results to the tune of several hundred million dollars, the share price took a big hit. The unravelling of Enron's finances had begun, as schemes that themselves depended on the unsustainable company share price came undone. What the numbers game gave, it also took away. The Enron stock price spiralled to nothing within a couple of months. Bankruptcy was declared on 2 December 2001 at a loss to investors of $70bn and to 20,000 employees of their jobs. Thousands who had been encouraged to invest their retirement savings in the company's shares lost everything.

Fastow co-operated with prosecutors and in 2006 began six years in prison for wire and securities fraud. Skilling is still serving a 24-year sentence for fraud and insider trading (having cashed in his shares for eight-figure sums before resigning five months ahead of the bankruptcy). Ken Lay was convicted of fraud but died before sentencing. Arthur Andersen & Co.'s demise wasn't far behind Enron's. Aware that a formal SEC investigation was in the offing, it began shredding documents. Both the firm and Enron audit partner David Duncan were convicted of obstructing justice. Those verdicts were overturned some time later on technicalities, but Andersen's conviction had disqualified it from auditing and shut the firm.

If Enron was the house that McKinsey built, it was also one that Arthur Andersen should have condemned. It didn't do so because keeping the corrupt edifice standing paid more. Many people and companies take a share of the blame for the Enron scandal, with its executives and bankers in the front row of culpability. But these people had legitimate profit motives, albeit ones they corrupted. Arthur Andersen ought not to have had such a motive. It was the watchdog that should have been checking and preventing the misleading and often illegal methods that were being used. It therefore failed most in its duty because it betrayed its core purpose and its higher professional responsibility. 'Show me one fucking transaction that the accountants and the attorneys didn't sign off on,' Jeff Skilling ranted after the bankruptcy.[42] He might not have been the best person to make it, but he had a point.

NOT GUILTY

Enron was one of dozens of major accounting scandals to emerge in the early years of the twenty-first century, as an economic downturn exposed the 1990s numbers game for the accounting scam it was. The Houston oil company wasn't even the largest. That distinction went to WorldCom, a telecoms company also audited by Arthur Andersen that brazenly misrepresented expenses as investments in assets before being exposed by another female accounting whistleblower, internal auditor Cynthia Cooper, who refused to be silenced by corrupt bosses. The company went bust eight months after Enron with the loss of 30,000 jobs and $180bn of investors' money. Demonstrating how the fallout from accounting fraud could spread, its competitor AT&T had not long before sacked 20,000 people in order to match WorldCom's bogus profits. Arthur Andersen & Co. could be blamed for those lost livelihoods too. It wasn't just Andersen clients either. Security company Tyco inflated income by $500m under PricewaterhouseCoopers' nose. All were playing the same stock market numbers game. The chief executives of these three companies went to jail, as did their chief financial officers (who, incidentally, had all been garlanded by *CFO* magazine just like Andrew Fastow).

The other big firms had their disasters too, notably Deloitte at cable TV company Adelphia and power company Duke Energy; Ernst & Young at corrupt healthcare company HealthSouth; and KPMG at photocopier company Xerox. They would, however, get away with paying some affordable civil penalties to the SEC without admitting wrongdoing. The regulator was typically damning and lenient at the same time in the Xerox case, finding that 'KPMG permitted Xerox to manipulate its accounting practices to close a $3 billion "gap" between actual operating results and results reported to the investing public ... Most of Xerox's topside accounting actions violated generally accepted accounting principles (GAAP) and all of them inflated and distorted Xerox's performance but were not disclosed to investors.' Deliberately breaking the accounting rules sounded pretty serious. But then came the generous resolution. KPMG had to cough up $22m in ill-gotten gains and penalties 'without admitting or denying the SEC's findings'.[43] Apart from Andersen, all the (now) Big Four firms thus emerged from the numbers-game era without guilt. A handful of individuals were fined and some suspended from practice. But when it came to the firms themselves, the prospect of one of them joining Andersen in whichever circle of bean-counting hell it now inhabited – reducing the profession to an untenable Big Three – ensured that the regulators backed off from alleging law-breaking.

With the WorldCom fraud emerging so soon after Enron, and European and other scandals demonstrating a systemic global failure in all the major firms, it was impossible any longer to deny that major change was needed in the accountancy profession. A few new rules did indeed emerge. But they didn't address the most dangerous fault line exposed and even entrenched by the age of scandal. Through their own misconduct and by selling out their heritage, the accountants had themselves become all but unaccountable. Responsibility-free bean counting was about to exact its heaviest price yet.

6

CRASH!

THE ROLE OF THE BIG FOUR IN
THE 2008 FINANCIAL CRISIS

Not long after most of the world's largest banks had been bailed out with trillions of dollars of taxpayers' money, one old lady in London wondered out loud: why had nobody seen the September 2008 financial crash coming?

A few months later, this senior citizen received an answer, possibly because she was the Queen of the United Kingdom, from some of the most eminent brains in the land. The British Academy gathered thirty intellectuals, central bankers and assorted great-and-good and identified some now widely accepted causes: an expansion of credit in response to a largely Chinese savings glut; financial engineering magnifying and hiding risks within the ensuing credit bubble; lax financial regulation; skewed and excessive incentives for bankers, and political indulgence of their methods. Overall, they said, there was a 'psychology of denial' and it was 'difficult to recall a greater example of wishful thinking combined with hubris'. This 'fuelled the increase in house prices both here and in the USA' and meant more loans to people without the means to repay them. When these 'subprime' borrowers began to default, the financial edifice built on their loans collapsed.

The British establishment was too polite to apportion blame. 'Everyone seemed to be doing their own job properly on its own merit,'[1] the authors generously concluded. That might have been some mitigation for the banker instructed to make bumper profits with no regard to future risks. But one group, who went unmentioned in the dispatch to Her Majesty, could have no such excuse. The accountants responsible for reporting on the financial system and the banks controlling it had 'professional scepticism' written into their job description. They should have warned of the gathering storm some time before it broke. It would have been possible.

SHORT OF EXCUSES

'While the whole world was having a high old party, a few outsiders and weirdos saw what no one else could.' So says the narrator at the beginning of the *Big Short*, the 2015 film based on Michael Lewis's book about a handful of traders who bet against the US housing market in the pre-crisis boom years. 'These outsiders saw the giant lie at the heart of the economy and they saw it by doing something the rest of the suckers never thought to do. They looked.'

It wasn't the first time the *Big Short*'s protagonists had looked at the subprime housing market, which mushroomed out of a dangerous combination of well-meant policies to expand home ownership to low-income groups across the States and the financial deregulation of the 1980s. Back in the mid 1990s, Steve Eisman, the most outspoken short-seller (renamed Mark Baum and played by Steve Carell in the film), had crunched the subprime numbers with the help of a disaffected young accountant he'd recruited from Arthur Andersen. Vincent Daniel had been trying to understand how investment banks made their money so that he could audit them properly, but had found Andersen uninterested. 'Vinny, it's not your job,' he recalled his boss telling him. 'I hired you to do XYZ. Do XYZ and shut your mouth.'[2]

Daniel's inquisitiveness was more valued at Eisman's New York brokerage firm Oppenheimer & Co. than it had been at

Enron-era Andersen. Tasked with examining data on every pool of subprime mortgage loans that the lenders were selling on, he found 'stunningly high delinquency rates'. When it came to their accounting, however, the mortgage companies were ignoring them. For the loans on their own books they were reporting exaggerated profits using the 'mark-to-market' accounting method that had prompted a champagne celebration in Enron Tower not too long before.[3] This allowed them to treat theoretically high income in the future – assuming no defaults – as profit today. They could then raise more capital to make more loans for which they could misleadingly record more profit. Eisman published a damning report on the sector in 1997, causing his desired 'shitstorm'. He was vindicated the following year when, in a nervous market following the collapse of the Long Term Capital Management hedge fund, many of the first generation of subprime lenders went bust.

The lesson of this episode was that with some curiosity and application, it *was* possible to identify looming disaster in the subprime market. It had taken Vinny Daniel six months to review all the pools of loans being sold. That was just half a bean-counter year. So when subprime mortgage lending began to grow again in the early 2000s, it was eminently feasible to assess the quality of the loans, and thus to account for them properly at more realistic values taking into account predictable losses based on past and current performance. While the financial crisis that would follow was triggered by a breakdown in complex markets built on the back of these mortgages, the underlying cause – overvaluing suspect loans – was quite simple. Identifying it should not have been beyond the major accountancy firms auditing the lenders, and billing them for *several* bean-counter years of work on every audit. All they had to do was look.

It was no surprise that Arthur Andersen at its fee-chasing worst had given Vinny Daniel and his difficult questions short shrift. But things were supposed to have changed since conflicted auditors played along with the 1990s numbers game. Governments round the world, even Britain's 'light touch' New Labour regime, had tweaked rules and codes to make it harder for auditors to cash in on their relationships with clients. In the United States, new laws piloted through Congress by Senator Paul Sarbanes and Representative Mike Oxley had imposed stricter requirements for the independence of auditors, including stiff restrictions on the consulting services that their firms could provide to a client. Moments before he'd signed the Sarbanes–Oxley Act into law on 30 July 2002, President George W. Bush had stood in the East Room of the White House and declared: 'The era of low standards and false profits is over.'

Bush hadn't reckoned with the fact that years of viewing clients as sources of consulting income had pulled the Big Four firms so far out of shape that, like overstretched springs, they couldn't be returned to the condition required to do their job. None of the early-twenty-first-century reforms addressed the fundamental changes in accountancy in the later part of the twentieth, such as the unrelenting motive to make more profit. Indeed, by 2004, the firms that had sold off large chunks of their consultancy arms not long before were so deeply back in the game – although they now called it 'business advisory' – that the Big Four were once again earning less than half of their income from auditing.[4] Then there was the limiting of liability for inadequate auditing in the 1990s. In 2003, Nobel-prize-winning economist Joseph Stiglitz wrote that 'there are plenty of carrots encouraging accounting firms to look the other way . . . there had been one big stick discouraging them. If things went awry, they could be sued.' But with the next boom beginning, he noted with great prescience, 'insulated from [law] suits, the accountants are now willing to take more gambles'.[5]

The casino they played in was the expanding world of finance. Bank balance sheets doubled from around $50 trillion in 2002 to $100 trillion by the middle of 2007, around twice world gross domestic product.[6] In addition, the so-called 'shadow banking system' – consisting of hedge funds and special investment vehicles – grew worldwide from around $26 trillion in 2002 to $62 trillion in 2007.[7] This hyper-financialized, over-leveraged world added up to some test for the bean counters. Would they think, as their antecedents had of Britain's nineteenth-century railway companies, that here was great commercial and economic risk requiring their scrupulous attention? Or would they see the oceans of new money as a chance for the best yet of many bumper paydays?

SUBPRIME SUSPECTS

The short-sellers knew their bets were going to pay off when, on 12 March 2007, shares in Californian subprime mortgage lender New Century Financial Corporation plummeted by 90% and were suspended from the New York Stock Exchange. Three weeks later the company filed for bankruptcy. It had been brought down by lending to low-income Americans to buy overpriced properties they couldn't afford. A year earlier, the house-price bubble had stopped inflating and interest rates had risen but New Century had carried on regardless, until rising defaults left it unable to meet the demands of its own funders.

The company's lending increased from $14bn in 2002 to $60bn in 2006. It had 'a brazen obsession with increasing loan originations', Washington DC bankruptcy examiner Michael Missal would later note, 'without due regard to the risks associated with that business strategy'.[8] Sales staff were trained at a centre called the CloseMore University and rewarded with escalating commissions. Their customers were offered loans without evidence they could pay and were enticed with misleading 'teaser' rates that before long flipped into unaffordable higher ones. The company's loans, in Missal's words, 'created a ticking time-bomb'.

Since New Century was 'securitizing' and selling off more than 90% of the mortgage loans it made, if the bombs exploded they would bring down more than the company; they would blow a hole in the wider financial markets. But as the ticks grew louder, the bean counters weren't listening.

By mid 2004, New Century's managers were aware of 'alarming and steady early repayment defaults'. According to Missal, they hid this unfortunate truth with 'at least seven wide-ranging improper accounting practices'. The main one related to a kind of returns policy for the mortgages that it sold on to banks and other investors. If repayments on these mortgages were missed, or became 'delinquent' in the jargon, New Century would buy the mortgages back. At any point in time, it needed to make sufficient provision for such future buy-backs. Instead, it deliberately set these reserves far too low. It also drastically overvalued the mortgages that it kept on its own books. There was nothing too esoteric about this. The short-sellers were already looking at the details of the mortgages and concluding that large proportions of them were going to end badly.

Others who should have been looking were the company's auditors from KPMG. But the firm seemed to be more concerned with maintaining its own dominant market position. It audited all of the top four subprime lenders: New Century, Countrywide, Wells Fargo and Option One, each of which would be plunged into its own scandal. KPMG had a rich interest in the shakiest part of the American financial system appearing sound, which might explain why – in the words of the liquidators who would sue the firm in 2009 – it 'assisted in the misstatements and certified the materially misstated financial statements' that concealed the ugly truth.[9]

On the ground this had a familiar look. KPMG's so-called 'engagement partner' on New Century was ex-Arthur Andersen partner John Donovan. According to bankruptcy examiner Missal, he and his assistant 'appeared unwilling to challenge the client and in some instances may have acted as advocates for the client'. When one of KPMG's specialists refused to sign off the way New Century was accounting for some important financial derivatives, Donovan attempted to talk him round. 'All we are going to do is piss everyone off,' he said, oblivious to the fact that this might be something a decent auditor needs to do every now and then.[10] Donovan was backed up by a superior from KPMG's New York headquarters and the accounts were given the all-important clean audit certificate minutes before the 2005 filing deadline. The echoes of Arthur Andersen audit partners enlisting their bosses to overrule accountants who had rumbled Enron's scams were unmistakable.

As market conditions worsened, the amounts New Century needed to set aside for repurchasing 'delinquent' loans from investors were going up. 'KPMG's workpapers showed that the number of loans [made in the last quarter of 2005] that New Century was going to need to purchase was approximately $140 million,' reported Missal, but its reserve for the amount was a mere $70m. 'KPMG had no explanation for this large discrepancy,' he noted. In 2006, the repurchase reserves were again manipulated, this time by more than $100m, by simply ignoring the expected costs of buying back defective mortgage loans. Several people the bankruptcy examiner interviewed 'claimed that KPMG actually recommended the improper changes', suggesting more than just negligence – although KPMG disputed this. Then the auditors allowed New Century to apply improper valuation methods to the loans that the company retained on its own books, resulting in a further $86m overstatement. As a result of these and a host of other lapses in bread-and-butter accounting matters, KPMG issued catastrophically misleading clean audit certificates on New Century's accounts for three years. When a new chief finance officer arrived at New Century in late 2006 and spotted the 'stunning magnitude of the forecasting failure on the repurchase reserves', bankruptcy was inevitable.

The stock of other subprime lenders plummeted on the revelation that this wasn't such a great market after all, forcing multiple rescues by larger banks. As the *New York Times* wrote in April 2008, still four months *before* the full-blown worldwide financial crisis: 'New Century's collapse ushered in a series of failures among mortgage lenders – ultimately rocking global financial markets, forcing banks around the world to write down or take losses on nearly $250 billion in mortgage-linked securities and sending the nation's housing market into a tailspin.'[11] It is reasonable to speculate that if the accountants had done their job, then either the subprime housing bubble would not have been inflated in the first place, or it would have been deflated much earlier. Instead, poor accounting allowed the business to grow exponentially: in 2000, $130bn of subprime loans were made; by 2005 the figure was $625bn.[12] Included in this total, wrote author Michael Lewis, was a loan to a 'Mexican strawberry picker with an income of $14,000 and no English, who was lent every penny he needed to buy a house for $724,000'. Subprime lending was a loss-making business made to look very profitable by bad accounting and bad auditing.

KPMG eventually paid a small price for its disastrous auditing of New Century in the form of $45m of compensation to ex-shareholders (which would have been far higher without the liability concessions won by the accountants in the previous decade). The firm also had to cough up $24m for failings at Countrywide Financial Corp, though it was spared the scrutiny of the bankruptcy examiner by Bank of America's bailout of this subprime lender. Further humiliation followed over its role at government-sponsored Federal National Mortgage Association ('Fannie Mae'), established in response to the Great Depression to guarantee and buy up responsibly provided mortgages. KPMG audited the body as it manipulated profits so that it too could wade into the subprime mire, from which it would eventually be hauled by the American taxpayer.[13]

The sad irony of KPMG's role in the subprime debacle was that the American side of the firm had been built on cleaning up dubious mortgage finance, not encouraging it. In New York in 1895, records the firm's historian, '[James] Marwick's first engagement was to audit the accounts of a mortgage finance company . . . [where he] found that some securities had been overvalued by as much as $350,000.'[14] When the directors of the mortgage company voted to ignore his suggested provision, the 'intrepid Marwick then turned around and wrote up an audit report in which he not only called attention to the excessive values at which the securities were listed but also stated that the directors had refused to make any provision to cover this deficiency'. Faced with such a determined bean counter, 'the directors gave in and unanimously voted to rescind their previous resolution'. One hundred and ten years later, James Marwick's successors, 'unwilling to challenge the client',[15] as the New Century bankruptcy examiner would put it, were the ones who gave in. In place of steadfastness and probity were surrender and self-enrichment.

PARTY TIME

By the early 2000s, most of the big investment banks like Lehman Brothers and Morgan Stanley were run by men who had made their names as 'big swinging dicks' on the 1980s trading floors. Although now a few lift-stops up in the boardroom, they were no less macho and certainly hadn't lost their appetite for the green stuff. So they couldn't get enough of the packaged-up mortgage loans that subprime lenders were churning out by the billions of dollars' worth every month, either holding them or spinning them on to other investors such as pension funds.

This demand in turn emboldened the subprime lenders to sell home mortgages more aggressively; to 'feed eagerly the wave of investor demands', in the New Century bankruptcy examiner's words. That in turn meant even lower-quality home loans.

The risks from the increasingly toxic raw material being fed into the investment banking machine weren't merely transferred from one set of financial institutions to another; they were multiplied. Where the 1980s bond traders had dealt in relatively straightforward bundles of loans – so-called 'mortgage-backed securities' – their twenty-first-century counterparts went one step further. They created the 'collateralized debt obligation' (CDO), in which the mortgage-backed bonds themselves were bundled up, often with other debts such as credit card bills or corporate bonds. The income from these CDOs could then be sold in 'tranches' carrying different risks. The riskiest would have to take the hit from defaults up to a certain amount, the next tranche up a subsequent loss and so on. A CDO could have up to fifteen tranches, each of which would be separately traded.

But that wasn't enough. The tranches could themselves be parcelled up into securities, so-called 'CDOs squared'. Then, multiplying the size of the market, all these instruments could be betted against using 'credit default swaps' (CDSs). This was a financial derivative equating to an insurance policy that paid out if a particular security or tranche defaulted, but without any requirement to hold the underlying asset (a bit like having fire insurance on somebody else's house). Finally, these CDSs too could be packaged up, re-sliced and sold on as 'synthetic CDOs'. With deregulatory governments egging on the industry creating this alphabet soup, about a trillion and a half dollars of subprime mortgages outstanding in 2007 translated into several trillions of dollars of the new exotic financial products.[16] All were laced with the poison of the underlying assets, which became more potent as it passed up the financial food chain. As Wall Street's predators gorged, it was essential that the watchdogs were watching. Their failure to have looked too closely at the subprime loans going into the investment banking machine made it all the more essential that they ensured the weird and wonderful stuff it turned them into was properly accounted for.

The bean counters' priorities were unfortunately somewhat different, as their presence at one industry event showed. At the annual Issuers' and Investors' Summit on CDOs/Credit Derivatives in New York in March 2006, senior accountants from all the Big Four firms sat alongside bankers from Merrill Lynch, Barclays, Bear Stearns, Goldman Sachs and other big Wall Street names. While the traders and investment professionals discussed the market's towering prospects in sessions such as 'CDOs for safe haven, CDOs for outperformance', the bean counters might have been expected to sound a note of caution. But their sponsorship of the event and pitches in the conference programme gave away other intentions. KPMG was proud that 'we are a team of professionals devoted to serving the needs of the CDO market'. Ernst & Young, which had bought up Arthur Andersen's structured finance group four years earlier, could advise on everything from 'optimal asset selection' to 'the ultimate transaction design'. It would be '"on call" 24 hours a day, seven days a week, to offer you the immediacy your transaction demands and the responsiveness you require'. PwC claimed to be 'clear-cut leaders in the securitization marketplace'. Deloitte had worked on 'more than 14,000 securitized offerings with an aggregate principal amount of more than $5 trillion'. It served 'leading players in the MBS [mortgage-backed securities], ABS [asset-backed securities], CDO [collateralized debt obligation] and CMBS [commercial-mortgage-backed security] markets' with 'state-of-the-art products and expert services in financial modeling, analytics, technology, operations, due diligence, accounting and tax'.[17]

Whatever Paul Sarbanes and Mike Oxley thought they had achieved in eliminating accountants' conflicts of interests with their post-Enron legislation, a major new one had emerged in the form of the Big Four's reliance on the financial markets. The patchy information released by the firms showed that in 2005, for example, KPMG's revenue from financial services businesses rose by 17% to $3.9bn, or a quarter of its total income. PwC could claim to be acting as adviser to 95% of all large companies in the banking, capital markets and investment management sectors.[18] All the firms had 'structured finance groups' to help the banks create vast numbers of financial products while auditing the books of the other banks that were buying them up. The relationship was particularly close at the firms' UK arms. PwC, for example, was now earning 30% of its revenues from financial services.

It paid the bean counters to think like the cheerleaders of the new financial order. The star turn at KPMG's 2007 conference on the world economy at London's swanky Claridges hotel was Alan Greenspan, the just-retired Federal Reserve chairman who bore no small responsibility for the freewheeling economic conditions that were so conducive to the subprime bubble. In 2003, he had claimed that 'the use of a growing array of derivatives and the related application of more sophisticated methods for measuring and managing risk are key factors underpinning the enhanced resilience of our largest financial intermediaries'.[19] He'd inflated the world economy after the dot.com slump and fiercely opposed moves to regulate trading in financial derivatives like the credit default swaps that cranked up the subprime system. All of which was now adding billions of dollars to the Big Four's own financial services profits. The 'rock star' central banker was their kind of guy.

The bean counters could more usefully have listened to one of Greenspan's predecessors. Back in the 1960s, Federal Reserve chairman William Martin had said that his job was to 'take the punchbowl away when the party gets going'.[20] The accountants ought to have played a similar role, at least pointing out just how drunk the banks had become on the financial cocktails they were sinking. But the modern bean counter, grooving along with the traders, wasn't going to poop this party.

SUB-STANDARDS

The accountants were also setting the rules of the party games, in ways that encouraged excess rather than restrained it. Since the 1970s, as their global empires grew, the major firms had been attempting to standardize accounting around the world, on the principle that cross-border investment demanded common accounting standards, or 'convergence' in the jargon. The vehicle for the project was an International Accounting Standards Board, which from the outset was dominated by veterans of the major firms that were also funding the project. By the 1990s, its main job was to agree new accounting rules for the myriad financial products that had transformed banking over the previous decade or two.

The key measure was International Accounting Standard 39, which made two critical changes to the way banks account. Firstly, with due deference to the markets, it enshrined the principle that assets held with a view to being sold on – so-called 'trading assets' – should be counted on the balance sheet at 'fair value'. This was a euphemism for the mark-to-market method common in American financial reporting. In 2005, the standard was duly adopted in Britain, aligning its banks' accounting more closely with that in the United States. But at a time of growing financial complexity, 'fair value' methods took accounting further into the realm of make-believe. The core principle was to value trading assets at what the market would pay for them. Now, however, large chunks of the world's financial trading were taking place 'over the counter', or away from exchanges that published market prices. Values couldn't simply be looked up. So the new standard allowed something called 'mark-to-model'. This meant that whatever valuation a bank's internal systems threw up, it would enter the accounts. The system came to be known, with good cause, as 'mark-to-myth'. Five hundred years earlier, the Father of Accounting Luca Pacioli had advised traders to 'make the prices rather higher than lower . . . so that you can make a larger profit'. Twenty-first-century computer models would prove adept at doing this. Some in the Big Four, mostly the technicians not let too near the clients, feared the dangers. In a May 2005 paper, one Ernst & Young partner described how mark-to-market methods 'bear little or no relation to cash flows, may cause confusion when unrealized gains are included and may produce valuations that fluctuate considerably year-on-year'. Moreover, the 'relevance and reliability' of accounts 'could be compromised by the use of mark-to-model calculated "fair values"'.[21]

The second major change brought in by International Accounting Standard 39 (IAS39) had equally profound consequences. It governed assets that weren't valued on 'mark-to-market' methods because they weren't owned with a view to being sold on. These were mainly loans to customers. Under the new rule, a bank would make provisions for losses on loans only when it was clear that it wasn't going to get its money back. Again, this was closer to the American approach.[22] Previously, if a bank made, say, £100m of loans to customers of a sort that experience said would default 5% of the time, it would set aside £5m for 'expected losses'. But under the new rule it didn't have to set aside anything until, at some point in the future, customers actually defaulted and it had 'incurred losses'. The justification was that accounts were a backward-looking report to shareholders of a bank's performance over a period. But the result was a rosy rather than a realistic picture. More financially meaningful statements would incorporate some measure of the present risks inherent in a business. Again, more thoughtful accountants spotted the risks. A 2004 PwC paper pointed out that there would be 'a risk of a shortfall' between the accountancy view of losses and the way financial regulators ought to measure them.[23]

The new rule neglected the interests of investors and regulators, who needed the full story, warts and all. In the era of highly leveraged financial institutions, a typical balance sheet might be 95% funded by borrowing, 5% by capital. A mere 5% off the value of the assets would wipe out the bank's capital. Ignoring it, as might now happen, could make a bank look sound when it was really a basket case. The chairman of one FTSE100 company reportedly thought the scope for abuse so great that the new standard was a 'rogues' charter'.[24] (And an academic study after the crisis would find that most finance professionals thought the standard 'had undermined UK financial reporting integrity before the credit crunch'.)[25] At precisely the wrong time, prudence became a poor accounting relation indeed.

THE FALLING ROCK

The first bank to fall as a result was Northern Rock. The solidly named bank that emerged from a building society set up in the nineteenth century for workers in the north-east of England was, by the early twenty-first, a less circumspect outfit. Its business model now entailed shipping out as many new mortgage loans as possible, using cash raised on the short-term money markets, securitizing and selling off the loans to repay the debt, and then repeating the process. The bank called it a 'virtuous circle strategy of high growth in high-quality assets and profits, with improving cost efficiency'.[26] Few questioned the hyperbole while the money flowed in ever-increasing volumes. In 2006 alone, the bank increased its lending by £33bn (or 23%) and its reported profits by

£59m (19%). It was, however, paying out almost all of the latter in dividends and operating on capital of not much more than 2% of its balance sheet. The slightest write-down of asset values would eliminate that. It was a risk of which its auditor PwC was certainly aware, based on what it had said in its 2004 paper, but one about which the firm now said nothing.

Northern Rock began to use the new IAS39 accounting standard at the beginning of 2005, a year earlier than most banks. It was no longer making provision for expected losses on mortgage loans. At the same time, the consequences of the markets' excesses were becoming real: 8,200 home repossessions across the UK in 2004 became 21,000 in 2006.[27] The interest rates the bank was having to pay in the money markets were steadily rising. Yet the prospect of greater defaults in the not-too-distant future was being ignored in both the accounts that Northern Rock was preparing under the new standard and, accordingly, the numbers used in its boardroom. As chartered accountant and former standard-setter Tim Bush told a later parliamentary inquiry, 'banks are run on key ratios from the accounts'.[28] And these accounts were giving chief executive Adam Applegarth, a 44-year-old maths and economics graduate who earned £30m in five years, the kind of ratios he liked – although even he admitted that nearly 50% profit growth in the first half of 2005 because of the new accounting method was 'faintly insane'.[29]

The madness had to end. As subprime mortgage defaults in the US spread into the mainstream banking system and credit became harder to come by, the market took a closer look at Northern Rock. In September 2007, it said 'no more'. The shunned Rock turned to the Bank of England for support. When the news leaked, the streets of Britain saw the first 'run' on a bank since Overend & Gurney a century and a half earlier. Hundreds of jobs went as Northern Rock was nationalized, with no compensation to investors, many of whom had spent their life savings on shares.

In a description applied to many of the banks a couple of years later by Financial Services Authority chairman Lord Turner, Northern Rock's returns had been 'illusory profits'.[30] Yet they justified huge payments to executives and shareholders, stripping the bank of any real capital. The episode proved that healthy numbers under new accounting standards could, as Bush later told a parliamentary inquiry, 'mask insolvency'.[31] Strong auditing might not have allowed them to. Whatever the rules agreed in a City boardroom a few years earlier, the auditors still had an overriding responsibility under company law to flag up concerns over whether a bank's accounts gave a 'true and fair' view and to report any 'material uncertainty' to its status as a 'going concern'. Certainly by 2006, a critical look at Northern Rock's loan book and minimal capital would have indicated that the bank was in peril. The new rules, however, provided auditors with a justification for turning a blind eye. They created a fool's paradise that the bean counters were only too happy to inhabit.

The evidence showed that the sooner a bank adopted the new IAS39 rules, the sooner it hit the buffers. There was also a remarkable match between countries adopting the standard and those suffering major banking crises. The UK, Ireland and Iceland took them up, while France resisted; in 2003, no less a figure than President Jacques Chirac predicted that the rules would have 'nefarious consequences for financial stability'.[32] The former countries had comprehensive banking crashes, the latter did not (until the later euro crisis). Australia adopted IAS39 but avoided disaster by prudently demanding its banks keep books on the old basis too. A retired leading partner in PwC, Northern Rock's auditor, hinted in a newspaper interview why IAS39 was so lethal: 'The rules allowed banks to pay dividends and bonuses out of unrealized profits, from profits that were anything but certain.'[33]

Four years after the run on the Rock, PwC's senior partner defended his firm with the time-honoured excuse that whatever went wrong was not the bean counters' problem. 'It's not the job of the auditor presently to look at the business model of a business,' insisted Ian Powell (who refused to be interviewed for this book). 'That is the job of management.' His firm 'did extensive work in auditing the year ending 31 December 2006 to make sure, assuming that the markets would continue as they did ... that that model would be sustained for the next 12-month period by the markets and by the continued rolling of the commercial paper [the short-term debt]'. This was the crux of the matter. The auditor had been prepared to accept heroic assumptions about the markets powering on – which had already looked questionable when the accounts were signed at the end of February 2007 – if that was what was required. The parliamentary committee questioning Powell, led by former cabinet minister Lord (John) MacGregor, was not impressed. They were 'astonished that PwC appeared not to recognize an amber light that flashed so brightly' and considered Powell's defence to be 'disconcertingly complacent'. Even if the auditors had 'performed their duties properly in a strictly legal sense' – a big if – they had failed 'in the wider sense'.[34]

This wider responsibility was important. Since the collapse of the Johnson Matthey Bank in the 1980s, legislation had been in place to ensure communication between a bank's auditor, with its inside knowledge of the books, and the financial regulator. The law required the auditors to report to the Financial Services Authority when a bank 'may not be, or may cease to be a going concern'.[35] As any half-competent bean counter would have realized that Northern Rock was in a precarious position and 'may cease to be a going concern' well before it crumbled, this obligation ought to have been triggered. Even if the auditors were shy of publicly expressing concerns over a bank's 'going concern' status for fear of spooking the markets, they should at least have put the regulator in the picture. Yet, throughout the whole of 2006, PwC and the Financial Services Authority did not discuss Northern Rock at all.

They had just one meeting and one phone call, far too late, in 2007. This, said the committee, was a 'dereliction'.[36]

The question hovering over the post-mortem was why the bean counters had been so credulous. They were certainly happy to pick up around £80,000 a time for signing off the securitization deals that were central to Northern Rock's flawed financial model and that pushed PwC's non-audit fees above its audit income from the bank.[37] When I discussed the affair with PwC's 'global head of assurance', Richard Sexton, in 2016, he said that the additional work was standard for an auditor. He also said that the 'going concern' status had been assessed properly and the conclusion correctly reached at all relevant times that it was valid. But he did confess that 'all of us in the system should have spoken a bit louder' about the emerging risks.[38] The first half of this comment seemed to betray the real problem. The accountants were part of 'the system' when they should have been standing outside it, monitoring it rather than indulging it. As Mr Sexton's job title implied, this intimacy with the bankers whom the bean counters should have been holding to account went beyond the shores of Britain. Northern Rock was merely the hors d'oeuvres to the real 'global' blowout.

GOSPEL ACCORDING TO MARK-TO-MARKET

Modern accounting wove lustrous new clothes for the early-twenty-first-century emperors of investment banking. If the market said the trillions of dollars' worth of CDOs and other financial instruments sloshing through the system were valuable (even if it didn't understand them), then that's how those on their books would be accounted for. The institutions holding them could show sound finances, borrow more and take yet more of the exotic products onto their balance sheets in pursuit of the double-digit returns they were promising shareholders. This in turn would generate more demand for subprime loans, and thus even more reckless lending practices, first across the US, then in the UK. Mark-to-market accounting was, as the economists say, 'procyclical'.

Much of the blame for this lethal cycle has been justifiably heaped on the credit rating agencies. They scored CDOs as highly unlikely to default when a look at their contents would have told them otherwise. (The root cause of this failure was similar to the auditors': the agencies were being paid by the issuers of securities and were thus similarly conflicted.) But the credit rating agencies' fallibility should not have been news to the accountants. The same agencies had rated WorldCom and Enron 'investment grade' as they faked profits for years, marking down the latter only four days before its bankruptcy. Soon afterwards, in 2003, they had been forced to downgrade hundreds of CDOs containing poor-quality corporate bonds. So although mark-to-market methods endorsed credit ratings by using the healthy values they gave to AAA-rated financial instruments in the banks' accounts, bean counters with 'professional scepticism' should not have taken the agencies' gradings as gospel when judging whether those holding billions of dollars' worth of the stuff were in any danger. For one thing, the burgeoning market in credit default swaps and the growing band of CDO short-sellers ought to have set alarms ringing.

Yet the bean counters *did* rely on misleading credit ratings as the world's largest banks multiplied their holdings of such instruments. Even when the ratings agencies demanded that, because of growing defaults from 2006 onwards, newly issued CDOs required greater 'credit enhancement' (i.e., bank guarantees) in order to achieve a AAA rating, the bean counters did not question the now obviously unmerited top ratings of existing CDOs made up of similarly unreliable subprime loans. All the major banks that would eventually go bust or be bailed out therefore received clean audit certificates on their quarterly and annual reports right up to the meltdown of late 2008. They were 'going concerns', said their auditors, with no material risk of insolvency. In reality, the banks were skating on the thinnest of ice. While engorged with the riskiest assets valued at unsustainable market prices, plus plenty more priced using fanciful 'mark-to-model' methods, they were also operating with the slimmest capital buffers against losses. In 2006, Lehman Brothers' was as low as 3%. But that was only what it was admitting to.

REPO MEN

Lehman actually had a far bigger balance sheet, and thus a proportionately smaller amount of capital to support it. But admitting this would have hurt its capacity to play in the great financial games of the time. So with the bean counters' help, it set about concealing assets and corresponding debts.

A 'repurchase agreement' technique known as 'Repo 105' became the most infamous of the deceptions. Just before the end of a quarter, for which it had to report to the stock market, Lehman would sell a batch of securities with a promise to buy them back a matter of days later. The cash generated paid off some debts, the bank looked less leveraged and investors were reassured. But then, as agreed, everything was reversed. Ordinarily such a ruse wouldn't work because the 'repo' commitment would itself count as debt. But by selecting the right assets, routeing the transaction through 'light touch' London and obtaining a favourable opinion from a City law firm, Lehman thought it could get away with it. A more obvious step might have been to *actually* sell some assets and permanently pay off debt that way. Most, however, were sitting on the books at 'mark-to-myth' and mark-to-market values exceeding what they would fetch in a large-scale sell-off. This could therefore crystallize potentially terminal losses. So cranking up Repo 105 it had to be.

At the end of 2006, assets and corresponding borrowings of $25bn were spirited off the books by Repo 105. A year later, the figure was $39bn. By the first quarter of 2008, it exceeded $50bn. The markets were impressed. '[Lehman] reduced gross leverage from 32× to 25× [improving its capital ratio from 3% to 4%],' beamed one analyst.[39] Internal Lehman emails told the real story. It was all 'basically window dressing', admitted the bank's financial controller. According to a senior colleague of his, Repo 105 was simply 'another drug we are on'. The auditors should have pointed out that the bank was hooked on it. But in return for fees of $150m between 2001 and 2008, Ernst & Young repeatedly signed off accounts that didn't mention the transaction. When a whistleblower alerted the bank's management and Ernst & Young to the deceptiveness of Repo 105 and other practices, the accountants buried the matter. In a meeting with the bank's audit committee the very day after discussing with the whistleblower his qualms about the $50bn, Ernst & Young's partners didn't even raise the subject.[40]

In a series of lawsuits over the affair, the bean counters desperately tried to wriggle out of responsibility. Ernst & Young had been repeatedly presented with evidence that Lehman's repos were spiking dramatically over accounting dates, a sure sign of manipulation that should have been investigated and highlighted in its accounts. Yet the firm claimed, according to one judge, that those suing the bank 'cannot prove that anyone at EY actually read the [relevant reports] containing information about Repo 105s, nor that anyone at EY had any duty to do so'.[41] Fifty billion dollars disappearing into the accounting ether was not, the auditors thought, something for them to concern themselves with.

Under men like Dick 'the Gorilla' Fuld, Lehman was always a high-risk bank indulging in all the era's financial vices. In Ernst & Young it found a firm that was prepared to look the other way. Five years after the events, the accountants coughed up $99m compensation for investors and paid $10m to settle accusations by

New York Attorney General Andrew Cuomo that its auditing was 'fraudulent and deceptive', but without admitting guilt.[42] This was peanuts for a firm with annual fees now reaching $32bn, more than a quarter of them from servicing the financial industry.

On 14 September 2008, after being forced to report multi-billion-dollar write-downs and with funders abandoning ship, Lehman Brothers became the largest bankruptcy ever. When the US government refused to throw it a lifeline, a full global banking crash followed and the world was brought to the brink of economic Armageddon. Without the deceptive accounting in which the bean counters were complicit, Lehman would not have reached the scale that it did or have been full of so much financially toxic waste. It might well have been saved, allowing for an orderly rather than chaotic resolution to the world's dysfunctional banking system.

DOUBLE STANDARDS

Within a day of Lehman's downfall, insurance giant American International Group (AIG) received the first taxpayer-funded bailout. Its AIG-FP financial products unit had badly misjudged the market by taking on huge exposures to the subprime market. Through the boom years it had been writing credit default swaps, insuring banks against losses on their holdings of subprime-laden collateralized debt obligations. When the CDOs began to falter and AIG's own credit rating was marked down, it was forced to hand over increasing amounts of collateral, or upfront cash on account of any final payouts, to the banks on the other end of the credit default swaps. After another rating downgrade on the day of Lehman's collapse, AIG's collateral needs rose to the point where it could no longer raise the cash demanded of it. To avoid another Lehman – with far-reaching consequences for all AIG-FP's other counterparties – the Federal Reserve stepped in with an $85bn bailout.

How had a once solid insurance company come to this? Hadn't the whole point of AIG and its financial products arm been that it could shoulder and manage risk? The US government's later Financial Crisis Inquiry Commission would pin the blame on 'its enormous sales of credit default swaps [which] were made without putting up the initial collateral, setting aside capital reserves, or hedging its exposure'.[43] In other words, AIG-FP had drastically underestimated its potential losses. Details that would later emerge of its dealings with its largest credit default swap counterparty, Goldman Sachs, revealed the helpful role of its auditor, PwC, in the under-reporting.

When the events of 2007 hit the value of Goldman's CDO portfolio, the bank had reckoned that the credit default swaps it had entered into with AIG-FP as insurance against such losses were going to have to pay out. It had therefore demanded that AIG-FP hand over more than $1bn of collateral on account of the eventual outcome. AIG-FP had taken a different view, insisting the contracts wouldn't have to pay out. As the dispute rumbled on, in several quarterly and annual reports to the markets AIG and Goldman gave widely divergent values to the swaps – which could really only have one value – and thus the collateral that ought to be handed over. Goldman was using a model that marked the contracts down by as much as 40% of their full value as it now expected to receive payments to offset the premiums it was paying. Which was fine with its auditors from PwC. AIG-FP, on the other hand, had no model at all with which to value the contracts and gave them full value with no discount. Its auditors, who also happened to be from PwC and were led by the firm's US financial services boss Tim Ryan, were fine with that, too. The world's largest accountancy firm thus sat back as two of its biggest and most systemically important clients, with its full knowledge, valued the same assets wildly differently.

If this could happen with the same auditor on both ends of

one deal, the mind boggled at what contradictory accounting involving different auditors might be out there. Warren Buffett's long-standing vice chairman at Berkshire Hathaway, Charlie Munger, voiced his exasperation in a 2009 interview: 'Two firms make a big derivative trade. The accountants on both sides show a large profit from the same trade [when the profit on one side must equal the loss on the other] . . . and nobody's even bothered by the fact that this is happening.' By way of explanation for a scenario that 'violates the most elemental principles of common sense', he offered: 'There's a demand for it from the financial promoters.' And they generally got what they wanted from the bean counters. The accounting profession, concluded Munger, 'is a sewer'.[44]

PwC did eventually prompt AIG to try to value the relevant swaps properly. But when the model it used to do so produced an unhelpful $5.1bn loss at the end of 2007, the company arbitrarily slashed the figure to $1.5bn. PwC nodded its approval. More flattering results duly appeased the none-the-wiser stock market analysts. Four months later, in February 2008, PwC told AIG that the move had been 'improper and unsupported', and that 'this deficiency was a material weakness'. The books had to be rewritten. 'Why the auditors waited so long to make this pronouncement is unclear,' the Financial Crisis Inquiry Commission would comment three years later, 'particularly given that PwC had known about the adjustment in November.[45]

Why the auditors played along with false accounting at key moments was in fact becoming obvious. Inflated profits and hidden losses were now the life support system for the financial system, from which the bean counters were profiting just like the bankers they were serving. In 2007, PwC worldwide earned $7bn of its $25bn revenues from financial services.[46] Hanging onto the major payers of these fees like AIG and Goldman Sachs was worth a little duplicity.

WRONGS AND RIGHTS

One month after Lehman's demise and AIG's rescue, the 281-year-old Royal Bank of Scotland in the UK collapsed into a heap of losses on toxic loans and financial products and had to be salvaged with what came to £45bn of taxpayers' money.

RBS had moved to second spot in the UK banking charts at the dawn of the new millennium, when its hungry finance director, Fred Goodwin, secured the bank's takeover of National Westminster Bank. Goodwin, a trim Paisley grammar school boy and Glasgow University law graduate, had become a chartered accountant at Big Eight firm Touche Ross in 1983. He'd achieved partner status within five years, at the tender age of 29, and gone on to make a name for himself with a leading role in the liquidation of BCCI bank. On this mammoth project he had reported directly to John Connolly, the man who in 1999, despite his role in the 1980s Barlow Clowes scandal, had become senior partner of what was now Deloitte & Touche. The pair were widely reported to have been close, the older man acting as mentor to the young Fred.

With the NatWest takeover complete, Goodwin, still just 42, had been promoted to RBS chief executive. Within a fortnight he'd replaced the bank's auditor, PwC, with the firm he had been working at until five years before, Deloitte. In the years ahead, the solid frame of his old colleague John Connolly would be seen beside RBS's directors at annual general meetings. As Goodwin set about turning the grand institution into a major player on the global financial markets, this was perhaps not the fiercely independent watchdog that it needed.

Central to RBS's expansion was the US investment banking business that came with the NatWest purchase, Greenwich Capital Markets Inc. Under Goodwin, this outfit became a force in the securitization and subprime markets, swallowing up mortgages and churning out securitized bonds and CDOs for the markets to play with. But as the operation expanded in the first decade of the twentieth century, the scrutiny it needed did not. Its auditors had something else on their minds: fees. Annual earnings from RBS of £9m in 2000 became £23m by 2005. Of this, £13m was for consultancy and accounting advice on the bank's largely ill-fated new ventures.[47] In the year that RBS finally collapsed, Deloitte would pocket £59m, taking its total earnings from the bank to more than £200m. But increasing his firm's fee income was what Connolly had been elected by his partners to do. Nobody could argue that he didn't deliver, from RBS and other clients. In the year of the financial crisis, *The Times* would report that he had 'steered Deloitte to a credit-crunch-busting 16% jump in 2008 pre-tax profits to £654 million'. His own pay vaulted 22% to £5.7m.[48]

Bean counters didn't make that kind of money by giving clients a hard time, and from the outset, a closeness with the RBS boardroom was apparent. 'The relationship between Fred Goodwin and Deloitte & Touche was inappropriate, ineffective and incestuous,' one senior RBS executive from the time later recalled.[49] Numbers that emerged in the wake of the crash certainly suggested this was one of the less demanding auditor–client relationships. When in 2011 the Financial Services Authority reported on the failure of RBS, it revealed that the bank had been consistently valuing CDOs and other asset-backed securities more generously than its peers. At the end of 2007, with the credit crunch now gripping the markets, European banks were assessing so-called 'super senior' CDO tranches (once considered safe) as worth 72% of their nominal value, while US banks were marking them at just 53%. RBS had them on its books at 90%. The regulator concluded that 'there was a bias to optimism by RBS senior management in its approach to CDO valuation issues at end 2007 and the start of 2008, and an acceptance of that optimism by RBS's auditors . . . which with hindsight is difficult to justify'.[50] This was, however, insufficient to warrant any sanction for the bankers 'in light of

Deloitte's sign-off of the accounts'. The comment made a broader point about how the banker–bean-counter double act kept itself out of trouble. The banks were excused because the auditors approved the numbers. The auditors were let off because the banks were responsible for the numbers.

Misplaced confidence in RBS's figures, thanks in part to Deloitte's silence, enabled the disastrous acquisition of the worst parts of Dutch bank ABN Amro to go ahead in late 2007. RBS's worldwide balance sheet ballooned to the point that at the end of 2007, a 'trading book' holding £470bn worth of assets for resale, including plenty of the era's more noxious products, was backed by just £2.3bn of capital. The 'banking book', holding mostly corporate and personal loans, was also harbouring losses running into tens of billions of pounds for which provisions of just a few billion had been made. For a bank dependent on short-term money markets, this was more than precarious. When Lehman folded and these markets froze, the only answer was the taxpayer's munificence.

Britain's Financial Services Authority passed no judgement on the bank's auditors in its 2011 report. Since its findings were based on earlier (unpublished) work commissioned from PwC, this wasn't surprising. An accountancy firm with skeletons in its own financial crisis cupboard might not have been keen to spotlight the role of the bean counters in the years up to the crash. Deloitte's performance on RBS, said the FSA, was a matter for its regulator, the Financial Reporting Council (FRC). This body was handed some papers and invited to investigate, but the case disappeared without trace. Five years on, when I tried to find out what had happened, the FRC told me it 'did not conduct a formal investigation into Deloitte's audit of the financial statements of RBS' and refused to say whether it had even performed an informal review. Some pressing questions hanging over the largest British banking collapse in history therefore weren't asked, never mind answered. Why hadn't Deloitte queried whether the highly leveraged institution was at risk of not being a going concern much earlier? Why had Deloitte talked just once to the financial regulators during the tumultuous year of 2007 and not at all in 2008? Why had Deloitte accepted overvaluations of the bank's assets? How close had Fred 'the Shred' Goodwin and his mentor John Connolly remained while the latter's firm audited the bank?

It was left to a group of RBS shareholders to shine a little light on Deloitte's work at RBS. They were seeking compensation for losses from a share rights issue in the spring of 2008, claiming they'd been lured into the deal on a false prospectus. In the document accompanying the invitation to buy shares, issued on 22 April 2008, the prognosis for RBS's troubled loan book and other assets such as CDOs was critical. A draft announcement, produced a couple of days before the final version, had addressed the point head on. Estimated losses would be '4.3bn net of tax . . . from write-downs in respect of credit market exposures in 2008', i.e., the whole year. This was more than a little misleading. The bank was then just three and a half months into what was always going to be a torrid year. US investment bank Bear Stearns had been bailed out by J. P. Morgan the month before, and RBS's own capital plans already anticipated further write-downs exceeding the £4.3bn. So Deloitte's lead partner on RBS, Steve Almond, responded to the draft by deleting 'in 2008'. The wording, he emailed, 'implies there will be nothing more [i.e., no further write-downs] in the next 8 months'. That wasn't all. 'Reference to "outlook" again implies write-downs are forward-looking,' he added. 'Not allowed under accounting rules and not what has been done.' Independent bankers from Goldman Sachs, also working on the deal, shared Almond's objections. But when he noticed that his amendments had been rejected in the next version, he simply wrote back that 'my comments that applied to the previous 2 drafts have not been acted upon so I assume [RBS] is happy to run the risk that the write-downs are interpreted by readers as including provisions for what may happen through to the end of 2008, notwithstanding that this is not what has been done and, of course, is not allowed under accounting rules'.[51]

The following day the rights issue was announced, on the terms that Steve Almond had objected to. It even received the thumbs-up from Deloitte. The financial information, complete with what Almond viewed as a misleading outlook for 2008, had been 'properly compiled', the firm certified. The investors piled in, only to lose almost all their money within a few months. Court documents would show that RBS's lawyers, Linklaters, had emailed Almond at 11.29 the night before the rights issue, recording that in an email earlier that evening he had agreed his concerns were 'not of a fundamental nature'.[52] Deloitte, it appeared, had not stood its ground against the wishes of an overbearing management. RBS eventually settled the legal action out of court for £200m.[53] The bean counters paid no price.

SCOT-FREE

Scotland's other main bank, the Bank of Scotland, had merged with former English building society Halifax in 2001 and embarked on its own aggressive strategy. This too ended with a rescue in the shape of a takeover by Lloyds Bank and an injection of taxpayer cash. The title of one of Parliament's post-crisis Banking Commission reports would sum up the affair: 'An accident waiting to happen: the failure of HBOS'.[54] It could have added: 'as allowed by the bean counters'.

A more detailed investigation by the Financial Conduct Authority (which replaced the failed Financial Services Authority in 2012) and the Bank of England in 2015 would set out the bank's descent into insolvency.[55] More than 10% of a loan book exceeding £500bn turned out to be bad. Yet in 2006 and 2007 HBOS had been setting aside less than £2bn (0.4%) a year for losses. Provisions for losses had grown more slowly than loan defaults and been consistently at the lower end of ranges agreed with auditors KPMG. The regulator's report was littered with concerns about whether the auditors had been tough enough with the bank. Although junior auditors had raised concerns about levels of provisions, they hadn't, for example, checked flawed procedures for moving loans from a so-called 'good book' to a 'bad book', where they would be more critically assessed. KPMG had nevertheless consistently vouched for growing profits and the absence of material threats to the bank's going-concern status.

The same bean counters had also played a heavily conflicted role in silencing dissent. In 2004 – early enough to have made a real difference – HBOS's head of risk, Paul Moore, had objected internally to the bank's unbridled risk-taking and inadequate controls. He'd been sidelined and then sacked. His complaints, though vindicated five years later, had been investigated and dismissed by none other than auditor KPMG.[56] The accountants had a certain interest in siding with the bank: in eight years, KPMG would earn £56m from auditing HBOS, plus a further £45m in consultancy fees.[57] Perhaps unsurprisingly, these amply remunerated auditors hadn't taken any concerns into the boardroom. As the bank's chairman Lord Stevenson would later testify, 'there were never any issues raised' in his personal meetings with KPMG's audit partners.[58] This was entirely in line with a telling comment from the lead partner on the audit, Guy Bainbridge, in his firm's 2007 annual report: 'Our focus is on creating the most constructive relationships.' Some destructive analysis of HBOS's unrealistic accounting might have been more useful.

Just as with the out-of-control subprime lenders in the States, the non-confrontational KPMG's name appeared on more clean audit certificates for the major failed UK banks than any other firm's. Bradford & Bingley, another former building society, overstretched itself in the buy-to-let market and underprovided for the risks before it too had to be taken over by the government. Even the ethical Co-operative Bank succumbed to the hubris of the times and faced the humiliation of a rescue by hedge funds. Both its intoxicated management and its auditor KPMG had ignored some of the worst of Britain's subprime loans when it had bought the Britannia Building Society in 2009.

NOTHING TO SEE HERE

Although suspect accounting was at the heart of the downfall of Britain's banks, the country's public accountancy regulator, the Financial Reporting Council (FRC), appeared reluctant to delve into it. The only punishment for the bean counters over their work before the crash came in connection with minor subprime lender Cattles plc. In 2016, PwC was heavily fined over the 'seriousness of audit failings in relation to the critical area of impairment provisioning [in 2007]'.[59] Yet the regulator ignored the same firm's work at Northern Rock, Deloitte's at RBS and – initially – KPMG's at HBOS. More than six years after the crisis, and having been told by the chairman of an influential parliamentary committee that the latter omission was a 'serious mistake', the FRC did open a file on the case but closed it just over a year later with the conclusion that KPMG's work, including on the critical question of whether there were material uncertainties over the bank's going-concern status, 'did not fall significantly short of the standards reasonably to be expected'.[60] The credibility of this conclusion took a blow when leaked minutes of a December 2007 meeting among leading accountants revealed that the accountancy regulator at least had been 'fully aware that there may be going-concern problems in relation to the forthcoming year-end and sectors such as banking'.[61] With Northern Rock already at the banking knacker's yard and HBOS looking likely to head there next, these doubts had almost certainly included the Scottish bank. But KPMG had taken the HBOS board's word that funding would continue to be forthcoming. That, decided the regulator, got the firm over the depressingly low bar required to escape any censure.

Regulatory indifference had already been apparent some years earlier. When the House of Lords committee looking at the banking crisis had questioned FRC chief executive, former civil servant Stephen Haddrill, one peer had asked: 'As a matter of interest, who were the auditors of Northern Rock?' That was in November 2010, just three years after the Rock had been bailed out with £20bn of public money. It might have been hoped that the accountancy regulator would have been deep into an examination of the part that accountancy had played in the crisis, including this key episode. A parliamentary report on Northern Rock had already criticized PwC's conflicts of interest. Yet the answer from Britain's top accountancy regulator had been: 'I can't recall, I'm afraid.'[62]

In the autumn of 2017, I met Mr Haddrill at a conference and asked him whether he thought his organization had responded adequately to the financial crisis.[63] He admitted some frustration at the time it had taken to examine KPMG's work on HBOS, but said this was because the findings of the banking regulators had to be looked at in conjunction with the auditor's files – which could be done only after those other regulators had finished their work. He agreed that this pushed his organization to the back of the regulatory queue, but argued that new powers to access company records would allow him to start investigations earlier in future. I wasn't persuaded, however, that they will transform Britain's accountancy regulator into one that really wants to unearth poor accounting at the most important institutions.

Post-crisis inaction wasn't confined to the UK's regulator. Ireland was hit harder than anywhere else by the crisis after its major banks made preposterous, sometimes criminal, loans and investments. Yet none of the accountancy firms that slept through it all were disciplined. In 2016, an exasperated Dublin judge presiding over legal action against Ernst & Young for its work on Anglo Irish Bank – scene of the most dramatic downfall – remarked: 'It beggars belief that Ernst & Young signed off on the accounts. How they signed off on the accounts as true and fair is a mystery to me.'[64] But the local Chartered Accountants' Regulatory Board had already declared there was nothing for them to see. Nor did the American regulators take any action against the auditors of Lehman or any of the other crisis-era accounting basket cases. It later emerged that lawyers working for the Financial Crisis Inquiry Commission had recommended referring PwC to the Department of Justice over AIG's 2007 misstatements, as they 'may be liable as aiders and abettors of the false representations'.[65] This was how serious it was, but neither the justice department nor the US accountancy regulators took any action.

The docility of regulators who should have been policing the rules and challenging the Big Four's performance in the wake of the crisis might be explained by their capture by those very firms. In the UK, the chairman of KPMG's public interest committee, former mandarin Sir Steve Robson, sat on the board of the Financial Reporting Council, as did the firm's recently retired senior partner, Sir Mike Rake (from 2007 to 2011). Alongside them were the former senior partner at Ernst & Young, Nick Land, and a couple of PwC partners. Another KPMG veteran was in charge of 'conduct', i.e., looking at whether to investigate firms like KPMG over its audits. This did not look like a body of (mostly) men that was going to ask the Big Four, run by their old colleagues and paying their pensions, too many searching questions. The chief accountant at the US Securities and Exchange Commission, who oversees the Public Company Accounting Oversight Board (PCAOB), has for twenty-five years been a former top partner at one of the (now) Big Four firms. Since the financial crisis, the job has alternated between veterans of Ernst & Young (of

Lehman infamy) and Deloitte (auditor of bailed-out Bear Stearns, Washington Mutual and Fannie Mae during the subprime crisis). Although the PCAOB has long been aware of the firms' shortcomings, reporting annually on a host of anonymized 'audit deficiencies', it too shied away from investigating the Big Four's performance in the financial crisis or any of its key episodes.

'The high standards of your profession will be enforced without exception,' George W. Bush had said to the bean counters at the White House in the summer of 2002. 'The auditors will be audited. The accountants will be held to account.'[66] A decade and a half and a global economic crisis later, the world is still waiting.

PEER REVIEW

If the regulators weren't going to look at the role of the bean counters in the crisis, there ought at least to have been some democratic scrutiny. But this, too, has been limited. In the US, the Financial Crisis Inquiry Commission's report made only passing criticisms of Ernst & Young's work on Lehman and PwC's on AIG, to no real purpose. The other Big Four firms, Deloitte and KPMG, simply didn't feature in the 530-page tome, despite their deep involvement. The averted gaze of the political establishment might just have been connected to a ramping-up of lobbying and political funding by the Big Four in the aftermath of the crisis. 'Time and time again Congress had the chance to call one, or all four, of the auditors of the major banks and investment banks that failed,' said leading American accountancy commentator Francine McKenna. 'They never did.' The reasons included 'a lack of understanding of the auditors' role in the capital markets, the revolving door between congressional staff roles and lucrative positions in the Big Four' and 'a long-standing reluctance of legislators to call some of their biggest and most reliable donors and active lobbyists to testify under adversarial conditions'.[67]

In the UK, the most searching probe came from a House of Lords committee set up in 2010 to look at the important but less urgent question of over-concentration in the audit 'market'. It soon realized it would serve a more useful purpose by asking why the accountants seemed to have failed so badly in the financial crisis. The peers faced well-rehearsed defensiveness from Britain's top bean counters. KPMG's senior UK partner, John Griffith-Jones, sat in the wood-panelled committee room and insisted his job was primarily to 'count the score' at the end of a period. 'So, for example,' he said, 'if you have a company that has leverage of 100 times [so capital of just 1% of its balance sheet] and a company that has no leverage at all [entirely funded by capital, with no debt], the audit report is the same.' As shown by simple arithmetic (the former company's assets would need to fall in value by just 1% for it to be bust), not to mention financial crises through history, extreme leverage has a decisive bearing on a company's status as a going concern and therefore the audit report. But on this point the bean counters thought they had a get-out-of-jail card.

Deloitte's top man, John Connolly, nonchalantly dropped the bombshell that the going-concern certificates for the banks' 2008 year-ends – in the teeth of the crisis – had been given after a meeting with Treasury minister and former asset manager Lord (Paul) Myners in December of that year. The minister then confirmed that he had reassured the Big Four firms that the government was 'committed to taking whatever action is necessary to maintain financial stability and to protect depositors and the taxpayer'. The accountants interpreted this to mean that the government would keep all banks afloat with the necessary multi-billion-pound bailouts. So, no matter how poor their finances, they remained going concerns. Committee member Lord Lawson, a former Chancellor of the Exchequer, called this 'astonishing'. The accountants told nobody that such support was critical to their clients' status, even though a nod and a wink from a junior minister fell well short of a cast-iron guarantee. And it was, of course, no excuse for failing to address going-concern doubts in earlier years. 'It cannot (or at least should not) be taken for granted by auditors that banks in difficulties will be bailed out by the authorities and the taxpayers,' concluded the committee.[68]

The peers hit another nail on the head when they looked at the role of the IAS39 accounting standard. By 'limiting auditors' scope to exercise prudent judgement', the new rules produced 'an inferior system which offers less assurance'. The bean counters protested that the long-standing 'true and fair' override remained, but the peers had no trouble seeing that IAS39 brought in a system in which 'a box-ticking approach is replacing the exercise of professional judgement'. Overall, they concluded, 'there was no single cause of the banking meltdown of 2008/09', but 'the complacency of the bank auditors was a significant contributory factor'. Two years later, the parliamentary commission on banking standards endorsed their view. 'Auditors and accounting standards have a duty to ensure the provision of accurate information to shareholders and others about companies' financial positions,' it found. 'They fell down in that duty.' The result was that 'accounts conspicuously failed accurately to inform their users about the financial condition of banks'.[69]

Others went further still. Tim Bush, the chartered accountant who was now representing institutional shareholders in major companies, said this was a 'crisis largely caused by accounting'.[70] Over in the States, veteran investor Charlie Munger argued that 'a majority of the horrors we faced would not have happened if the accounting profession were organized properly'.[71]

ONWARDS AND UPWARDS

After the City of Glasgow Bank collapse in 1878, Britain's chartered accountants had stepped in to clean up bank accounting. In doing so, they had enshrined auditing as an essential safeguard at the financial heart of capitalism. One hundred and thirty years later, it failed badly, and its twenty-first-century custodians had much to answer for. But by now they had created a world for themselves in which, even amid economic carnage, they would not face accountability. Quite the opposite, in fact. Those who audited the banks in the years leading up to the crisis have since been promoted to some of the most senior positions in accountancy. Those above them, who led the Big Four and set their cultures, have been garlanded and appointed to the boards of the world's most powerful companies, including its largest banks.

The worldwide chairman of RBS's auditor Deloitte until 2007, William Parrett, moved swiftly onto the board of Swiss bank UBS to run its audit committee. The firm's UK senior partner and Parrett's successor internationally until 2011, John Connolly, became chairman of controversial outsourced public service provider G4S. He in turn was succeeded as Deloitte worldwide chairman by Steve Almond, the lead auditor on Royal Bank of Scotland between 2005 and 2009.

PwC's British leader in the years up to and after the Northern Rock collapse, Kieran Poynter, retired in 2008 and glided into the boardrooms of British American Tobacco and the holding company for British Airways. The firm's US boss while it signed off multi-billion-dollar discrepancies in values of derivatives for AIG and Goldman Sachs, Dennis Nally, became its worldwide chairman in 2009. When he retired in 2016, he moved onto the board of investment bank Morgan Stanley. Meanwhile, Tim Ryan, the man who ran the financial services practice as it approved different values on the same contracts for AIG and Goldman Sachs, continued his rise up the ranks and in 2016 became chairman and senior partner of PwC in the US.

Ernst & Young's top dog during the Lehman debacle, Jim Turley, became a director of a bank that was bailed out in the ensuing mayhem, Citigroup. (He also took the helm at the Boy Scouts of America, who it must be hoped guard their 'Be Prepared' vow more carefully than EY did.) William Schlich, Ernst & Young's lead audit partner on Lehman, who ignored the $50bn Repo 105 scheme, remains its 'global banking and capital markets' leader.[72]

But it is the top bean counters at KPMG who have fared best of all. The firm's international chairman until 2007, presiding over a multinational accountancy firm that mis-audited the subprime lenders and stood by as HBOS lent its way to catastrophe, was Mike Rake. He was soon hopping in and out of several boardrooms as Sir Mike, lending an air of assurance to companies including Barclays Bank, as deputy chairman, and the parent company of credit rating agency Standard & Poor's. The chairmanship of BT and a raft of worthy public positions – including a directorship of the Financial Reporting Council, the accountancy regulator – would also add to his glittering CV. Under Rake, the man who led KPMG's auditing practice as the American subprime lenders ran riot in the early 2000s was Timothy Flynn. He became the firm's US chairman in 2005, then a couple of years later its worldwide chairman, until 2012. Retirement into some plum boardroom positions, including one at investment bank J. P. Morgan, followed five years later.

The British establishment also embraced the bean-counting veterans of the crisis. KPMG's senior UK partner until 2006, and thereafter European leader, while it audited HBOS, Bradford & Bingley and the Co-operative Bank, was John Griffith-Jones. In 2012, Chancellor George Osborne rewarded the Old Etonian with the chairmanship of Britain's new financial regulator, the Financial Conduct Authority. Somewhat embarrassingly, Griffith-Jones was repeatedly forced to leave the boardroom when the scandals that broke on his bean-counting watch at KPMG were discussed. More recently, when KPMG came to elect a new British chairman in 2017, its partners chose Bill Michael. He had been in charge of auditing financial services companies such as HBOS and the Co-op Bank in the critical period from 2005 to 2009.[73]

These men had all made millions from the expansion of their firms through the boom years leading up to the crash, much of it from the banks themselves. Yet none ever had to account for his organization's performance or his own record in setting the priorities, the incentives and the tone of the 'professional services' firm he ran. I invited the British leaders during those years – Rake, Connolly, Poynter and Griffith-Jones – to be interviewed for this book. All declined.

Given the trillions of pounds, dollars and euros that the financial crisis and its ongoing fallout have cost economies and taxpayers, some contrition might have been expected from the bean counters. But then hitting the taxpayer in the pocket was not something that bothered them unduly. They had been doing so, more directly and deliberately, for quite a while.

PART II
FALSE PROPHETS
The Price We Pay for the
Failure of the Bean Counters

7

DUTY FREE

TAX AVOIDANCE: A TOXIC INDUSTRY OF
THE BEAN COUNTERS' CREATION

Tax avoidance is not new. The bricked-up facades of old English houses tell of eighteenth-century reluctance to pay window-tax bills. Rudimentary levies in the earliest civilizations doubtless had their dodgers too. But it was in the second half of the twentieth century that the practice changed from a relatively amateurish minority sport into a worldwide industry in its own right. The pioneers of this revolution were the bean counters.

When income tax was introduced in the United States in 1913, accountants like Arthur Andersen who sought to advise on it encountered suspicion from the lawyers, who considered the new levy a strictly legal matter. In 1946, the New York County Law Association went so far as to persuade a court that a local certified public accountant was illegally practising as a lawyer by advising on a tax matter. It wouldn't be long, however, before the bean counters conquered much of the territory. They had recently proved their worth measuring incomes for the 'excess profits tax' on companies that had prospered from the war economy. Post-war business expansion was turning tax advice into a more commercial discipline and the lawyers were soon forced to relinquish their monopoly. A radically new tax code in 1954 brought in a raft of measures on matters such as stock valuation and depreciation and, according to Price Waterhouse's historians, 'catapulted accountants into a central, interpretive role'.[1] So broad-ranging and complex was the new code that the firm's young tax department issued 'over 3,000 copies of memoranda analyzing specific parts of the new code' as it 'maximized its opportunities'. Ominously, noted the authors: 'As the code's provisions became more familiar, the PW tax department moved into planning and shelter work.'

'Tax shelter' became the American euphemism of choice for tax avoidance, and the bean counters were ideally placed to advise on it for their large audit clients. As the hunt for fees intensified in the 1970s, tax was to prove one of the more lucrative lines, and soon all the major firms had scores of partners dedicated to advising clients on the subject. By 1975, they were generating around a fifth of the Big Eight's US income.[2] The cost of their efforts to federal and state funds went largely unnoticed until the Washington government discovered in the mid 1980s that dozens of the top US companies were paying no tax at all. 'I didn't realize things had gotten that far out of line,' said President Ronald Reagan, shocked that his all-American one-time employer General Electric was among the non-payers.[3] The tax code was once again rewritten through a 1986 Tax Reform Act that closed many of the shelters and tightened up the loophole-riddled laws. No legal draughtsman, however, could be a long-term match for the creativity of the modern tax accountant. The now deregulated economic system allowed the big firms to turn tax avoidance into one of their most effective gambits.

For the right clients, the big accountancy firms would go to extreme lengths. Just how far would become clear in 2004, when former SEC chairman Richard Breedon reported on the looting of publishing group Hollinger – then owner of the *Telegraph* newspapers in the UK and the *Chicago Sun-Times* – by its later-jailed proprietor Lord (Conrad) Black. Under arrangements sanctioned by KPMG, around $400m of the public company's profits were stripped out between 1997 and 2003 into tax haven companies controlled by Black and his associates. These companies, claimed the Canadian press baron, owned his uniquely valuable management expertise and deserved the hundreds of millions of dollars they received. So-called 'transfer pricing' rules dictate that payments for goods or services by related companies should be at levels that would be agreed between independent parties operating at 'arm's length' from each other. This is to prevent profits being artificially shifted into lower tax areas by, for example, overpaying fees to a tax haven company. Yet KPMG, doubling up as Hollinger's tax adviser as well as auditor, chose to compare Hollinger's fees 'with the venture capital business because it was the one industry against which [its] fee structure would favorably compare'. Under 'more traditional methods', KPMG would admit to investigators, the management fees 'were substantially in excess of an arm's-length price'. For the right fees, the Big Four firm was prepared to subvert the now long-established golden rule of international tax.[4]

Thanks largely to the bean counters' cross-border machinations, of which Hollinger was just a rare publicized example, between 1990 and 2005 the share of US corporate profits made in tax havens almost doubled. While the headline federal tax rate remained steady, the effective rate paid by US corporations consequently fell from 30% in the 1990s to 25% in the 2000s.[5]

It might have been expected that things would be different in Britain, where the accountants had built their reputations ensuring a business's numbers were right for both its shareholders and the tax authorities. As Professor Lee Seidler had written in his 1969 comparison of American and British bean counters, while American accountants were 'proud of their ability to minimize clients' taxes', their British counterparts 'appear to display little enthusiasm for such tactics'.[6] Since then, however, British accountancy had become part of the global bean-counting business and had less time for old-fashioned notions like public responsibility.

PLAYING CHARADES

As the 1990s post-Big Bang City of London created new financial instruments to enrich itself, amenable governments adapted antiquated tax laws to accommodate them. But new laws meant new loopholes. A low, rumbling level of UK corporate tax avoidance became an all-out assault by the bean counters on the national coffers.

The firm with the most substantial American heritage, Ernst & Young, was at the forefront. One of the few schemes to become public knowledge, in a country that liked its tax system kept as secret as possible, showed just what contortions the firm was prepared to put clients through to avoid tax. This was its 'tax-efficient off-market swap' arrangement, aimed at exploiting the new laws in a way that, the firm knew full well, no legislator would ever have intended. Ernst & Young's specialist tax accountants had found what they gleefully called an 'asymmetry between the [new] foreign exchange and financial instruments regimes'. This could be engineered into a complex 'currency swap', under which interest and repayments on loans in different currencies are exchanged between two parties. In Ernst & Young's clever variation, such a swap would be agreed between a client and a bank but at non-market prices for the exchange. It would, of itself, be a bad deal for the bank but a good deal for the client. To compensate, the latter would make a payment to the former 'in consideration' for 'entering the transaction'. It was like a punter paying £3,000 for a car worth £5,000 and handing over another £2,000 to the salesman on the side 'in consideration' for doing the deal. The fiscal magic, or 'tax law asymmetry', suggested the accountants, was that the extra payment would be deducted from the client's taxable profits whilst not being taxable when received by the bank.

Ernst & Young's slickest bean counters toured Britain's major boardrooms in 2001 flogging the scheme. Of the thirty buyers, who between them would have avoided £1bn in tax (or several new hospitals), it was insurance company Prudential that ended up in the courts as a test case a couple of years later. It had signed up for schemes involving payments totalling £105m to Royal Bank of Scotland and Goldman Sachs for 'entering into' the off-market currency swaps. These would have cut its tax bill by £30m and enhanced otherwise weak earnings by several crucial percentage points. For its trouble, Ernst & Young pocketed £200,000 from the Pru, with a further £300,000 'success fee' in the offing. The latter didn't, alas, materialize as tribunals and courts ruled that the payments were all part of the deals, not separate ones for entering into them – just as the £2,000 would really be part of the price of the car. Ernst & Young's description of the payment, said one judge, was 'a misnomer, a deliberate mislabelling'.[7] Now Britain's bean counters, it was clear, were happy to misrepresent transactions in pursuit of a tax break for their clients and a payday for themselves.

In the words of the UK's most senior tax official at the time, Ernst & Young was 'probably the most aggressive, creative, abusive provider' of avoidance schemes.[8] By this stage it wasn't alone, however. It had been some time since the Big Four firms with more British roots – PwC, KPMG and Deloitte – had guarded their respectable reputations by eschewing tax avoidance. The money was too good to resist. A 2001 study by one of the main pushers, Deloitte, reported that 52% of multinationals used 'novel tax planning ideas which they would expect the Revenue to challenge and/or test in the courts'.[9] Official figures confirmed this and indicated that three quarters of tax-avoidance schemes were 'purchased from the big accountants'.[10] When Chancellor Gordon Brown noticed the toll that the epidemic was taking on his finances in the first years of the twenty-first century, he required tax advisers to disclose their schemes to the authorities. Within two years from 2004, the Big Four admitted to having flogged 353 of them, each generally to dozens of clients.[11]

The richest individuals had became hungry consumers of the bean counters' products, too. Deloitte specialized in schemes that pushed bankers' bonuses through offshore companies from which the money would re-emerge as dividends or loans in order to reduce personal tax bills. In 2003, the firm corralled Deutsche Bank's 426 top earners in London into one such ruse. It didn't, however, withstand legal scrutiny. The scheme, said the Supreme Court some years later, had 'no business or commercial purpose'.[12] In fact, while the Big Four firms' adventures in artificial tax avoidance were great for their partners' pay packets, they usually turned out badly for clients. This reflected not so much the bean counters' incompetence as their willingness to sell schemes that they knew were legally tenuous (aided by equally unscrupulous lawyers ready to take a nice fee in return for an unduly optimistic legal opinion).

In the late 1990s, KPMG launched its own series of specious schemes for rich clients looking to shirk their tax dues, only to be repeatedly humiliated in the courts. A 'round the world' plan was supposed to enable customers to sell assets through a trust that, it was claimed, moved in a single tax year from Jersey to Mauritius and back to the UK to get through a loophole in the relevant tax law. When ungrateful businessman Trevor Smallwood used the scheme to dodge a bill on a large windfall on shares in a privatized rail company, he ended up as a test case. A judge concluded that his trusts had never actually left KPMG's Bristol office.[13] A string of other ruses sold by the firm around the turn of the century eventually received their own contemptuous judicial dismissals, ranging from 'entirely artificial' to 'acting out a charade'.[14]

William Deloitte, James Marwick and the firms' other founders, who had established their practices to present reality and expose charades, would no doubt have taken a dim view. But at least the British bean counters had not been accused of crossing the line into illegality (although this was partly because their enduring status and closeness to government headed off such difficult questions). The same could not be said of their US counterparts.

MAKING TAX CRIME PAY

'Accountants and attorneys should be the pillars of our system of taxation,' said Internal Revenue Service (IRS) boss Mark Everson as he unveiled a $456m fine for KPMG one summer morning in 2005 in Washington DC, 'not the architects of its circumvention.' Under pressure from a congressional committee run by Democrat Senator Carl Levin, Everson's staff had just investigated the firm's tax practices and found conduct that 'passes from clever accounting and lawyering to theft from the people'. KPMG, he announced, 'has admitted that it engaged in a fraud that generated at least $11 billion in phony tax losses which, according to court papers, cost the United States at least $2.5 billion in evaded taxes'.[15]

Of its five hundred 'active tax products', KPMG's four main ruses went under the acronyms BLIPS, FLIP, OPIS and SOS.[16] All were designed to generate tax losses that wealthy Americans could set against income they should have been taxed on. In the most actively sold BLIPS scheme, the customer would put a relatively small amount, say $1m, into a shell company. It would also borrow a larger amount, say $50m, from a bank. On this it would pay an excessive interest rate and in return receive an upfront premium of, say, $20m. The company would then set up a supposed investment fund, which would be assigned the $71m. Financial 'swaps' ensured the bank quickly got its premium back and was broadly flat on the deal. But when the whole structure was unwound within a few weeks, the $71m put into the fund had shrunk to $50m. Exploiting rules that linked the fund's loss to the ultimate owner, the tax dodger could claim to have lost $21m – and thus save several millions of dollars in tax – when he had actually expended just $1m (which made its way to the bank and KPMG as fees).

The complexity of the structures – BLIPS was one of the more straightforward ones – hid a simple truth: that these were little more than shams. KPMG knew tax losses were available only for real investments involving commercial risk, not the circular artificial arrangements it was selling to thousands of clients. Yet it misled clients into believing that they would be effective and then covered up what it was doing, 'fraudulently concealing the shelter losses and income on tax returns', according to the IRS.[17] It also flouted laws requiring tax avoidance schemes to be disclosed to the IRS, cynically calculating that the penalties for not doing so were worth paying. 'Based on an analysis of the applicable penalty sections,' ran one internal email, 'we conclude that . . . our average deal would result in KPMG fees of $360,000 with a maximum penalty exposure of only $31,000.' The penalty was worth paying because, without the subterfuge, 'we will not be able to compete in the tax advantaged products market'.[18] Fat fees came before complying with the law.

A network of up to 125 'business development managers' was established explicitly to 'help create an aggressive sales culture'. In came hard-sell techniques more usually associated with boiler-room fake share scams. One memo suggested that a good time to call a reluctant client was 'at or near estimated tax payment time when the [customer] is making or has made a large estimated tax payment and is extremely irritated for having done so'. The firm's own name was pimped out, the national head of tax acknowledging that KPMG's 'reputation will be used to market the [BLIPS] transaction. This is a given in these types of deals.' Commissions could triple the salary of a salesman hitting his target, while the more successful scheme-peddlers enjoyed a 'Performance Club 1999' trip to California.[19]

There were dissenting voices. One partner in the firm's

personal financial planning group, Mark Watson, repeatedly pointed out the artificiality, and therefore legal ineffectiveness, of the BLIPS product. But in an organization geared to profit, in which those with fewer scruples progressed to the upper ranks, he was countermanded – in graphic terms. 'It's time to shit or get off the pot,' said KPMG's deputy chairman Jeffrey Stein, irritated by the doubters. 'I vote shit.' The firm's head of 'professional practice' twice objected to the failure to disclose the schemes, Levin's Senate committee would report, 'only to be overruled each time by the head of the entire tax services practice'. Another KPMG tax expert said of the illegal concealment of the losses on tax returns (by improperly netting the artificial losses against income instead of reporting them separately), 'the whole thing stinks'.[20] He, too, was ignored.

A significant part of KPMG had become a semi-criminal enterprise in which corruption reached very close to the top of the organization. Nineteen individuals were indicted over the affair, including deputy chairman Stein. A blunder by the justice department, refusing defendants access to KPMG funds, let Stein and twelve others off the hook. A handful nevertheless received lengthy prison sentences. KPMG itself escaped the prosecution that would have brought it down, but only because this would have reduced an already over-concentrated Big Four to a Big Three. Notes of a meeting between KPMG and the US Department of Justice shortly before the 2005 settlement revealed how critical this was. 'If we go under, that will disrupt not only KPMG clients but also the national economy,' KPMG's lead lawyer Robert Bennett told US Deputy Attorney General James Comey (who would be sacked as FBI director by Donald Trump in 2017).[21] The comments confirmed what a whistleblowing ex-KPMG lawyer named Mike Hamersley had told senators two years before: 'There was a "too few to fail" attitude, that all of the firms, the Big Four and Big Five accounting firms, are doing this and they cannot shut down all of us.'[22]

Indeed, KPMG hadn't been first with the new style of tax products. It had stumbled across them in 1997 when going through the books of Ernst & Young ahead of a proposed merger (which didn't come off), and decided to catch up. But, having come to the party late, said one former partner, 'we drank more, and we stayed longer'.[23] Ernst & Young ended up paying a $123m fine of its own. Overall, the US government's official auditor estimated, from 1993 to 1999 between $11bn and $15bn per year had been lost to 'abusive tax shelters' at the hands of the big firms.[24]

The bean counters responded to their disgrace with a modicum of contrition for PR purposes, but more significantly, a desperate defence of their money-spinning ways. 'I'm extremely embarrassed by what some of our guys did,' said Mike Rake, KPMG's £3m-a-year British international chairman, after the 2005 fine was announced. His priority, however, was self-preservation and avoiding another post-Enron-style clampdown on providing non-audit services, so he added with no apparent logic: 'This confirms that from a quality of service point of view firms should continue to offer a full range of services and retain a multi-disciplinary approach.'[25] The abuse had occurred 'in a small part – a non-core part – of our tax business'.[26] The money involved – including KPMG's $115m fees from just the BLIPS, FLIP, OPIS and SOS schemes – suggested otherwise, as did the fact that by 2002, KPMG in the US was generating a remarkable 38% of its income from tax advice.[27]

In later criminal proceedings it would emerge that the dodgy business was encouraged from the very top. A March 1998 letter from KPMG US's chief executive set out the firm's shift of emphasis from traditional business to more profitable areas like tax shelters. 'The rationale for our thinking is clear,' wrote Stephen Butler. 'Clients buy products.' There was, he went on, 'an incredible opportunity to continue the aggressive growth curve we've seen over the past 18 months'.[28] Contrary to Rake's suggestion, this was not the work of a rogue unit; it was how the world's third-largest accountancy firm at the time did business.

NEW HAVENS

The *really* big money for the accountants was still in broadly legal corporate tax avoidance, and it was set to grow out of all recognition. The ease of sending money across borders in the age of financial liberalization allowed multinational companies to break up their businesses and park the more profitable parts where they would be only lightly taxed. By the mid 1990s, retailers like Gap and Nike, as well as major food and drinks companies, began selling to customers around the world from the Netherlands and other tax-efficient locations. Pharmaceutical companies such as Pfizer and GlaxoSmithKline made sure that rights to blockbuster drugs were held in fiscally friendly locations: Singapore, Switzerland, Puerto Rico. A new form of competition opened up among countries bidding to host the valuable financial capital and intangible assets that companies could now locate anywhere in the world. In return for small local contributions, these territories would enable the world's largest companies to avoid far larger amounts of tax in the countries where they really did business. The bean counters would show them how to do it.

Ireland had been offering tax breaks in an attempt to attract industry into its troubled economy, mainly from the UK, since the 1950s. Its success was limited until the late-twentieth-century era of deregulation. In 1987, at the suggestion of businessman and one-time Price Waterhouse accountant Dermot Desmond, and with the help of a study from his old firm, Irish premier Charles Haughey had established Dublin's International Financial Services Centre. Companies providing banking and treasury services for major multinationals from the city's declining docks area would enjoy a tax rate of 10%, far lower than the rate of 35% at the time in the UK, from where plenty of diverted income came. Within a year or so, fifty international banks had set up outposts in the zone.[29]

The accountants never strayed too far from the legislator's elbow over the following years. When the giants of the internet age came looking to shrink their tax bills in the late 1990s, the bean counters ensured that Ireland's fiscal system was just what they needed. No accountant was more supportive than Price Waterhouse tax specialist Feargal O'Rourke, the scion of a political dynasty who had flirted with a political career. 'There's a fair chance you can end up running the country,' he would recall a Price Waterhouse mentor telling him, 'or you can end up running here, but you can't do both.'[30] It was a mark of the importance of tax consulting in 1990s Dublin that he stuck with the firm, becoming the go-to tax adviser for successive Irish governments. One former senior official behind the country's corporate tax laws told reporter Jesse Drucker how, when he wanted to know about 'tax and how it operates in the real world', he would 'naturally pick up the phone and ask him [O'Rourke]'. So did Charlie McCreevy, Ireland's finance minister from 1997 to 2003, as the country sucked in the big US tech companies: 'I used to use him to get advice on technical tax issues and he'd give that advice freely.'[31]

The outcome is that, for over a decade, the major US tech companies like Google and Facebook have been selling products outside their home country through Irish companies that earn huge incomes but make minimal taxable profits. They manage this by paying royalties for using the genius behind their products to other Irish companies that own the relevant patents and know-how and claim to be tax-resident somewhere like Bermuda or the Caymans. The money usually flows through a Dutch company to avoid a 'withholding tax' on payments directly to a recognized tax haven. This is the infamous 'Double Irish' (with 'Dutch sandwich') scheme. It relies on multiple flaws in tax law of the sort that other countries have long corrected but with which Ireland determinedly persists. As Drucker discovered, with pressure on the Dutch government to stop functioning as a tax-avoidance conduit, in 2010 O'Rourke successfully lobbied for withholding taxes on royalties paid out of Ireland to be scrapped altogether.

Google, to pick one of O'Rourke's clients, thus pays a tax rate worldwide of around 17%, not much more than half the average of the rates where it really makes its money.[32] By 2013, largely thanks to these offshore structures, the average tax rate paid by US corporations had fallen to 20% (compared to 30% fifteen years earlier, when headline US rates were no higher).[33] When a UK parliamentary committee looked at Google's dismal corporate tax payments in its second largest market – a total of $16m for five years up to 2011 despite UK sales of $18bn, thanks to the Irish structure – it concluded: 'The big accountancy firms sell tax advice which promotes artificial tax structures . . . which serve to avoid UK taxes rather than to reflect the substance of the way business is actually conducted.'[34] The bean counters were twisting the world tax system and everybody else was paying the price. Yet Ireland wasn't the only, or the most prolific, new tax haven. Indeed, the British politicians' interest in big companies dodging their dues had been piqued a couple of years earlier by a scheme designed by PwC for UK mobile phone company Vodafone using a country right at the heart of Europe: the Grand Duchy of Luxembourg.

From 2000, Vodafone had been channelling billions of euros and dollars of its profits into Luxembourg by using subsidiary companies there to lend to real businesses within the group in Europe and America. The Grand Duchy profits were taxed at less than 1%, reducing the multinational's overall tax bill by hundreds of millions of pounds every year. So central was (and still is) PwC's Luxembourg scheme to Vodafone's success that its finance director would later admit that 'a reasonable proportion of the group's free cash flow [around $7bn a year at the time] obviously does come from the tax efficient structuring we have got'.[35] The British tax authorities initially challenged the scheme through the courts, claiming that the Luxembourg profits should be taxed back home. In 2010, however, they reached what the company's finance director called a 'very good' settlement after discussions between the country's most senior tax official, Dave Hartnett, and the UK chairman of Deloitte, David Cruickshank. So close were the top taxman and the Big Four boss, it would later emerge, that the pair settled many cases together and met on 48 occasions in five years, before Cruickshank gave Hartnett a post-retirement job at Deloitte in 2013.[36]

The Vodafone saga – a huge offshore tax scheme created by one Big Four firm and generously settled with the help of another – sparked a street protest movement, UK Uncut, and long-overdue scrutiny of corporate tax avoidance in Britain and elsewhere. But the depth of the bean counters' role in the business and their capture of the new havens still wasn't fully appreciated. That would all change when a new scandal exposed scheming so prolific that it shocked even the most jaundiced observers.

BLOWING THE WHISTLE

One afternoon in late 2010, Antoine Deltour, an auditor in PwC's Luxembourg office, went searching for training materials in his firm's chaotic IT system. Before he found what he was after, he stumbled across hundreds of secret 'advance tax agreements' between his firm's clients and the Luxembourg tax authority.

The slight 29-year-old Frenchman was staggered by the scale of the tax avoidance before his eyes, running into billions of euros and created for some of the biggest companies in the world, including Pepsi, IKEA, HSBC and Deutsche Bank. All were intricately detailed by his colleagues in PwC's tax department. Diagrams set out how millions – and in many cases billions – of euros, dollars or pounds would flow into and out of Luxembourg. In one case British pharmaceutical company GlaxoSmithKline would borrow £6bn from a Luxembourg subsidiary, which itself would sign up to a complex financial instrument called a 'zero coupon convertible bond', or ZCCB, with another Luxembourg company. The UK company would pay hundreds of millions of pounds in interest on its loan, reducing GlaxoSmithKline's taxable profits by tens of millions of pounds annually. (See Figure 8, taken from the ruling application itself.) But the effect of the ZCCB, PwC suggested in the documents, would be to eliminate any net taxable income in Luxembourg. Expenses associated with the ZCCB would be deductible from the profits of the Luxembourg company paying them, while the corresponding income of the other Luxembourg company receiving them would not be taxable. For their trouble,

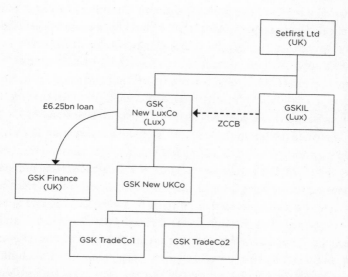

Figure 8: Extract from PwC's application for a ruling on a tax-avoidance scheme for GlaxoSmithKline, summarizing the scheme for which the firm sought approval

the Luxembourg authorities would tax an 'acceptable' 1/64% (or 0.016%) of the £6bn, leading to just a six-figure local bill. It was complicated, but it had to be: the Grand Duchy was a member of the EU and couldn't just offer tax haven rates. To get the desired tax dodge demanded something cleverer, which – as in Ireland – was where the Big Four bean counters came in. The overall result – a massive saving for the client, some useful income for the Grand Duchy and a big fee for the bean counters – suited everyone. Except, that is, the citizens who paid the price.

Almost all the dossiers that Deltour looked at followed a similar pattern. First was a covering letter addressed to director Marius Kohl of the Luxembourg Bureau d'Imposition Sociétés VI, the authority's company tax division. It contained a summary of the scheme, which was then detailed over twenty or thirty pages. Crucially, the documents included PwC's own verdict on how Luxembourg's tax law applied to them. Central to this was the farcically low taxable margin that it thought appropriate for the funds washing through the Grand Duchy and for which it sought Kohl's approval. Finally came the taxman's boilerplate response: 'I find the contents of [your] letter to be in compliance with current tax legislation and administrative practice.' More often than not, it was stamped the same day as the letter coming in from PwC.

'Appalled by their content', he would later explain, Deltour copied more than 500 rulings involving 350 companies. He sat on them for a year until, with post-financial-crisis protest movements growing around the world, he made contact with a French TV reporter. Edouard Perrin had exposed a number of financial scandals through a series called *Cash Investigation* and realized he had a new scoop: the orchestration of tax avoidance on a grand scale by the world's largest corporate auditor, with the connivance of a founding member of the European Union. But he was no tax expert and needed some help understanding how exactly the schemes worked. What, for example, was the purpose of the 'zero coupon convertible bond' deployed between two GlaxoSmithKline companies in Luxembourg? Why would billions of dollars be routed by the then *Financial Times* publisher Pearson to its United States businesses via a Luxembourg branch of an English company? As a tax inspector some years before, I had spent many hours scratching my head over such questions, so, through a matchmaker at the Tax Justice Network campaigning group, Perrin enlisted my help.

That December, the pair of us spent three days traipsing the grey streets of Luxembourg checking out some of the companies that, according to the documents, were handling trillions of dollars of the world's largest companies' funds. In fact they barely existed beyond the local corporate registry. When Perrin's film was aired in May 2012 under the strapline '*Les petits secrets des grandes enterprises*', it featured plenty of unanswered questions into tinny intercoms, plus a fractious encounter with a man supposedly administering a group of companies owned by Pearson in a single room above a sports shop. All were the cogs in an elaborate clandestine tax-avoidance operation that was saving the multinational tens of millions of dollars a year.

In Britain, my own magazine, *Private Eye*, and the BBC's *Panorama* programme exposed the PwC tax-avoidance factory at the heart of Europe, but with limited impact.[37] Until, that is, more than two years later, when Edouard Perrin passed the documents to the Washington-based International Consortium of Investigative Journalists, which had already co-ordinated some agenda-setting offshore-leak stories. On 5 November 2014, 'LuxLeaks', as it became known, dominated headlines and news bulletins around the world. '*Konzerrne ertricksen sich in Luxemburg Miliarden an Steuern* [Corporations gain billions in Luxembourg through trickery],' ran Germany's *Suddeutsche Zeitung*. '*Luxembourg, plaque tournante de l'evasion fiscale* [Luxembourg, tax evasion hub],' said *Le Monde*. 'Luxembourg tax files: how tiny state rubber-stamped tax avoidance on an industrial scale' was the splash on the *Guardian*'s front page.

Governments could no longer ignore the scandal, and from Britain to Australia launched official investigations. So did the European Commission. It found that Luxembourg's tax agreement with Fiat breached 'state aid' laws preventing governments giving special favours. It also put many other deals, including those with Amazon and McDonald's, under investigation. The European Parliament established a special investigatory committee to get to the bottom of the scandal on its doorstep, estimating that corporate tax dodging – of which Luxembourg now looked like the largest single source – was costing the continent between €50bn and €70bn every year.[38] The Organization for Economic Co-operation and Development (OECD), the steward of the international tax system, upped the pace of reform efforts to prevent multinationals shifting profits into tax havens. The Luxembourg ruling system was all but shut down overnight. As one member of the European Parliament put it, LuxLeaks was the 'game-changer'.[39]

The leaks were also a serious assault on a major financial player in the Grand Duchy. PwC was the country's sixth largest employer and a regular provider of economic, health and other consultancy services to its government. Its place at the heart of the Luxembourg establishment was symbolized by a monolithic new office, Crystal Park, dominating the skyline on a hill to the south of Luxembourg City. When the building was 'inaugurated' three weeks after LuxLeaks exploded, PwC's local leader, Didier Mouget, was joined in the ribbon-cutting line-up by both Luxembourg's prime minister, Xavier Bettel, and finance minister Pierre Gramegna. The local newspaper reported how the premier 'stressed that the building, and PwC Luxembourg itself, are synonymous with the growth of the country'.[40] This was certainly true. For a decade – as Luxembourg acquired the highest world GDP per capita by offering light regulation and tax avoidance[41] – PwC's top man in the Grand Duchy had sat on its Haute Comité de la Place Financière, advising the finance ministry. 'Transparency and innovation are the key words of this achievement,' Mouget said of the new building, 'and these two values best characterize our firm.'[42] But when real transparency arrived in the shape of LuxLeaks, it was not so welcome. PwC's dirty secrets were those of the Grand Duchy itself. They hit back hard.

On 12 December 2014, Antoine Deltour was indicted for 'theft, violation of professional and business secrecy, laundering and fraudulent access to a system of automatic data treatment'. It would later emerge that PwC had made a criminal complaint to the Luxembourg police more than two and a half years earlier, after the original French TV exposé. But with the affair having gone fairly quiet, it had hoped that the episode would be forgotten. After LuxLeaks, the bean counters needed to demonstrate that those who threatened the secretive workings of its tax haven operation would be punished. They would come for another whistleblower even more ferociously.

PHONEY CALL

Back in May 2012, Raphaël Halet was sitting at home in the Moselle region of France, a hundred kilometres south of Luxembourg, watching the latest episode of *Cash Investigation*. Halet was a 36-year-old support office manager at PwC's Luxembourg office, responsible for processing the documents that, to his rising horror, now appeared on his TV screen. 'I understood that what I was doing wasn't just administration,' he would later tell me. 'I was part of the tax avoidance system.' Deciding he would rather be part of the effort against it, he contacted Edouard Perrin to offer yet more information. The details he could provide of the Luxembourg tax returns of major companies, including Amazon, ArcelorMittal, Disney and Koch Industries, demonstrated just how the ruling system translated into billions of dollars' worth of tax avoidance. Perrin reported this new information in a second film in 2013, at which point PwC knew there must be another whistleblower. Still trying to contain the scandal, however, it kept its suspicions to itself. It was only when LuxLeaks broke the following year that the firm moved.

On the morning of Friday 28 November 2014, three weeks after LuxLeaks, Halet was in hospital in Metz receiving treatment for a long-standing medical condition. He received a call from the local police saying that his home had been broken into and his car stolen. His wife Sophie, at work nearby, was given the same message. Panicked, both raced home to discover that house and car were untouched. It had been a lie, a ruse to get them back so that Raphaël's home computers could be examined and seized on the orders of a French judge.[43]

The welcoming committee for Halet comprised a bailiff, two policemen, PwC lawyer Marc Vandemeulebroeke, a locksmith and a computer expert. Apart from the police, all were being paid by the accountancy firm. The bailiff held a warrant that was remarkable in its implications: 'Take copy of the incoming and outgoing emails from the computer equipment since 1 January 2010 until now relating to the professional activities (PwC or its clients) of Mr Raphaël Halet, including any email, and any part and attachment, addressed to or received from a journalist.' This blatantly flouted well-established press freedom laws protecting journalistic sources. It had been written by PwC and signed by an incompetent judge in Metz, who had accepted the respectable accountancy firm's drafting. She would later admit on camera for a 2016 French TV documentary on the affair that, given a second chance, 'I would without doubt delete this sentence.' (At the end of 2017, in the course of legal action taken by Perrin against PwC, even the French public prosecutor would acknowledge that the warrant violated laws protecting journalists' sources and formally retract it – albeit after the damage had been done.[44])

After entering the house, the bailiff and PwC's Vandemeule-broeke went to Halet's study, the former telling Halet to log onto his email account and enter 'Edouard Perrin' in the search bar. Up came correspondence with the journalist, for the PwC lawyer to see. 'Raphaël , you have shared information with a journalist!' Halet's wife Sophie recalled the PwC man exclaiming. 'Is this true or false? Eh, is it true?' The whole operation had been co-ordinated so that once the computers had been accessed and seized, Halet could be confronted by PwC Luxembourg's tax boss Wim Piot and its human resources director Vinciane Istace. They had been sitting 30 metres away in a black 4×4, waiting for the call to the house. Over several hours they interrogated Halet – who had no lawyer present – with the advantage of having unlawfully accessed his emails and knowing full well that he had not been in good health for weeks. 'They taunted him, they jabbed him, they brutalized him with words,' recalled Sophie.

Four days later, Halet attended a meeting with his wife at PwC's Metz office. 'It was explained to him that he would serve years in prison,' recalled Halet's lawyer, Bernard Colin. 'That he would end up almost, I think the word used by one of [PwC's] members was that if he didn't co-operate he would end up homeless.' At 3 a.m., after eight hours with senior PwC officials led by Luxembourg boss Didier Mouget, Halet was pressured into signing a confidentiality agreement. Should he ever speak of the affair, he would be liable for €10m damages – PwC's estimate of the cost to its business – and the loss of his house. In return, PwC's and Halet's lawyers agreed verbally that the firm would not pursue a prosecution. A fortnight after inaugurating their shiny new offices in Luxembourg with the promise of 'transparency', PwC had silenced Raphaël Halet.

Or so it thought. A couple of weeks later, the first whistleblower, Antoine Deltour, appeared before a Luxembourg judge and pointed out that he had not leaked all the information. There must be another source. PwC tried to conceal the identity of this second whistleblower, claiming that the man they had just tied up with a €10m gagging agreement was unimportant. The judge replied firmly that she would decide that for herself, and demanded to know his name. When told, she summoned Halet to the Grand Duchy. There, in January 2015, he was charged with similar offences to Deltour. Three months later, Edouard Perrin's name was added to Deltour's and Halet's on the charge sheet, as 'co-author, if not an accomplice, in the infractions committed by a former employee of PwC'.

THE RULING CLASSES

For several days in the spring of 2016, Court TL 1.10 of Luxembourg's Tribunal d'Arrondissement became home to the two whistleblowers and the journalist who had exposed PwC's tax-avoidance factory. As fate would have it, Perrin would take the stand on World Press Freedom Day. But it was Raphaël Halet who, having seen the tax ruling system close up, would reveal most about its inner workings. When he stood in front of Judge Marc Thill, raised his right hand and promised to tell 'la verité', the truth he was about to speak explained why PwC had been so anxious to silence him.

Halet's evidence revealed just how hand-in-glove PwC and the Luxembourg tax office had been. To partly shocked, partly amused disbelief in the packed courtroom, the former clerical manager recounted how one Wednesday every month around 1.30 p.m., PwC would take thirty to forty applications for tax rulings, many involving billions of euros' worth of transactions, to director Marius Kohl's office. He would approve most of them by 5 p.m. the same afternoon. The process was so comprehensively controlled by PwC that the firm retained the letterhead of Monsieur Kohl's tax division. It would draft not just its applications on behalf of clients but also the taxman's agreement letters. Kohl would have to do no more than add his signature – an efficient single straight line – and bang down the rubber stamp. It was not something Kohl or his superiors wanted aired in a criminal court. When the trial arrived, he submitted a doctor's note excusing himself for two weeks. His boss, Guy Heintz, director of the Luxembourg tax authority, did turn up but refused to answer the most basic questions about the operation of his department on the grounds of official and commercial secrecy.

In June 2016, Antoine Deltour and Raphaël Halet were convicted and handed fines and suspended prison sentences. Edouard Perrin was acquitted. A year and a half later Luxembourg's highest appeal court would quash Deltour's conviction but uphold Halet's on the grounds that he did not meet the Grand Duchy's definition of a whistleblower.[45] More importantly for the bean counters, however, PwC had shown anyone tempted to reveal its secrets that it would seek to criminalize them. But it could not take away from

Figure 9: The man who first blew the whistle on PwC's Luxembourg tax avoidance business, Antoine Deltour, facing charges in a Luxembourg courtroom, April 2016

the public service the three men had performed. Nor could it any longer suppress the tawdry details of its tax scheming.

A few months after the trial, intrigued by how a Big Four firm could effectively run a crucial part of a sovereign state's tax authority, I met Raphaël Halet at a café on the outskirts of Metz. Released from the shackles of confidentiality by his prosecution and vindicated by the international response to LuxLeaks, the former administrator looked considerably more relaxed than he had in the Luxembourg courtroom. He set about explaining to me the secrets of the tax-ruling production line.

PwC Luxembourg's tax advice practice had five main divisions: real estate; private equity; banking; and two units called International Tax Structuring 1 and 2. The latter was devoted to UK and US multinationals. On 'tax ruling' Wednesday every month, one partner from each unit would assemble the papers that explained the schemes for which they wanted Marius Kohl's consent. Each would take a handful of schemes, with accompanying documents detailing often highly complex transactions. They would also be carrying, for every case, a ready-drafted ruling

Figure 10: Raphaël Halet, who blew the whistle on how PwC Luxembourg's tax avoidance operation operated

notice on the Government du Grand Duchy de Luxembourg headed paper, complete with the red lion national symbol. After a ten-minute taxi ride from the bean counters' office on the main road to Belgium, the first partner would enter Kohl's office at 1.30. 'It was like meeting the doctor,' said Halet. After just half an hour or so going through his schemes, this partner would finish and the next one would traipse in. And so on until all five were done. They would leave with around 75% of their cases cleared, on Halet's estimation. The other quarter would be left with Kohl for him to chew over, generally getting their clearance in the following days. Rarely, if ever, were applications refused. Back at the office, PwC would then scan all the approved documents, put the PDF files on a USB stick and send it back to Monsieur Kohl's office so that he had records of what he'd done. At one point, recounted Halet with a smile and a shake of the head, the sticks started going astray. So PwC streamlined the process further by setting up a platform on its IT system for Kohl's office to access the documents – his own clearance notices – directly.

There was a similar rigmarole for the other Big Four firms, who had their own monthly sessions but were not so active. Where PwC had obtained around 400 clearances every year, the other firms had managed about 150 each. PwC's partners had therefore enjoyed an especially close relationship with the man known in tax circles as 'Monsieur Ruling'. As Halet told me, clients had paid PwC 'for the tax advice and also the proximity to Marius Kohl'.

INDUSTRIAL LANGUAGE

PwC had exploited its expertise, international networks and influence to siphon off billions of euros from hard-pressed economies, with an impunity denied to those who had exposed them. The closest the bean counters came to facing any accountability at all over the affair was in the British parliament, in front of the committee that had led the way in scrutinizing tax avoidance.

A couple of years earlier, when the Big Four firms had been summoned in the wake of revelations about Starbucks, Google and Amazon, PwC's UK tax boss, Kevin Nicholson, had protested that his firm 'was not in the business of selling [tax avoidance] schemes'. Following LuxLeaks, which contained schemes for British clients that would have had extensive input from PwC in London, this was no longer credible. The bean counter was recalled and accused of having lied. He denied it as only an incorrigible loophole-hunter could, claiming that since each arrangement was tailored to a company's needs, they were not 'schemes'. Members of Parliament, led by the Labour Party's Margaret Hodge, on a crusade to expose the sophistry of the tax avoiders, were having none of it. They concluded that Nicholson had indeed misled them earlier, given what it now called PwC's 'industrial scale' promotion of tax avoidance.[46] No sanctions, however, followed for the untouchable bean counters.

PwC's tax-avoidance secrets extended round the world. While Margaret Hodge tore into them in London, over in Washington DC the veteran scourge of tax avoiders, Senator Carl Levin, was examining another huge scheme designed by the firm for equipment group Caterpillar. A whistleblower from within the company had revealed the plan to shift several billion dollars of its taxable profits to Switzerland by routeing sales of parts through companies that had negotiated low tax rates in the canton of Geneva. When a change in US tax law had threatened the arrangement in 2008, two partners at PwC had discussed how to keep it working. 'What the heck,' one had emailed. 'We'll all be retired when this audit comes up [for review by the tax authorities] . . . Baby boomers have their fun, and leave it to the kids to pay for it.' For adding to the economic woes being inherited by (other people's) kids, PwC's baby-boomer bean counters picked up fees of $55m.[47]

PwC had a ready-made public relations strategy to cover its tax embarrassments. Back in 2005, after Britain's Labour government had reacted against the tax scheming led by the Big Four, PwC had decided to focus attention on what their large business clients *did* pay. Ever since then – even with its Luxembourg avoidance factory spewing out its noxious products – the firm has produced an annual 'total tax contribution survey'. (The brains behind the idea was one of its higher-profile partners, John Whiting, who would go on to run the government's Office of Tax Simplification and become a non-executive director of Her Majesty's Revenue and Customs: HMRC.) The survey adds together all taxes paid by the one hundred largest British companies: on profits and as an employer, plus indirect taxes such as excise duties and VAT. Then it lumps in the amounts companies collect and hand over to government on behalf of others, largely their staff's income tax. And hey presto! For companies controlling a large chunk of the economy, the numbers are large. The public is invited to be grateful.

This dubious gloss on reality, now extended to the US, Australia and elsewhere, in fact has little more credibility than a burglar pleading: 'Look how many houses I *haven't* broken into.' But it receives official endorsement. Just two days after LuxLeaks broke, Britain's Treasury minister responsible for tax, David Gauke, stood in the firm's offices and pronounced himself 'delighted to be joining you here today for the launch of PwC's 2014 Total Tax Contribution Report'. That the industrial-scale tax avoiders could enlist government support for their PR operation in the immediate aftermath of a global tax scandal of their making reflected the success of the Big Four firms' other strategy: getting as close as possible to power.

INSIDE JOB

In a political climate that had turned against tax-avoidance schemes following the financial crisis, the bean counters sought to shape legislation itself in ways that would provide similar opportunities but without having to exploit loopholes. Ernst & Young brazenly set up its own 'tax policy development team', run by a former special adviser at the Treasury. Its sales pitch was that 'where there has been considerable media coverage of particular "tax avoiders", policy development offers a low-risk alternative'.[48] Let us know what laws you want, in other words, and we'll persuade governments.

The Big Four's fingerprints could be found all over changes to the UK corporate tax system that enabled their clients to reduce their tax bills while legitimately claiming that they were not avoiding tax. In 2013, KPMG sent secondees into government to advise on controversial 'patent box' tax breaks for research and development (which had to be reined in after international objections) and on relaxations to laws governing offshore companies of the sort the accountants were setting up for clients in Luxembourg. Once their stints in government were over, the KPMG bean counters would then advise clients on how to make the most of these changes. During a 2013 investigation for *Private Eye*, I posed as a corporate adviser and called one of the KPMG ex-secondees to discuss the offshore changes he had worked on in the Treasury. When I put it to him that a major change in the so-called 'controlled foreign companies' laws allowed a multinational company to get tax relief twice for a single expense, he cheerily replied: 'Yes, exactly.' Another KPMG tax director advised that if I used the arrangements for my clients, 'you'd be left with a sort of minus 15 [per cent tax rate]'.[49] His counterpart at PwC told me of arrangements to achieve tax rates of 'a very small fraction of a per cent', boasting of 'a number of different structures ... there's more than one Luxembourg structure for example'.

Having engineered the right rules – so that they can reduce clients' tax bills without resorting to tax-avoidance schemes – the accountancy firms can now affect an air of great probity. Offering clients 'minus 15 [per cent]' tax rates, for example, does not stop KPMG from spearheading a 'responsible tax' campaign.

KERRCHING!

The Big Four's leading role in trashing the tax system over recent decades is no bar to them cashing in on the gargantuan international effort to put it back together again. New rules emerging from the OECD's reform programme have become serious fee-earners. All major companies, not just those that want to avoid tax, require extensive advice to comply with them. It's another service line over which the Big Four have cartel-like control. Between 2010 and 2016, while economies reeled from the consequences of their scheming over a couple of decades, the Big Four's worldwide income from tax services rose by 32% to $29bn.[50] Immediately after LuxLeaks, PwC Luxembourg itself simply won more business. 'In the tax space we grew by nearly 17% in 2016,' droned Wim Piot (giving the lie to the firm's earlier claim that Raphaël Halet's actions would cost it $10m).[51]

Not only have the accountants' finances emerged from the great tax swindle in good shape. Somehow, so have their leaders' reputations. Most of the senior bean counters responsible for the schemes and scams in this chapter have gone on to bigger and better things. Stephen Butler, the KPMG US boss who pushed for the 'aggressive growth' provided by its fraudulent BLIPS, FLIP and other schemes, retired in 2002 and took a series of non-executive directorships, including with Ford Motor Company. Mike Rake, senior UK partner while the firm promoted its highly artificial avoidance schemes and from 2002 the global chairman who played down the American frauds, retired in 2007 and, along with top directorships, took government advisory jobs, trusteeships, including at the Prince of Wales's charity, and a position with the Oxford University Centre for Corporate Reputation. His former colleague Ian Barlow, head of the UK tax team that dreamt up the 'round the world' plan and other 'charades', became KPMG's top man in the UK before also retiring into plum corporate positions. Then in 2012, he made a leap that Evel Knievel would surely have balked at, from tax avoider to chairman of Her Majesty's Revenue & Customs. Remarkably, the appointment came just weeks after Britain's Chancellor of the Exchequer, George Osborne, had described aggressive tax avoidance of the sort Barlow had peddled as 'morally repugnant'.

Nick Land, Ernst & Young's UK leader throughout its 'aggressive, creative, abusive' heyday – in the words of Britain's most senior tax official at the time – became a director of Britain's accountancy regulator, the Financial Reporting Council, where he now chairs its Codes and Standards committee. Richard Collier-Keywood, PwC's 'global tax leader', presiding over the Luxembourg tax ruling factory for a few years, was promoted to become the firm's worldwide vice chairman and now champions its 'corporate responsibility' programme. The firm's top Luxembourg tax partner since 2005, Wim Piot, remains resolutely in place, boasting how his firm now mostly helps companies comply with the tax law. 'Just five years ago,' he told one reporter in 2016 with a straight face, 'it was the complete opposite.'[52] His scheme-denying colleague, top UK tax partner Kevin Nicholson, remains at the helm in Britain. In the supposed age of responsible tax, 'industrial scale tax avoidance' is no black mark on a bean counter's CV.

After the 2008 financial crisis, even some of the top bankers, not an over-punished breed, were frozen out of boardrooms and corridors of power. Honours were removed and reputations tarnished. Yet the top accountants, who were behind so much of the tax dodging that also defined the era, didn't just escape accountability; they actually grew in status, influence and, of course, wealth. It was a measure of just how deeply the Big Four had worked their way into the fabric of the establishment.

8

GREAT BRITAIN, LLP

THE BEAN COUNTERS MARCH
DOWN WHITEHALL

The same late-twentieth-century economic forces that transformed the big accountancy firms into 'professional services' businesses making most of their money from consulting also turned taxpayers into their most lucrative clients. But since the consultants generally have their own rather than the public's interests at heart, it is a relationship that comes with a heavy price.

The Chicago School-inspired shrinking of the state gave Britain its 1980s wave of privatizations. But once these had run their course and the windfalls had been spent, the low taxes that were here to stay demanded yet more 'efficiency'. There was nowhere better to find this, ran the orthodoxy, than in the methods of the market. In place of selling off state-owned companies and utilities came the commercialization and outsourcing of public services.

The accountants' way into the consultancy bazaar that this became was largely opened by McKinsey, the firm that had itself been born out of the accountancy profession. As early as the 1970s, the McKinsey management consultants had been fomenting the near-permanent revolution that still afflicts the country's National Health Service. When this produced the 'internal market' in 1990, with hospitals competing in the name of efficiency, the NHS became a prime target for the accountancy firms now also hunting for consultancy income in Britain. Their finance expertise and IT systems, they told the new NHS trusts, would provide the all-important competitive edge. Not everybody was persuaded, however. In 1994, the Labour Party's shadow health spokesman Alan Milburn condemned 'more trading in healthcare, and more PR specialists and management consultants', who were 'all looking to make a killing in the new environment'.[1] This distaste for consultancy was not destined to last, however.

Milburn's party had already been rebranded as New Labour. It was moving away from socialism towards a broad acceptance of the economic doctrines of the Thatcher–Reagan years. As it became increasingly likely that the party would return to power under the refreshing leadership of Tony Blair, so the consultants became more helpful. Andersen Consulting provided free services to the party's mid-1990s Social Justice Commission through a consultant called Patricia Hewitt, who would go on to become a cabinet minister. Sister firm Arthur Andersen & Co.'s specialists began shaping the party's economic and tax policy and drumming up essential support in the City. One of Hewitt's Andersen Consulting colleagues, a 26-year-old named Liam Byrne, played a major role in organizing the party's campaigning and in 1996 held a seminar at an Oxford University college for 90 MPs on how to run a government. (Old Labour wasn't overly impressed. 'These management consultants are just making money out of suckers,' harrumphed former Chancellor Denis Healey.)

In government the following year, the appeal of the consultants to New Labour was twofold. They were more malleable than civil servants, who, Blair would claim a couple of years later, blocked change and inflicted 'scars on his back'. And, of more immediate value, they were adept at the financial engineering of which he and his Chancellor Gordon Brown had urgent need.

PRIVATE PARTY

Central to New Labour's election victory was renouncing high taxes and committing to sound public finances. These twin new commitments were enshrined in a self-imposed limit on government debt. But the party had also distinguished itself from the Tories by promising to improve public services that had been starved of investment. This created a fiscal conundrum. How was the extra spending to be funded without extra borrowing? The answer was something called the private finance initiative (PFI), which had been devised by the previous government but used only to a limited extent for some road extensions and a couple of prisons. The new government would put all its infrastructure eggs in the PFI basket, no longer paying for major projects out of taxes or borrowings. Consortia of banks, construction companies and service providers would borrow the money, construct the school, hospital or other facility and then make it available to the relevant public service under a long-term agreement. The magic in the scheme was that the taxpayer's commitment to pay fees for using the new infrastructure every year, typically for thirty years, would not usually count as government borrowing. The scheme would be 'off the books'.

Under cautious government rules, such helpful accounting was strictly possible only if the taxpayer was not on the hook if the scheme went wrong. The Tories had accordingly insisted that the private companies bear all the risks of any deal, which had limited PFI's appeal to the bankers and builders on whose involvement the scheme depended. So when he took office, anxious to deploy PFI for hospital- and school-building programmes, Gordon Brown set about making it more attractive to them. Under a special task force containing two consultants from Price Waterhouse and one from Coopers & Lybrand working on the all-important accounting, the rules were relaxed.[2] Private companies would be able to shoulder fewer risks, while the government would keep its essential off-the-books accounting. Not for the first – or last – time, the bean counters had written the rules of a game they would go on to play very profitably.

The other knotty problem was that, under a long-standing parliamentary principle, large projects could be signed only if they gave value for money. This was tricky when the price to be paid to the private PFI consortia had to include profits large enough to persuade them into lengthy deals and cover private borrowing costs, which were always higher than the government's. PFI was inevitably far more expensive than the alternative of conventional government funding. To get over this hurdle, a series of spurious reductions would be applied to the sum of future PFI payments when comparing the cost of a proposed scheme with paying for it through government borrowing and taxation. Many were highly subjective, involving estimates of the likely costs of vague matters such as 'operational risk'. Then there was an adjustment for 'optimism bias', on the soon-discredited assumption that traditional procurement ran significantly more over-budget than PFI. There was even a large discount for tax payments that the private companies operating PFI schemes would supposedly make but in reality did not. It was devised by KPMG at the same time as the firm was advising the PFI companies on how to avoid their tax liabilities. This usually involved treating the costs of building schools or hospitals not as an asset on the PFI company's balance sheet but as an ongoing expense, which attracted greater tax relief. Many of the country's largest new hospitals were thus taken off both the government's and the PFI companies' books, dispatched to an accounting fourth dimension. One Tory MP (and chartered accountant) taunted Gordon Brown with some justification that he had become the 'Enron Chancellor'.[3]

The fiddles achieved the desired result. Over Labour's first two terms in government, more than 400 deals for infrastructure worth £25bn were signed (the figure now stands at about £60bn worth, costing £10bn a year for another generation).[4] The complex contracts required the services of financial consultants, almost always from KPMG, PwC, Deloitte or Ernst & Young, on each side. Public bodies such as NHS trusts or local education authorities, for whom each deal was a once-in-a-generation event, were especially dependent on their expert advice. The Big Four would ensure that their value-for-money calculations gave the 'right' answer and that they kept their scheme 'off the books'. One accounting academic who advised the Treasury on PFI, later explained: 'There became an industry in cosmetic presentation of projects.'[5] A rich industry it was too, with fees for all advisers coming in at around £3m for an average contract, around half of which would typically go to one of the Big Four firms.[6] By 2014, the same academic reckoned that the Big Four had earned £1bn from the private finance initiative. Small wonder they had been so keen to push it in the first place.

Conflicts of interest proliferated, the bean counters often advising public bodies on signing deals with companies that were also their clients for auditing and consulting services. And with the government's task force recommending 'success fees' for advisers, including the major accountancy firms represented on the task force, the incentive was to get the deal done. There is no trace of any advice that a scheme wouldn't be such a smart idea.[7] Getting the contract through often involved blatant manipulation, with the cost of a PFI deal usually ending up just a few pounds better value than the publicly funded alternative. In one case reported by the National Audit Office public spending watchdog, a new £130m hospital at West Middlesex had at first appeared to be more expensive to build under PFI. But the trust's adviser, KPMG, had convened a series of 'risk workshops' to identify some more convenient risks associated with the public sector alternative. Hey presto, the PFI deal came out slightly cheaper.[8]

The accountancy firms naturally became highly protective of their new golden goose. When critics attacked the early hospital deals – on which financial engineering took precedence over design quality, and extra costs immediately led to fewer beds for the sick – New Labour's friends at Arthur Andersen & Co. stepped in with a study, in 1999, concluding that PFI schemes came in cheaper than others. It was soon discredited, mainly because it ignored large cost escalations after schemes had been agreed but before they were signed.[9] The leading PFI consultant, PwC, rode to the rescue with another supposedly 'independent' report. It was no more than a summary of testimonials from officials who had signed PFI contracts and were not about to admit they had thrown the taxpayer's money away. Yet it became an official endorsement. When Prime Minister Blair was confronted in Parliament in 2002 with PFI's shortcomings, he simply referred his questioner to 'the PricewaterhouseCoopers report on the PFI, which found that it was excellent value for money'.[10] It certainly was for the bean counters, who as so often were paraded as independent authorities on areas from which they were getting very rich.

Meanwhile, the holder of the national public purse strings, Gordon Brown, was ensuring that Whitehall's biggest investment decisions would be taken by PFI consultants from the Big Four firms rather than civil servants who might be more circumspect. KPMG's head of infrastructure, Dr Timothy Stone, a former physical chemist who moved into consulting through Arthur Andersen and was known by some as the 'sage of PFI', became especially powerful. He could be found variously in the Department of Health's commercial directorate, at the education department advising on the schools rebuilding programme, on the government's 'sustainable procurement' task force and as permanent adviser to the Ministry of Defence on the biggest PFI scheme of them all, a £10bn project for in-flight jet-refuelling aircraft. 'I wear many hats,' the KPMG man would later admit.[11]

Special PFI units inside the key government departments across Whitehall were all handed to consultants on secondment from the Big Four. In 2005, PwC bean counter Richard Abadie took over the central Treasury PFI Unit for a couple of years, delivering a 30% growth in the number of deals signed.[12] A few years later, back running PwC's private finance practice (and having been succeeded at the Treasury by a Deloitte bean counter), Abadie was summoned by a sceptical committee of MPs. Would he 'be willing to submit some aggregate numbers for the amounts of money [PwC] have earned on PFI in this country over the last 10 years?' asked one. 'Probably not,' replied Abadie. 'I believe that is commercially confidential.'[13] Just like the other accountants' ramps, even if the public were paying a heavy price, PFI was a private affair.

DISASTER MANAGEMENT

In 2008, after a five-year delay, the jet-refuelling scheme on which KPMG's many-hatted Dr Stone had advised eventually went ahead. It soon became clear that the 27-year Future Strategic Tanker Aircraft contract had lumbered the armed forces with overpriced planes that weren't even fit for 'high-threat areas': something of a drawback in military aircraft. The fiasco prompted one of the National Audit Office's most damning reports on a major public contract, complete with the 'not value for money' black spot. The deal, said the watchdog, had been struck 'without a sound evaluation of alternative procurement routes to justify why the PFI route offered the best value for money'.[14] Since KPMG's top PFI man had been in charge, this wasn't too surprising. In 2010, the outcome was summed up by the chairman of Parliament's public accounts committee at the time, Sir Edward Leigh. 'By introducing a private finance element to the deal,' he concluded, 'the MoD managed to turn what should have been a relatively straightforward procurement into a bureaucratic nightmare.'[15] Still, a 'bureaucratic nightmare' is a consultant's dream, and with the taxpayer handing over £10m for 'finance, tax and accounting advice', once again the bean counters led by Dr Stone came out on top. Nor did the affair harm the head of the MoD's PFI unit who had signed off the deal, Nick Prior. By the time the extent of the waste was exposed, he had stepped through the well-oiled revolving door between Whitehall and the PFI industry to be Deloitte's 'global head of infrastructure'. There he rejoices in the role of 'lead client service partner' for the Ministry of Defence.[16]

Even with PFI and the big accountancy firms' role in it largely discredited, the scheme remains another gift from the taxpayer that keeps on giving to the bean counters. When hospital trusts saddled with overpriced PFI contracts inevitably ran into trouble after a few years, the Big Four would be back on the scene selling remedies for the ill-effects of their own snake oil. By 2013, the biggest health PFI scheme, a £1.1bn redevelopment at St Bartholomew and Royal London, was eating up £120m a year of the trust's budget, plunging it into a deficit of around £50m and forcing thousands of job cuts. In came PwC as 'turnaround' specialists, even though the same firm had advised the trust on signing the PFI deal in the first place seven years earlier. Back then, even the trust's chairman had admitted: 'If this was the private sector, you'd be in jail. This is what got Enron into trouble. It's all off the balance sheet. It's cloud-cuckoo land, Alice in Wonderland stuff.'[17] Yet not only did PwC go on to earn fees for the remedial financial advice, they then sold the hospital a 'sustainable operational efficiency and improvement programme'. While the hospital cut thousands of jobs, the firm was shortlisted – without irony – for a Management Consultancies Association award in the 'performance improvement in the public sector' category.[18]

Across Britain, the bean counters continue to clean up from the financial mess left by PFI bills that will demand payment before doctors', nurses', teachers' and armed forces personnel's wages for another generation. In 2013, six years after PwC told Peterborough hospital that a £400m PFI scheme was 'competitive, robust and demonstrate[s] value for money', the public accounts committee labelled it 'catastrophic'. By this time PwC was back in there earning £3m a year from telling the trust how to deal with the £45m annual deficit caused by the contract.[19] Up in Northumbria, Deloitte advised the trust running Hexham General Hospital on how to buy itself out of a financially ruinous PFI deal that KPMG had advised it on back in the late 1990s. So expensive had the contract turned out that the trust could pay the PFI company tens of millions of pounds in compensation and still save money.[20]

PFI became a huge public sector money-spinner for the Big Four accountancy firms and played a key role in ensconcing them in Whitehall. Once inside, they began creating a more enduring legacy. It would go well beyond the bricks and mortar and into the transformation of public services themselves.

UNHEALTHY COMPETITION

A central plank of New Labour's 'NHS Plan', unveiled in 2000 by its second health secretary, Alan Milburn, was 'choice' for patients. This meant extending the internal market to external private sector health providers and, in the process, giving a greater role to the management consultants at the heart of the health service. Although much of the early thinking came from McKinsey and Boston Consulting, the accountancy firms soon became the main drivers of the reforms. Within a couple of years a former consultant at what was now PwC, Adrian Masters, was running the health team in prime minister Tony Blair's delivery unit, while over at the Department of Health itself, another ex-PwC consultant, Simon Leary, was in charge of strategy. From there they ushered in changes including independence for trusts under 'foundation' status; 'independent sector treatment centres' run by private companies; and more marketization, pitting one NHS 'purchaser' of services against another 'provider'. The bureaucracy of the pseudo-market quickly became a headache for the health service but a field day for the consultants. Total spending by the NHS on consultants rose from around £10m in 2002 to £600m just four years later.[21]

More important than the cost was what the consultants were doing to the service. They were re-engineering the NHS in the same way they did large companies. By 2007, while McKinsey were advising on 'creating a commissioning market', PwC had been brought in to set up a framework for 'contracting and procurement', with predictably expensive results. 'Whatever the benefits of the purchaser/provider split,' a parliamentary committee would report in 2010, 'it has led to an increase in transaction costs, notably management and administration costs.' Confidential NHS research showed its administration costs had risen to 14% of its budget, more than double the level before the 1990s reforms.[22]

Just as with PFI, the fragmentation of the health service created huge demand for advice from 'purchasers' and 'providers' unfamiliar with how to contract competitively in a health service built on co-operation. The same consultants who created this inchoate matrix naturally stood ready to help. Soon after the Department of Health's 'Director of Commissioning' Mark Britnell had produced a 'framework for securing external support for commissioners', which included KPMG on a list of firms able to provide this support, he left to take over the health practice of . . . KPMG. He was very quickly joined at the firm by his successor at the health department, Gary Belfield. After the 2010 general election, Britnell was regularly back in Whitehall as an informal adviser on new prime minister David Cameron's 'kitchen cabinet'. This inside track allowed Britnell to tell a 2011 conference in New

York, in a session titled 'Reform Revolution', that 'the NHS will be shown no mercy and the best time to take advantage will be in the next couple of years'.[23]

The cause of the KPMG man's glee was yet more upheaval. The 'purchasers' of healthcare were being broken up into smaller units still, this time groups of local family general practitioners. The 'clinical commissioning groups' into which they were corralled, unable to manage complex commercial arrangements and run their practices at the same time, were soon inevitably funnelling more millions into the consultants' pockets. When NHS England produced a report called *Mapping the Market* in 2013, KPMG's Belfield could boast that his firm was advising a quarter of the more than 200 clinical commissioning groups, plus two thirds of the major 'commissioning support units' across the country. The other Big Four were similarly enthusiastic. Deloitte predicted that 'given the considerable financial pressures facing [clinical commissioning groups] we anticipate that our restructuring and turnaround services will continue to be in demand'. PwC's 250-strong health team was working with more than one hundred of the groups.[24] The health service that they had broken up and marketized was paying the accountancy firms back handsomely. It promises to continue to do so. KPMG also designs courses for the NHS Leadership Academy to teach senior executives 'global best practice in healthcare management'.[25] A new generation of health-service leaders learns through the consultants' eyes, and will surely send more public money their way.

Having positioned themselves as health-market experts, the Big Four now advise on major reorganizations, not always successfully. When, for example, struggling Hinchingbrooke hospital in Cambridgeshire became the first NHS hospital in the UK to hand its services over lock, stock and barrel to a private company in 2011, it relied on PwC confirming that the figures looked fine. The hospital trust would make the required savings and the hedge-fund-controlled Circle Health would get its financial return. Four years later, with the deal proving unviable, Circle pulled out.[26] Just up the road in Cambridge, a £725m deal struck by a clinical commissioning group with a consortium of other health trusts to provide all adult community care in the area collapsed within months because of miscalculations in how much the contract would pay.[27] The advisers this time were Deloitte.[28] Both its and PwC's work for the NHS continue undisturbed, prompting one former Department of Health clinical director to remark that such firms 'are unaccountable and can walk away from bad or damaging advice with no consequences'.[29]

With no accountability for mistakes, the gravy train steams on. Although NHS spending on consultants halved to around £300m between 2006 and 2010 – thanks to a backlash against New Labour's consultancy splurge – the coalition government's reforms doubled it again to £640m by 2014.[30] The result is permanent, destructive revolution. No sooner has one set of changes bedded in, and become less fee-generating, than new upheaval is recommended. It is an essential part of the Big Four's model. Public sector consulting, like other areas of their business, has to make its contribution to the firms' targets for fee growth. This means selling ever more advice to clients, including the public sector, which in turn means creating the demand for it.

Disrupt. Cash in. Clean up. Repeat. This is the perpetual consultancy machine of the Big Four. In 2016, less than four years after the last wholesale NHS reforms, PwC's ex-health minister Alan Milburn took to the airwaves and newspaper columns to plug yet another blueprint for change. This time it was his firm's plans to merge healthcare and social care.[31] The likely mechanism will be regional bodies much like the 'accountable care organizations' run by the Big Four's private health company clients in the US. It's a fair bet that, whatever direction the health service takes, it will be big business for the Big Four. Twenty-two years after Milburn accused the management consultants of 'making a killing', there is no end in sight to the bloodshed.

AT YOUR SERVICE

David Cameron had come into office in 2010 promising 'an end to government by management consultant'. And while overall consultancy spending across Whitehall did fall during his time as prime minister – largely through reductions in spending on wasteful IT projects – the Big Four still prospered. The parliamentary committee that was looking into their tax avoidance activities asked, out of interest, how much the firms were earning from the taxpayer. In 2011/12, it emerged, they had earned £490m (around 6% of their UK income) from the taxpayer. Two years later, with the accountancy firms having found their way round a new government and the fragmentation of the health service providing opportunity aplenty, this had risen by more than 50%. PwC doubled its public sector income to £333m. As public spending was slashed everywhere else in austerity Britain, the taxpayer cash lavished on PwC continued to grow as fast as the queues at the nation's food banks. In 2015/16 it hit £440m.[32]

The consultants' overwhelming financial incentive when advising government is to tell it what it wants to hear, untrammelled by the more objective traditions of the civil service. The consultants don't have the heritage of 'speaking truth to power' instilled in the civil service in the nineteenth century. Financially motivated, they can be kept to heel more easily. When a Deloitte memo pointing out gaps in the government's Brexit preparations was leaked in 2017, the firm was put in the public sector contract sin bin for six months. Causing political embarrassment warrants stiff punishment – unlike real public service cock-ups – and the message to the Big Four is clear: don't upset the government paymaster.

This unspoken understanding goes a long way to explaining why an 'independent' financial endorsement from a Big Four firm will be found behind most politically driven government-sponsored projects. The 2012 Olympic Games was one example. When a London bid had been contemplated ten years before, it had gone ahead only on the basis of its modest price. Early estimates, produced by PwC with supposedly 80% certainty, were that the public cost of the games would be up to £2.1bn. Since this could be met by lottery players and London council taxpayers without raiding central government coffers, a sceptical Chancellor of the Exchequer was won round. 'Gordon [Brown] was absolutely clear,' recalled the then sports and culture minister Tessa Jowell. 'He knew what the forecasts for the economy were and knew we would not be in a position to put huge amounts of government money into it.'[33] A few months before the bid was made for the games in 2004, the costs rose to £4.5bn. Again, said PwC, there was an 80% chance of them coming in within 10% of this. Then the price escalated even more dramatically. By the time the budget was finalized, the public cost had hit £9.3bn.[34] If PwC's experts had looked at previous Olympics bids, they would have realized that their early optimism was always wildly misplaced (and 'optimism bias' in public projects was one of the adjustments they used liberally to justify PFI schemes). The value of the 'independent' bean counters, however, was that they would look at what their paymasters considered convenient. Visions of Jessica Ennis and Mo Farah atop the podium may now shroud the Olympic financial fiasco in happy sporting imagery. Other bean counter-justified plans, however, are unlikely to be remembered so warmly.

One of the most critical problems facing Britain today is how to reinvigorate a largely post-industrial north. It's a huge challenge, requiring well-crafted but not individually transformational investments in industry, education, technology and local transport networks. But in Westminster politics, this isn't sexy enough. So at least £50bn is instead to be invested in a single high-speed rail link between London and Birmingham and from there on to Manchester and Leeds. To justify 'HS2', in the face of loud public and parliamentary opposition, in 2013 the government took the now standard step of commissioning an 'independent' report from one of the Big Four accountancy firms. Unsurprisingly, KPMG concluded that the new link would generate major economic benefits, to the tune of £15bn a year. A few months later, greatly helped by the claim, the scheme was voted through Parliament.

Among those without a political or commercial interest in HS2 going ahead, the KPMG report met with criticism verging on ridicule. The BBC's then economics editor Robert Peston blogged that 'some would say [there] is a flaw the size of Greater Manchester in its analysis – because KPMG is ignoring one of the fundamental causes of lacklustre growth in many parts of the UK, which is a shortage of skilled labour and of easily and readily developable land'.[35] When a committee of MPs came to examine the report, academics lined up to rubbish it. 'I don't think the statistical work is reliable,' said a professor of statistical modelling at Imperial College, London. 'They [KPMG] apply this procedure which is essentially made up, which provides them with an estimate,' added a professor of economic geography from the London School of Economics. 'It is something that really shouldn't be done in a situation where we are trying to inform public debate using statistical analysis.'[36]

Noting that HS2 'stands or falls on this piece of work', the committee's acerbic chairman Andrew Tyrie summoned the report's authors.[37] One exchange with KPMG's Lewis Atter (a former Treasury civil servant) spoke volumes for the bean counters' role in lumbering the taxpayer with monothilic projects:

Tyrie: It [the £15bn a year economic projection] is a reasonable forecast of what we might hope to get from this project?

Atter: We believe so.

Tyrie: The reason I use the word 'forecast' is that I note that in several places you caution that a key part of your analysis is, and I quote, 'prepared for illustrative purposes only and does not constitute a forecast', and a moment ago you told me that this considered estimate is a forecast.

Atter: It is a considered estimate.

Tyrie: But it is no longer a forecast?

Atter: I think it is clearly a forecast.

Tyrie: Even though you are making clear that it does not constitute a forecast in your own report.

Atter: No, I think you are looking at our standard disclaimer.

Tyrie: This is a standard disclaimer?

Atter: Yes.

Tyrie: So if you are forecasting that tomorrow the sun will rise, you will nonetheless put a disclaimer on and say that is only a projection?

Atter: I think the conversation with Risk and Compliance might be a little more straightforward, in that case, but yes.

Tyrie: This is to stop you being sued?

Atter: Correct.

KPMG had, in other words, produced some numbers that its client could call a forecast for political purposes without actually making a forecast. It could say anything it liked, demand a nice fee (£200,000 in this case) and abrogate responsibility. Three years later, with KPMG now earning even larger fees from the project itself on the back of its own forecast (or maybe non-forecast), and with one of its directors having become HS2's programme director, Andrew Tyrie alerted a new transport secretary to the shaky foundations. 'HS2 has the weakest economic case of all the projects within the [government's] infrastructure programme,' he wrote, 'yet it is being pursued with the most enthusiasm.'[38]

In 2017, the first contracts for constructing HS2 were signed. By this time, a senior figure had been appointed by the publicly owned company delivering the project, HS2 Ltd, to ensure the taxpayer's money would be well spent. Sue Kershaw described her role on the £50bn-plus deal as being 'effectively the eyes and ears of government within the project'.[39] Remarkably, she was a director at KPMG. Such is the power, without accountability, of the bean counters.

SHADOW STATE

With their 'can do' attitude – often when the correct advice would be 'don't do' – it's no surprise that consultants and bean counters from the Big Four are preferred to sceptical civil servants. All the firms accordingly have active practices in every area of public policy, with expertise in everything from health to education, transport to housing, criminal justice to social justice, defence to international development. Using the insights of former officials, they can mimic the machinery of government. EY's tax policy team, run by a former Treasury special adviser, boasts of 'developing technical policy options in a form used inside government . . . This ensures proposals can be implemented with the minimum of delay . . . and have the maximum chance of adoption.'[40] The Big Four thus play the role of shadow civil services without the corresponding constitutional or operational responsibilities.

Whereas Whitehall has to deal not just with policy but with all the drudgery of the state – the administration, the scrutiny, and clearing up the mess when things go wrong – the Big Four can simply lap up the cream, charging rates that would cause uproar if paid to civil servants. This gives them the resources to assert influence in important ways. Countless studies by the Big Four present the world as they see it and showcase the expertise that they can then sell to create it. The practice was pioneered to great effect by management consultants in the States in the 1970s, and is now packaged as 'thought leadership'. At the time of writing, PwC's healthcare website advertises reports on various hot topics, among them 'Road to recovery: addressing NHS financial challenges' and 'The role of hospital chains in the future NHS'. KPMG's defence page has its 'Global aerospace and defense [sic] outlook', while its international development site has a 'Sustainable development goals matrix' through which it parades its understanding of the developing world.

If these are the firms' brochures, then conferences and hospitality for ministers and officials are the sales events. When, after much resistance, I forced the Cabinet Office to reveal details of hospitality provided to the most senior board-level civil servants, it emerged that in 2007, the Big Four accountancy firms had entertained them – usually to lunch or dinner – on 104 separate occasions. KPMG had treated the permanent secretaries (the most senior mandarins) at the business department, the Home Office and the Cabinet Office each to a day at the Chelsea Flower Show.[41] Other top civil servants went to the opera, sports events and art exhibitions with the bean counters. The junketing has been greatly curtailed after the revelations brought damaging publicity and forced the publication of hospitality registers, but the closeness remains. At the very top of government, the leaders of the big firms have long been valued companions on overseas trade promotion tours and prime ministerial business councils. Ernst & Young's UK chairman, Steve Varley, beamed in one interview in 2016: 'I've been lucky to go to 10 Downing Street many times over the last few years. It's a real privilege to be in this role, in this job and at the heart of our country's government.'[42]

The Big Four's deep pockets pay for other routes into Whitehall. Ernst & Young, for example, sponsors the annual Civil Service Awards (none of which has yet been given for plans to reduce reliance on consultants). KPMG, meanwhile, sponsors the annual Civil Service Live conference, complete with a challenge to 'reimagine' services. The deal complements a contract to deliver training to all 400,000 civil servants (on KPMG's possibly exaggerated estimation) on 'topics as diverse as leadership and management, customer service, finance and policy', using 'technology and intellectual capital at KPMG'.[43] Regular secondments into government further align Big Four and official thinking. A 2013 report by lobbying watchdog Spinwatch found that at least fifty people had been seconded to government departments by the Big Four firms in three years.[44] Most were in the Cabinet Office, the Treasury and the Department for Business, the centres of power where policies governing everything from corporate taxes and financial markets to industry and the shape of public services themselves are determined. Other bean counters from PwC were providing free assistance to several of the Labour Party opposition teams (until Jeremy Corbyn's less consultant-friendly regime brought the arrangement to a close).

ARMED CONFLICT

When formulating their advice, whether as secondees into government, across a restaurant table or through a formal contract, the major accountancy firms are fundamentally conflicted. Certain outcomes – fragmenting services, outsourcing others, expensive procurement – provide them with their future paydays. Other more economical and effective incremental changes – never mind the status quo – do not. There's no money in stability. The companies that benefit from the consultants' advice to government bodies by providing the duly outsourced services certainly appreciate the importance of the Big Four. The former lead UK partners of Deloitte (John Connolly) and PwC (Sir Ian Powell) are now chairmen of two of the largest outsourced public service providers, G4S and Capita respectively. When the latter announced its catch in 2016, it was struggling with badly performing public service contracts and a tumbling share price. Powell, it reassured shareholders, had 'led PwC's interactions with the UK government and other public sector organizations'.[45] His contacts both in Whitehall and in the accountancy firm advising it clearly made him the man to have at the helm.

While advising government, the Big Four firms will invariably also be acting for others interested in their advice: not the citizens who depend on the services in question, or the people who deliver them, but the large corporations who form the bean counters' core clientele. The danger is twofold. Firstly, advice to government that benefits these companies is likely to lead to more work for the consultants in future. And secondly, the ongoing closeness to corporate clients with vested interests in the relevant services is bound to skew the consultants' thinking. In 2014, KPMG proudly reported two developments. It had 'secured strong client wins, including working with Lockheed Martin [the world's largest weapons maker]', announced consultancy partner Richard Gosling. He then added that a 'standout area of growth for us in the year was our government work, particularly defence, where we are of strategic importance to the Ministry of Defence'.[46] The obvious, and some might think fatal, conflict of interests went unmentioned. Lockheed, incidentally, would win major MoD contracts the following year. Acting for government and business can even constitute a form of policy insider-trading. EY, for example, is unabashed about how its work advising government 'gives us the insight and experience to help our clients maximize competitiveness'.[47]

Perhaps the MoD didn't notice, or care about, such conflicts while it paid the strategically important KPMG £70m over a couple of years. Nor did the health ministers and NHS managers pouring millions into KPMG's pockets seem to mind that another of the firm's 'strong [consultancy] client wins' was Imperial Tobacco.

The evidence shows that the government will employ the Big Four even when the most unobservant official might be expected to spot the conflicting interests. In 2009, the Treasury brought in Deloitte to review whether companies were using Britain's tax havens for tax avoidance (conclusion: not too much to worry about). The same firm had not so long before been pushing major tax schemes through the territories and, bizarrely, had advised the Inland Revenue to sell 650 of its tax offices to Bermuda under a PFI deal so that the company involved could avoid capital gains tax.[48]

New challenges bring new opportunities for government to enlist the bean counters' dependably flexible support. With the country's exit from the European Union certain to dominate economic policy for years, they are on the front line of the debate. A couple of months before the June 2016 referendum, prime minister David Cameron appeared at PwC's London office to unveil the firm's 'independent', eye-watering estimates of the cost of leaving the EU. Once the vote had been lost and Cameron's successor Theresa May adopted a hard Brexit line, the firm produced a more helpful report. 'The UK could grow faster than most other large EU countries in the long run, despite the medium-term drag from Brexit,' it now said. The report was seized on by the 'Brexiteers'.[49] KPMG, also a strong 'remain' supporter before the vote, was soon affecting optimism too. 'Our country's spirit of entrepreneurialism, mastery of technology and renowned business environment all point to a long-term collective ability to rebuild our economy after Brexit,' wrote the firm's 'head of Brexit'.[50] As Deloitte's ban from public sector contracts not long before over its unhelpful memo on Brexit had shown, keeping on the right side politically is a shrewd commercial move.

While their main Brexit-era task is to advise their multinational clients on the upheaval, the Big Four are also helping an ill-prepared government machinery on this one. Secondees from all the Big

Four have made their way into the Department for Exiting the EU. 'As with all crises,' KPMG's senior partner Simon Collins had mused a couple of days after the vote, 'there will be opportunities for professional services firms.'[51]

NUCLEAR CON-FUSION

The greatest long-term policy challenge – addressing energy needs in the age of global warming – is also providing one of the greatest consultancy paydays. When, in 2013, the British government made yet another controversial investment decision with far-reaching consequences – this time to build the first nuclear power station in Britain for three decades, at Hinkley Point in Somerset – the advice of KPMG was again central. A previous government had been won round to the idea of a new generation of nuclear plants five years earlier, thanks largely to the efforts of Dr Tim Stone, head of infrastructure at KPMG. As well as running the accountancy firm's major projects practice, covering such matters as nuclear power station construction, Stone had been chair of the government's office for nuclear development from 2007. The following year it had decided that new plants could indeed be affordably built and, ahead of making the Hinkley Point decision, had again been advised by KPMG's consultants.

The new power station would depend on promising the French/ Chinese consortium building and running it a minimum price for its output. To determine how much this should be, the energy department brought in the KPMG bean counters and paid them a couple of million pounds over two years. The outcome was a deal that will cost more than twice the current electricity price (plus inflation) for thirty-five years. It will also commit the taxpayer to underwriting the consortium's debts and, above a certain amount, the costs of dealing with the waste from what most nuclear experts consider an overpriced project based on flawed, out-of-date technology.[52] Once the financial terms were agreed, the civil servant responsible for nuclear energy advice to government ministers, Simon Virley, left the government on a five-year 'career break' to become 'head of power and utilities' at none other than KPMG. The firm pronounced itself 'delighted' with its new man, trumpeting his experience with 'overall responsibility for advice to the UK Government on renewables, nuclear, oil and gas, shale, carbon capture and storage, and UK energy security issues'.[53] Needless to say, KPMG has a long roster of corporate clients in these areas, including the French company behind the Hinkley Point deal, EDF, and others that are standing by to capitalize on any nuclear building renaissance that it might mark.

The Big Four firms can win such vast consultancy contracts, and sway major government decisions, precisely because of their size and all-encompassing 'professional services' proposition. No sooner had KPMG successfully advised the British government on a suitable price for the Hinkley Point C deal than it was pitching for a large contract to advise on the 'final investment decision' phase – effectively deciding whether its own previous advice gave a good deal. Its bid stressed that it was the government's 'incumbent financial adviser' and could offer a 'seamless transition as opposed to bringing a new adviser up to speed'. It had 'worked very closely to date with [an unnamed official] as part of our current work on [Hinkley Point C]' and had 'advised on over 400 infrastructure programmes'. KPMG could offer 'the full spectrum of accounting, tax and major projects advisory skills', plus a special 'competition economics team' to address thorny European 'state aid' questions. The Big Four's size, their entrenched position in Whitehall and the sprawling range of their services, in other words, give them an unassailable edge in winning public contracts.

On the back of their accounting heritage, the Big Four have become one-stop consultancy shops. Outsourcing large areas of public policy analysis and decision-making to them becomes an easy decision for governments. It may be far easier than building an objective, competent civil service, but it is corrosive of good government and over time compounds the dependency on the consultants. Despite the omniscience of which KPMG could brag in its contract bids, in 2017 Sir Amyas Morse, the normally restrained head of the National Audit Office, called the Hinkley Point C deal 'high cost and risky'. He pointed out that 'less favourable, but reasonable, assumptions about future fossil fuel prices, renewable costs and follow-on nuclear projects would have meant the deal was not value for money'.[54] The next generation of electricity consumers will pay a high price for KPMG's capture of government nuclear policy.

REVOLVING DOOR

The routine exchange of senior personnel, typified by Simon Virley's move from civil service director to KPMG consultant on the same patch, brings a closeness that breeds a uniform, market-oriented view of the public realm within Whitehall. So frequently and smoothly does the revolving door spin that it creates a realistic hope among ministers and mandarins that, subject to keeping them happy, the Big Four firms will present later career opportunities or some consulting fees to supplement their pensions. Taken with the closeness between those who have stepped through the revolving door and their former colleagues, the effect is to melt away the healthy tension that should exist between government and commercial interests. The riches on offer are generally kept secret, but the odd glimpse shows how attractive the well-connected can be to the Big Four. When former international development secretary Andrew Mitchell took a consultancy position with EY in 2016, as a serving MP he had to declare that the firm was paying him £30,000 a year for five days' work. For a possible £6,000 a day it's worth keeping in with the

Big Four, especially in the later, most influential, years of a public sector career.

Below is a small sample of the most senior officials and ministers who have left to find a nice payday among the bean counters.

Official or minister	Government job	Big Four job with year appointed
Peter Mandelson	Trade and industry secretary, 1998	Consultant, EY, 1999
Alan Milburn	Health secretary, 1999–2003	Chairman, PwC Health Industries Oversight Board, 2013
Charles Clarke	Education secretary, 2002–4 Home secretary, 2004–6	Consultant, KPMG, 2008
Jacqui Smith	Home secretary, 2007–9	Consultant, KPMG, 2010
Ian Pearson	Economic secretary to the Treasury, 2008–10	Member, PwC Advisory Board, 2011
Lord (Jack) McConnell	First minister (Labour), Scotland, 2001–7	Member, PwC Advisory Board, 2011
Lord (Gus) O'Donnell	Cabinet secretary and head of the civil service, 2005–11	Chair, PwC Public Interest Board, 2015
Lord (Jonathan) Evans	Director general, MI5, 2007–13	Member, KPMG Public Interest Committee, 2017
Lord (John) McFall	Labour MP and senior member, Treasury select committee, until 2010	Senior adviser to KPMG on regulatory and corporate governance, 2012
Sir Steve Robson	Second permanent secretary, Treasury, Financial Services, until 2011	Chair, KPMG Public Interest Committee, 2012
Dave Hartnett	Permanent secretary, Tax, HMRC, to 2012	Consultant, Deloitte, 2013
Sir Nicholas Montagu	Chairman, HMRC, to 2005	Member, PwC Advisory Board, 2004
Simon Virley	Director general, Energy, Department of Energy and Climate Change, to 2015	Head of power and utilities, KPMG, 2015
Sir Leigh Lewis	Permanent secretary, Department of Work and Pensions, until 2011	Member, PwC Advisory Board, 2011
Sir John Scarlett	Head of MI6, 2004–9	Advisor, PwC, 2010

Lord Strathclyde	Leader of the House of Lords, 2010–13	Advisor, PwC, 2010
Paul Kirby	Head of No. 10 Policy Unit, 2011–13 (having previously been KPMG consultant)	Head of government and public sector, KPMG, 2013
Neil Sherlock	Special adviser to the deputy prime minister, 2012–13	Head of reputational strategy, PwC, 2013
Lord (Norman) Warner	Health minister, 2003–06	Strategic adviser, Deloitte, 2008
Mark Britnell	Director general, Commissioning, NHS, 2007–09	Head of KPMG health services, 2009
Mike Farrar	Chief executive, North-West Strategic Health Authority, 2006–11	Chair, PwC Public Sector Health Board
Sir Peter Westmacott	UK ambassador to United States, 2012–16	Non-executive, EY, 2017
Andrew Mitchell	International development secretary, 2010–12	Consultant, EY, 2016
Mats Persson	Special adviser on EU to David Cameron 2015–16	Head of international trade, EY, 2016
Paul Skinner	Chairman, Infrastructure UK (part of HM Treasury), 2009–13 Chairman, Defence Equipment & Support, 2014–present	Member, PwC Advisory Board, 2015
Jon Pain	Managing director, Supervision, Financial Services Authority, 2008–11	Partner, regulatory practice, KPMG, 2011
David Strachan	Director, Financial Stability, Financial Services Authority, 2008–11	Head of regulatory strategy, Deloitte, 2011
Margaret Cole	Managing director, Enforcement & Financial Crimes, Financial Services Authority, to 2012	Chief risk officer and general counsel, PwC, 2012

REGULATION ISSUE

If the bean counters get a good deal from Whitehall, it's nothing next to their treatment from the regulators that they have also captured.

By the time the world needed to respond to the early-twentieth-century crisis of accounting epitomized by Enron and WorldCom, Britain's New Labour government was in thrall to the bean counters-turned-consultants now strolling the corridors of power reforming public services. When the accountants lobbied, the government listened. A 1997 New Labour manifesto commitment to more independent regulation of the accountancy profession was soon dropped. 'Light touch' regulation became a selling point for 'UK plc'. Set up your companies here or list on our stock exchanges, was the message, and we won't probe your accounts or those who audit them too closely.

Britain's public accountancy regulator, the Financial Reporting Council, was set up in 1990 in the wake of the 1980s scandals like Barlow Clowes, but had soon become the vehicle for this indulgence. While the accountancy profession largely self-regulates through its chartered institutes and associations, the FRC is supposed to examine disciplinary cases of serious public interest. But its priorities appear to lie elsewhere. Its chairman, Sir Win Bischoff, is a banker who lobbied against tighter controls on the Big Four in the wake of the 2008 financial crisis, while its chief executive since 2009 has been non-boat-rocking former civil servant and insurance industry lobbyist Stephen Haddrill. Two of its other three executive directors, covering 'corporate governance and reporting' and 'audit', are accountants from KPMG and PwC, while Big Four veterans chair other committees supporting their work.[55]

More important perhaps is the regulator's lack of firepower. In 2016/17, the FRC's total budget was £33m, and it spent just £4m on 'enforcement'.[56] Even after a recent recruitment drive, its enforcement division contains just 30 staff (mostly lawyers and forensic accountants).[57] Towards the end of 2017, it had only 24 cases under investigation, covering almost a decade of widespread accounting malpractice. It routinely turned down high-value apparent accounting failures for investigation as not meeting the FRC's 'public interest' threshold. Yet when I talked to Stephen Haddrill in 2017, he told me that he did not consider his organization's enforcement effort to be under-resourced. It didn't seem the most ambitious stance for an enforcer. It did, though, match the FRC's response to the 2008 financial crisis, which had amounted to investigating just one major banking failure – and then only after Parliament had forced it to.[58]

Even when the regulator achieves some success, it doesn't capitalize on it. In 2017, the FRC fined PwC £5.1m for misconduct in the audit of RSM Tenon, a dubious accountancy company that had gone bust four years earlier. Yet rather than retaining the funds to seriously bolster its investigatory efforts – perhaps by recruiting more forensic accountants – the regulator handed the millions to the bean counters' own professional body, the Institute of Chartered Accountants in England and Wales (ICAEW), 'in recognition of their funding of FRC cases'.[59] The ICAEW then set about spending the money on training, which they should have been doing anyway.

Paying for investigations into their own conduct and receiving the income from any fines, the bean counters enjoy one of the cosiest disciplinary systems around. Even following a review of the FRC's powers in 2017 after mounting criticism, recommending potential fines of £10m or more in the most serious cases, penalties for substandard auditing remain minor business costs for multi-billion-pound-earning firms.[60] Successive governments remain unmoved by calls for real reform, even when – perhaps especially when – the accounting scandals mount. The bean counters have become too important, too few and too close to power to be confronted in any meaningful way – even when they overlook the most egregious financial scandal.

9

CRIME AND VERY LITTLE PUNISHMENT

THE BEAN COUNTERS PLAY ALONG WITH CORRUPTION

The accountancy profession emerged in the nineteenth century from the need to root out fraud and the misuse of money in the early years of the modern company.

One particularly pernicious abuse has always been the payment of bribes to win business illicitly. It exposes a company to risks of which its shareholders are unaware and defrauds the other companies and public bodies whose officials are persuaded to make uncommercial decisions. Where governments are the customers, it sustains corrupt political leadership and loots often already impoverished nations. And it distorts the competition on which successful market economies depend. Unearthing corruption is one of the most important tasks entrusted by society to its accountancy watchdogs.

It isn't always easy to spot a bribe. It might be a small fraction of a company's expenses and will be entered in the books as something innocuous. Auditors can't be expected to examine every line. As the accountants are keen to remind those who accuse them of overlooking corrupt payments, in 1896 a Court of Appeal judge famously characterized an auditor as 'a watchdog, not a bloodhound'. The same bean counters are less likely, however, to quote the part of the judgement that said: 'If there is anything calculated to excite suspicion, he should probe it to the bottom.'[1] Precise rules and standards would vary over the years, but this is what the bean counters ought to have been doing. Where corruption exposes clients to material risks, such as serious legal action or loss of business, failing to say so would not be giving stakeholders a 'true and fair view', according to the British test. In the US, it would not be presenting the company's financial position 'fairly' in accordance with accepted standards.

That the bean counters weren't probing suspicious activity, never mind to the bottom, first became obvious after the Watergate-era revelations of illegal campaign donations by American companies. A 1975 congressional study identified $306m shelled out in 'questionable business practices' by just twenty companies.[2] None had been queried by their auditors. Two thirds of the payments had been made by arms and aircraft maker Lockheed alone, largely in bribes to win contracts supplying jets to Saudi Arabia. This was far from a purely American problem, however. Bribery was an open secret in official British circles. But with the Saudi arms trade viewed as essential for foreign earnings and post-imperial influence 'east of Suez', exporters were tacitly allowed to do whatever it took to clinch the deal.

When the British government had brought in an industrialist to increase the UK's share of this market in the mid 1960s, he had confided that 'it was often necessary to offer bribes to make sales'.[3] A special 1977 directive from the Ministry of Defence instructed officials involved in deals, which were strictly signed between governments with the arms companies as contractors, not to make 'over-extensive enquiries' into dubious payments.[4] The missive was certainly followed when the country's largest-ever weapons contract, for the supply of Tornado fighters and other services by British Aerospace, was negotiated in 1985 between the UK and Saudi governments. More than thirty years on, the al-Yamamah deal has been repeatedly renewed. It has so far earned BAE Systems (as the company became in 1999) around £50bn, despite reports of corruption having appeared as soon as the ink was dry on the first contract. Before 1985 was out, a *Guardian* headline had announced: 'Bribes of £600m in jet deal', based on documents obtained by an Arabic newspaper. A couple of years later, subcontractors on the deal, including Rolls-Royce, admitted that they'd paid large bribes.[5]

The least worldly bean counter ought to have harboured suspicions about British Aerospace's repeated deals with Saudi Arabia. Yet its auditor, KPMG, approved the company's accounts year after year with no mention of bribes or the many offshore subsidiary companies that it would transpire they were passing through. KPMG's determined indifference didn't do it any harm, of course: in 2003, for example, the firm earned £3.7m for auditing the group and a further £5.2m for consultancy services. By then the scale of what the auditors were overlooking was already beginning to emerge. Using a web of shell companies centred on the British Virgin Islands, BAE Systems was operating slush funds to pay for prostitutes, yachts and even luxury homes for Saudi sheikhs. It had created what the *Guardian* reporters who exposed the affair would later call 'an entire money-laundering system, an enormous worldwide network of secret cash payments amounting to literally billions of dollars that had gone on for years with the connivance of the British government'.[6] The wheels of business everywhere, from Hungary to Tanzania and South Africa, were oiled with bribes, paid for by then overcharging often impoverished nations for equipment they might not even need.

BAE Systems famously escaped from the scandal relatively unscathed after prime minister Tony Blair halted a Serious Fraud Office prosecution of the company in 2006.[7] The UK's accountancy regulator, the Financial Reporting Council, didn't even begin looking at KPMG's work until 2010, more than three years after the fraud investigators closed their file. Another three years later, the FRC concluded that any investigation would be too historic and would not be in the public interest. KPMG denied any wrongdoing. Once again, the bean counters faced no consequences for their shortcomings. By this stage, domestic and international clampdowns, such as an anti-bribery convention from the Organization of Economic Co-operation and Development to which the UK signed up in 1999, had already made it clear that this was a critical matter for auditors to examine and highlight in their reports. And no business carried more risk of corruption than contracts with the Saudi regime. Applying the 'professional scepticism' expected of them – summed up by their professional body as 'being alert to conditions which may indicate possible misstatement due to error or fraud'[8] – the bean counters should have been looking very closely indeed for corruption on these contracts. They had been warned.

COMMISSION IMPLAUSIBLE

Details of corruption become known only in exceptional cases. In 2011, five years after the BAE file had been closed, another case did emerge into the daylight thanks to a whistleblower inside a company delivering a $2bn military telecommunications contract between the UK and the Saudi Arabian National Guard.

In February 2010, Ian Foxley, a 54-year-old former lieutenant colonel in the Signals regiment, became programme director at a British subsidiary of the Airbus group called GPT Special Project Management. He quickly discovered that his new employer, the contractor on the so-called SANGCOM contract, was making regular payments for what were delphically labelled 'bought-in services' to a couple of Cayman Islands companies called Simec International Ltd and Duranton International Ltd. These transfers were the largest single expense on the contract he was running and were routinely signed off by the company's directors and the local Ministry of Defence team supervising the project. Yet neither Foxley nor his staff knew of any services actually being 'bought in' at all, from the Cayman companies or elsewhere. 'And if we didn't,' he would later ask, 'then who were they and why were we paying them so much money?'[9] He eventually discovered that over a three-year period, GPT had made 27 payments totalling 86m riyals, or around £14m, to the companies through HSBC bank accounts in London and New York. On top of these, there had been gifts for senior Saudi officials of Rolex watches and top-of-the-range cars. He also found out that a previous financial controller at the firm had raised concerns internally, only to be told by the international compliance officer of the Airbus division of which GPT was part: 'I am prepared to accept some corruption because I like my company better than ethics.'[10]

When I began investigating this story for *Private Eye* magazine, the history of SANGCOM confirmed all suspicions. The first phase of the deal had been signed back in 1978 between the UK and Saudi governments, initially with Cable & Wireless as the contractor. Documents unearthed by arms trade historian Nicholas Gilby showed commissions to companies including the first incarnation of Simec adding up to 15%. This, the head of the defence sales arm of the MoD had said at the time, 'although described as "technical consultancy" amounts in practice to the exertion of influence to sway decisions in favour of the client'.[11] They were bribes, in other words, which I would later discover made their way to a group of important Saudis referred to within the company as 'the Club'.[12]

It was obvious that GPT and Airbus had their own interest in keeping the arrangement quiet, while the government that had approved it all those years ago was still signing off the payments for political reasons (in defiance of its public position on corruption). But the auditors ought to have had no motive other than exposing the misuse of money and giving users of the company's accounts a 'true and fair view', including whether they were 'materially free from misstatement due to fraud or error'. These assessments should have encompassed whether 'bought-in services' were exposing them to major legal and financial trouble. Somehow, however, the auditors appear never to have probed what was behind a category of payment amounting to 15% of a company's total expenses and in some years all of its profits. Documents that I would later see showed that the 'bought-in services' were simply added at the bottom of each request for payment from the Ministry of Defence (which would then be reimbursed by the Saudi customer). It would not have taken a bloodhound to scent something suspicious here.

The auditors changed with the ownership of GPT over the decades. Coopers & Lybrand had the job until 1998, then Deloitte until 2007. When GPT was acquired by Airbus (or EADS as it was known until 2013), KPMG took on the job. Throughout the period, effective auditing was expected to pick up improper payments on the 'material' scale that GPT's certainly were. Some fraud 'risk factors' included in auditing standards could have been written with GPT in mind: 'use of business intermediaries' and 'significant bank accounts or subsidiary or branch operations in tax-haven jurisdictions' where in either case 'there appears to be no clear business justification'.[13] Yet all the accountancy firms signed GPT's accounts as giving a true and fair view, certifying that they had obtained 'all the information that we considered necessary . . . to give reasonable assurance that the financial statements are free from material misstatement, whether caused by fraud or other irregularity or error'. Such statements were hardly credible. That three of the Big Four firms gave them showed the blindness of the bean counters to corruption.

It wasn't until three months after Ian Foxley had taken his cache of evidence to the Serious Fraud Office (and, maybe equally importantly, the press) that KPMG first qualified GPT's accounts. 'Certain allegations have been made in connection with the company's contracts with a subcontractor group,' said the accountants on 15 April 2011, noting that 'the relevant sub-contracts have been terminated'. The possible misuse of the shareholders' money meant there was no guarantee that the company was a 'going concern' or that the numbers it presented gave the all-important 'true and fair view' of its finances. Decades too late, and only because whistleblowers had taken drastic action at great personal risk, the bean counters finally said something.

COVER-UP

While the Serious Fraud Office (SFO) began its investigation into the affair, Airbus shifted into damage-limitation mode. Helpfully, the same accountancy firms that should be rooting out malpractice are happy also to play it down. Airbus turned to PwC for what it called an 'independent review relating to GPT Special Project Management Ltd'. The remit was conveniently secret and almost certainly heavily circumscribed: the standard formula for an exculpatory bean counters' enquiry.

The accountants predictably reported that 'in the period under review and based on the work they undertook, nothing came to PwC's attention to suggest that improper payments were made by GPT'. This was world-class blind-eye-turning. One person familiar with PwC's work on GPT told me how the accountants had arrived at the company's Faisaliah Tower office, asked for evidence of the purpose of the 'bought-in services' payments and been told there was no paperwork. Rather than reaching the obvious conclusion that un-evidenced payments for non-existent services paid to mysterious offshore companies might just be suspicious, the PwC Sherlocks reported that they hadn't seen or heard anything amiss.

PwC and KPMG now have altogether different priorities to their scandal-busting founders Edwin Waterhouse and James Marwick.

As Andrew Gordon, 'global forensics leader' for PwC and the partner who was in charge of the GPT review, writes on the firm's website: 'We will fight the threats to your brand and bottom line – anywhere and everywhere, at a moment's notice.'[14] Both firms have extensive interests in the kingdom of Saudi Arabia. PwC is a member of the Saudi British Joint Business Council – on which KPMG's senior partner until 2016, Simon Collins, also sat – and boasts of being 'business advisers to the [Saudi] government'.[15] Since it is an article of faith in British government and business that the grubby secrets of Anglo–Saudi trade must not be revealed, such firms are always unlikely to speak out. The bean counters are not going to rock a boat to which their interests are so firmly tethered. When I discussed the major accountancy firms' performance with a lawyer who works on internal anti-corruption reviews, sometimes alongside the bean counters, he told me: 'There are always plenty of them, but they don't know what they're doing; they don't know what they're looking for.'[16]

The blind eye is not confined to the arms trade. A look at the cases currently being investigated by Britain's Serious Fraud Office suggests that few if any arose from the auditors informing the authority of concerns. All of the Big Four refused to tell me how many cases they had reported to the SFO in recent years, while the agency turned down my freedom-of-information request for numbers. My guess is somewhere not much higher than zero. What little comes out suggests that the prosecutors no longer have much faith in the bean counters anyway. When, in 2016, British-based oil services company Petrofac was accused of bribery (which it denied), it brought in KPMG and a law firm, who found no evidence of corruption. Later, the company was forced to admit that 'the SFO has informed Petrofac that it does not accept those findings'.[17]

The accountants rarely pay for their role in allowing corruption to fester. KPMG was fined €7m in the Netherlands in 2013 for actively helping construction firm Ballast Nedam to cover up bribes on Saudi contracts, but that is as far as its censures go. UK accountancy regulators have declined to examine the auditors' work on the GPT case while the Serious Fraud Office prosecutors examine it, raising the prospect that, just as with BAE Systems, it will eventually be dismissed as too old.

Accountancy failure allows corruption to go unnoticed for years, because the auditors are the ones who should have been doing the noticing. It silently rots business from within and only occasionally erupts into public view. When it does, however, it can be spectacular.

CAUGHT OFFSIDE

Six a.m., 27 May 2015. As the sun rose over a serene Lake Zurich, plain-clothed Swiss police officers walked into the adjacent five-star Hotel Baur au Lac and woke seven of the world's top football officials up with arrest warrants. A few hours later, US Attorney General Loretta Lynch stood before the press in New York and unveiled a 161-page indictment against these and other FIFA officials, covering offences from bribery to racketeering and money laundering over a couple of decades. 'They were expected to uphold the rules that keep soccer honest,' said Lynch. 'Instead they corrupted the business of worldwide soccer to serve their interests and enrich themselves.'

Reporters pored over the indictment for details of the crimes. Who had paid the bribes? To whom? What accounts had they used? Which football tournaments had been corrupted? How much had been plundered? But one question was largely overlooked. How had the governing institution of the biggest sport on earth got away with so much corruption for so long? A large part of the answer was that the bean counters had allowed it to. In fact, a look at the game's history showed they had actively set it on its crooked path.

Corruption conquered world football forty years earlier when aristocratic Brazilian Olympian João Havelange was elected FIFA president with the help of a few brown envelopes left in the hotel rooms of wavering voters. His benefactor was the head of the Adidas sports clothing group, Horst Dassler, a charismatic Bavarian who was pioneering the business of selling TV and marketing rights linked to the world's great sporting events.

To exploit his assets in the world of sport, such as his man at the top of world football, Dassler set up International Sport & Leisure (ISL) in the Swiss lakeside city of Lucerne, where nobody need see a company's accounts, and bribes were looked on indulgently by the authorities. It was complemented by a chain of companies and foundations in nearby Liechtenstein and the more distant British Virgin Islands. Through these, millions of Swiss francs would wend their way into the bank accounts of brass-plate companies and foundations controlled by the FIFA executives who would be instrumental in awarding TV and sponsorship rights.[18] ISL was duly awarded the World Cup TV and marketing rights, selling them on to broadcasters and sponsors around the world, all the way up to the 2006 finals in Germany. British journalist Andrew Jennings, who over twenty years prised open the closed world of FIFA corruption, caught what was going on in a 2006 BBC *Panorama* film. When he asked a former ISL accountant what the payments were for, the bean counter replied, 'Well, in common language, it's obviously corruption.' 'Bribes?' prompted Jennings. 'Yes.'[19]

By this time ISL had already gone bust, after messing up a tennis TV rights deal. The liquidation process led to a criminal investigation and, in a 2008 Zug courtroom, the prosecution of Havelange and some ISL executives. Their trial revealed both the scale of the bribery – an estimated $66m in twelve years up to 2001 – and the system's expert design. At one point a former ISL chief executive told the court that: 'The concept has been developed by [a major Swiss law firm] . . . in cooperation with KPMG and has also been approved by the federal tax [authorities].'[20] Here was KPMG again, not promoting financial probity, but pushing at the limits of the law in the most venal interests of its clients. (It also happened to be ISL's auditor, signing off accounts covering the payments.) Havelange and most of the ISL executives were acquitted on the grounds that bribery was not specifically outlawed in Switzerland at the time, but they weren't exonerated. The judge described the payments as 'immoral' and demanded that they be repaid. As the enablers of the bribery at the heart of FIFA's commercial operation, KPMG thus knew all along exactly how world football was being run. So when the firm was brought in by FIFA itself in 1999 as its first auditor – partly in answer to existing concerns over the organization's governance – it should have been ready to give its new client some especially close scrutiny.

When KPMG first reviewed the FIFA books in 1999, it did indeed find irregularities, a few of which it set out in confidential management letters. The previous year, for example, new president Joseph 'Sepp' Blatter had repaid the Saudi football federation for their support in his 1998 election with a payment of CHF 470,000 (about £200,000) to an unidentified recipient 'without the authorization of the finance and executive committee'.[21] It was just one of many failings of control. Blatter, like Havelange before him, had '*Einzelunterschrift*' status, allowing him to sign off payments as sole signatory. Lavish expenses were paid without appropriate checks. Debts from overseas federations were written off improperly, including a large one from the Caribbean and North African confederation run by the legendary exploiter of the game, Trinidadian Jack Warner. So were amounts owed by the old boss, João Havelange. The following year, KPMG's review reported loans of CHF160,000, thought to have been in cash, to 'the president of a national association'. Then there was an Enron-style transaction through which FIFA had pawned its income from the forthcoming 2002 and 2006 World Cups for $420m.

It was effectively a loan to finance a shortfall caused by all the misuse of funds and generous grants to the national federations whose leaders, it so happened, had elected Blatter as president. The upfront money was accounted for, however, as immediate income. KPMG described the accounting as 'misleading' and said that it gave a 'false picture of FIFA's earnings position'. But the firm let it pass as it scraped through Swiss, if not international, accounting rules at the time.

These shenanigans all said that this was a high-risk, institutionally corrupt client. As much was confirmed in 2002, when Blatter's number two, secretary general Michel Zen-Ruffinen, took the floor at a FIFA executive committee meeting and blew the whistle on FIFA's 'general mismanagement, dysfunctions in the structures and financial irregularities'.[22] Yet its auditor remained silent, protecting those at its head, for another thirteen years.

CLEAN AUDITS FOR A DIRTY GAME

Every year accountants from KPMG's Zurich office, led by a quiet silver-haired bean counter called Fredy Luthiger, signed off FIFA's accounts as free from any material misstatement. Sitting proudly on the podium alongside the FIFA top brass at its annual congresses, Fredy would declare that each annual report gave a 'true and fair view' of its affairs.

The 2009 congress, over a couple of balmy spring days in Nassau, Bahamas, was no different. Accounts for the previous year showed that stronger Swiss laws against bribery had not troubled world football's governing body. FIFA's audit committee, which it had set up in response to the ISL scandal, could also testify on the strength of work performed by KPMG that new laws demanding internal controls – in line with worldwide post-Enron measures – had been met. KPMG's Mr Luthiger pronounced himself satisfied: 2008 had been yet another clean year.[23]

59TH **FIFA** CONGRESS NASSAU, 2 AND 3 JUNE

Figure 11: KPMG partner and lead auditor for FIFA from 1999 to 2011, Fredy Luthiger, at the 2009 congress of world football's governing body

That's how it appeared, anyway, until Attorney General Loretta Lynch set out her indictment in New York in May 2015. There, on page 83, were three payments: $616,000, $1,600,000 and $7,784,000, totalling exactly $10m, wired from FIFA accounts in Switzerland in 2008 to Caribbean Football Union accounts at the Bank of Trinidad and Tobago controlled by Jack Warner (since banned for life from the game). Large parts of the $10m were then diverted by Warner to his own accounts. It was all part, said the Department of Justice, of a scheme going back to 2004 to bribe Warner into voting for South Africa's (successful) bid to host the 2010 World Cup. The ultimate payer of the bribes was the South African government. But, unable to use taxpayers' funds directly, its officials had arranged for FIFA itself to make the payments and later deduct a corresponding amount from support payments to South Africa for organizing the tournament.

Payments heading anywhere near Jack Warner's sphere of influence, never mind to accounts directly under his control, should have been earmarked for the closest scrutiny. International standards, to which Switzerland was now signed up, explicitly required 'professional scepticism' from auditors and a focus on areas of business especially susceptible to fraud. Some of the thuggish Trinidadian's scams had been laid out by Jennings in his landmark 2006 exposé *Foul!*, while a report submitted to FIFA the same year by Ernst & Young estimated that Warner's family had made at least $1m from illicit ticket-selling operations.[24] The following year, he was exposed asking for a cheque to be paid into his personal account for Trinidad and Tobago's appearance at a match against Scotland.[25] No shade of red was bright enough for the warning flags on a deal involving Jack Warner. Yet neither FIFA's internal control system nor the auditors from KPMG picked up on $10m going to him in a single year. This certainly called into question a claim by FIFA in its 2009 accounts that 'KPMG as external auditors have a very detailed picture of the FIFA [internal control system] following the in-depth audits that they have performed.'[26] When an audit misses unexplained payments of $10m to accounts run by a known corruption risk, the only thing 'in-depth' about it is how far the bean counters have stuck their heads in the sand.

After the 2015 raid at Baur au Lac, one or two commentators began to ask questions about the auditors. Some of KPMG's defenders thought that when corrupt payments totalling tens of millions of dollars went through FIFA's own accounts, they would not be 'material' for a $1bn-turnover organization and therefore not something for the auditors to flag up. Yet FIFA's total budget for development paid to local federations and confederations was just $133m, made up of hundreds of small payments.[27] Individual transfers of $0.6m, $1.6m and $7.8m to the Caribbean ought to have been spotted by the most somnolent bean counter. The former chief of the United Nations anti-corruption task force, Robert Appleton, who knew a thing or two about graft from examining corruption on the infamously corrupt Iraq oil-for-food programme, looked at the events and remarked: 'There were sufficient red flags of improper and highly suspicious payments, as well as money transfers to and from officials . . . coupled with a history of similar issues, that should have been identified and caused the auditors to highlight and report on them internally and recommend further investigation.'[28] That they did nothing of the sort for so long suited both the KPMG bean counters and the bosses of world football. Every four years, FIFA announced that 'renowned international audit company KPMG' would continue to check the books (for fees that would never be revealed).

In the absence of the control for which KPMG consistently vouched, breathtaking greed came to grip FIFA HQ. A week after the May 2015 raid, lawyers brought in by FIFA reported on 'a co-ordinated effort by three former top officials of FIFA to enrich themselves through annual salary increases, World Cup bonuses and other incentives totalling more than CHF 79 million [around €70m] – in just the last five years'.[29] They revealed how, just before Christmas 2010, Sepp Blatter, secretary general Jérôme Valcke and his deputy Markus Kattner had sat in Blatter's office in the hills above Zurich with the president's friend and finance committee chairman Julio Grondona and awarded themselves astronomical payments. Blatter had unilaterally signed off a CHF 9m 'World Cup' bonus for Valcke, before passing the pen to Valcke and Grondona. They'd then approved Sepp's CHF 11m bonus, before he and Valcke had completed the golden triangle by putting their names to Kattner's CHF 3m. Within a few months, Blatter had indemnified Valcke and Kattner against the increasingly likely costs of future civil or criminal proceedings and had guaranteed them CHF 17.5m and CHF 9.8m pay-offs respectively. The external lawyers thought the arrangements unlawful, and both men were later sacked. Blatter resigned. But the KPMG auditors, for whom the payments had been in plain sight for years and who had annually rubber-stamped FIFA's manifestly inadequate internal controls, had not batted an eyelid. In October 2017 the Swiss auditing regulator announced that it had found 'shortcomings' in KPMG's work between 2008 and 2014, and that it had formally reprimanded one, unnamed individual.[30]

'For the Good of the Game', runs FIFA's slogan. For a decade and a half KPMG had allowed it to be corrupted. But nobody had ever really found out how and why. In an effort to do so, I tracked down some insiders from the day in 1999 when FIFA had first brought in KPMG as adviser and auditor.

INSIDE FIFA

KPMG's first job, alongside McKinsey, had been to review FIFA's administration. Its terms of reference, one senior FIFA insider from the time told me, came 'directly from the President's office, because the President has some specific views as to what the result should be'. Blatter told the advisers what they should find, according to my source. 'I want you to come back with such [specified] suggestions,' he said, 'and they were listed and they [KPMG] had no choice but to do that.' The accountants were already doing what they were told.

The consequences became clear when I spoke to the man who had taken a stand against 'financial irregularities' and resigned from his position as FIFA secretary general after his explosive intervention at that 2002 executive committee meeting. Michel Zen-Ruffinen, now a 58-year-old lawyer in the French-speaking south-west of Switzerland, recalled only too well the financial

Wild West that FIFA's Zurich HQ had turned into.

There had been an important rule within FIFA, he told me. When Blatter was elected president he secured a special budget for his presidential office, which was placed outside the usual financial controls. Instead of having the use of this budget signed off by the finance committee, a separate 'Bureau of the Finance Committee' comprising just Blatter and his cronies Jack Warner and Julio Grondona would be responsible for it. 'It was not possible for anyone but the Bureau. . . to question the details of the budget', Zen-Ruffinen told me. When I asked if KPMG went along with this arrangement, he replied: 'Definitely, for sure, otherwise there would have been a problem.' That KPMG should accede to this arrangement, putting the executive president beyond control at the same time as vouching for the adequacy of the organisation's financial controls, was serious enough. But the firm's acquiescence appeared to go even further. Senior sources within FIFA at the time alleged that there was also a tacit understanding between FIFA and KPMG that audits would not be too intrusive. One told of discussions 'as to the way [KPMG] should execute their mandate, meaning, you know, when you get a mandate of such an importance you should not be too problematic. . .'.

As for the man who wasn't being too problematic, Herr Luthiger, he 'was always in FIFA'. The unassuming accountant 'was travelling with us, he was sitting in the first rows, he had the best tickets at the World Cup, he had the VIP treatment, something that is against all compliance rules'. At FIFA congresses, often just before major tournaments, 'Blatter would call Luthiger to answer any questions if there were any.' With the business over, often the bean counter 'didn't travel back as he was supposed to but he stayed and watched the matches in the VIP area. And that is already in conflict [for an] auditor.' Blatter's former number two, Zen-Ruffinen, concurred that the KPMG team 'were considered as being members of the FIFA delegation and invited to matches and inauguration ceremonies, et cetera, for sure . . . which is a conflict of interest, absolutely, but this is the way things were organized at that time'.

With the accountants' complicity, football ceased to be the people's game and became a criminal one. Some of the world's poorest countries have been deprived of the grass-roots facilities they should have had, either because the funds disappeared or because commercial rights were sold too cheaply while officials pocketed their pay-offs. In the rich world, no doubt the millions playing *FIFA 18* on their screens are paying more for the privilege too. Other consequences are more bizarre, but still diminish the game. The day after the December 2010 bonus-fest, Sepp Blatter pulled a card from an envelope and beamed: 'The winner to organize the 2022 FIFA World Cup is . . . Qatar!' Elation from the Gulf state's delegation mingled with incredulity around the rest of Zurich's Messezentrum conference centre. The world's most important football matches would be played in a country with no history in the sport and precious few fans, in stadiums built on near-slave labour at temperatures above 40°C.

Such an outcome could have been possible only from a rigged selection process. Which was exactly what it turned out to have been when the *Sunday Times* obtained a leak of documents and emails behind the bid. 'Plot to buy the World Cup', read its front-page splash on 1 June 2014. Millions of dollars' worth of dubious payments and schmoozing had secured the vote for Qatar. The country had won through backhanders paid to influential figures in the voting process, foremost among them Jack Warner.

If the auditors from KPMG had been doing their job many years earlier, this could not have happened. When the 2022 football season is thrown into turmoil to accommodate a ludicrous World Cup hosting decision many years earlier, a chunk of the blame will belong with the bean counters.

BANKING ON THE BEAN COUNTERS

If the world's favourite game became riddled with dirty money under the bean counters' noses, so too, on an even grander scale, did its banks.

It came as no shock that several of the payments on the indictment against FIFA went through accounts at British bank HSBC. In December 2012, the bank had paid record $1.9bn fines in the US for money-laundering failings so pervasive that, it admitted, 'at least $881 million in drug trafficking proceeds, including proceeds of drug trafficking by the Sinaloa Cartel in Mexico and the Norte del Valle Cartel in Colombia, were laundered through HSBC Bank USA without being detected'. The cartels had made boxes specially 'to fit the precise dimensions of the teller windows' at HSBC's Mexican branches, said one lead prosecutor.[31]

Since 1991, every significant HSBC operation had been audited by the local arm of KPMG (of which the bank's chairman Douglas Flint had been a partner until becoming HSBC finance director in 1995 in a classically conflicted accountant-to-director move). As KPMG's fees from HSBC rose – to £78m in 2010 – so did the incentive not to upset the client too much. HSBC Mexico's accounts were repeatedly signed off by KPMG Cardenas Dosal, which made the standard claim to have tested the 'evidence' behind the figures without ever appearing to have asked whether hundreds of millions of dollars in cash from Colombia might be at all dodgy. Although the rampant money laundering was exposing it to major risks that should have been reported, the 'clean' accounts didn't mention any. In the US, where the dollars were being sent, and where some of KPMG's finest might have been expected to question the source of such large sums, no suspicions were raised either.

For direct financial cost to the public, HSBC's money laundering was eclipsed by its involvement in tax evasion. A huge leak of data from its Swiss private banking arm, which found its way into the media in 2015 through the International Consortium of Investigative Journalists, revealed that it was home to thousands of undeclared accounts, used mainly for tax evasion or concealing illicit money – often with the bankers' encouragement. When HSBC director Rona Fairhead, chair of HSBC's audit committee at the relevant time, answered questions on the affair in Britain's Parliament, Labour MP Austin Mitchell put to her: 'You were audited by KPMG [who] do not seem to have noticed that there were basic control weaknesses, which allowed all this illegality to go on. They collected £53 million in fees.' Fairhead could only sigh: 'I look at what we did in both internal audit and external audit and I wonder why those things were not identified.'[32] The truth was that KPMG wasn't really in the identifying business; it was in the fee-earning business.

Some cases showed that, for the large fee-paying banks, the Big Four were prepared to do more than just look the other way. They would actively assist in the deception. In 2013, Deloitte was fined $10m for having watered down part of a report into how Standard Chartered Bank had hidden £250bn worth of illegal transactions with Iran. The regulators found that Deloitte had failed to 'demonstrate the necessary autonomy and objectivity'.[33] Once the watchwords of accountancy, these qualities were now set aside for the right fee. This criticism of Deloitte was mild, however, next to the same regulator's finding a few months later against PwC over a rigged report on sanctions-breaking transfers by the US branch of Bank of Tokyo-Mitsubishi. The accountants had excised from their report the fact that the bank had a policy of 'stripping' incriminating information from wire transfers and thus hiding the money's origins or destination. It had also deleted references to 'wire-stripping', 'enemy countries' and the use of out-of-place characters such as '#' and '-' in text so that automatic filters would not pick up words associated with the illegal transactions.[34]

The bean counters had wanted to limit the damage to the bank, rather than expose its wrongdoing. 'On numerous occasions', ran the settlement agreement imposing a $25m fine, one PwC director had 'made statements in emails to PwC partners and employees that elevated his apparent concern for client satisfaction over the need for objective inquiry'. He had warned that looking for more illicit transactions than had already been found 'can only raise questions', and suggested other lines of enquiry were dropped because they would 'open up a whole other can of worms at this point'. The PwC man had even resisted one suggestion on the grounds that 'if we do find information [and] it points the finger at another bank, it will not make [Bank of Tokyo-Mitsubishi] any more friends'. Significantly, no partner or senior figure at PwC had 'reprimanded or even told [the] director that his comments were inappropriate'. The firm, concluded the regulator, lacked 'objectivity, integrity and autonomy'.[35]

With money laundering estimated at 2–3% of world gross domestic product, or somewhere in the low trillions of dollars every year, the costs of the accountants' indifference – paid by victims of drug cartels, those impoverished by kleptocratic rulers and others – are huge.[36] But the banks are too important as clients to be asked awkward questions. This was why PwC had a dedicated relationship partner for maximizing the firm's revenue from the Bank of Tokyo-Mitsubishi even though it wasn't even the bank's auditor. It might also have explained why the bean counter who had played down the sanctions violations was promoted to become a PwC partner.[37]

Global banks like HSBC, Standard Chartered and Bank of Tokyo-Mitsubishi, operating in scores of countries, were the archetypal multinational enterprises for which the accountancy profession had itself become globalized. If accountants from a single network of firms could audit all the dispersed parts, improved accounting would follow. Or so the bean counters had reasoned. In reality, despite their protestations, everywhere the bean counters went, they became concerned more with keeping worldwide fee-earners happy than with rooting out financial abuse.

10

FAR FROM HOME

THE REST OF THE WORLD GETS THE BIG FOUR TREATMENT, AND PAYS A HEAVY PRICE

Ever since Edwin Waterhouse remarked that 'an American connection was springing up' and sent two young bean counters across the Atlantic in the 1890s, international coverage has been central to the major accountancy firms' business model. When New York-based James Marwick met William Peat from London on a liner in 1911, the Peat, Marwick, Mitchell & Co. that emerged could satisfy the accounting needs of corporate clients in a new age of transatlantic communication and trading. Many such companies now had operations elsewhere around the world, too, which also needed auditing. Usually this meant their home auditor teaming up with bean counters who had already made their way to some far-flung part of the British Empire. In India, for example, firms set up by English accountants in the 1870s and 1880s in the capital of the Raj, Calcutta, became business partners of Price Waterhouse and William Peat at the turn of the twentieth century.[1]

Closer to home, expansion was more direct. The Anglo-American firms were particularly keen to entrench the profession in Germany to serve emerging industrial giants like IG Farben and Daimler-Benz. Most set up offices in Berlin in the mid 1920s, Price Waterhouse cornering the market in auditing the country's steel industry on the back of its experience with US Steel. But it was here that the leading accountants showed how their eagerness to serve these masters could blinker them to more important moral questions. In September 1938, the International Accounting Congress, bringing together many of the international profession's leading lights, controversially gathered in swastika-bedecked parliamentary rooms. They flattered their Nazi hosts, who had already banned Jews from entering the profession. As accounting history professor Steve Walker put it in his account of this episode, the accountants 'behaved in a placatory manner in order to protect their own interests and those of American and British capital'.[2] In doing so, they exhibited a narrow world view and a reluctance to ask the hard questions that would linger over the decades.

It was soon after the Second World War, in a new phase of international trade growth, that the major firms began realizing the full potential of more organized, connected multinational networks. Price Waterhouse set up a new international co-ordinating company in 1946, bringing together senior partners from its US and British firms with a handful from Europe, South America and Australia. Thirteen years later, the firm's US arm was proud to say that it was 'part of what is today probably the largest professional organization in the world, having offices in 134 locations in 43 countries'.[3] During the 1950s and 1960s, all the big names established scores of overseas firms, often by acquiring the local practices with which they had previously had looser co-operation agreements but which multinational clients were now outgrowing. In the words of Arthur Andersen & Co.'s official historians, 'by the mid 1950s, developments justified full-scale offices'. While the aggressive American firm had nothing like as many overseas arms as Price Waterhouse, it did lead the way in providing, as one Price Waterhouse partner enviously put it, 'the same quality of work done everywhere in the world'.[4]

A critical move to the East came in the form of alliances with Tokyo accountancy practices following the admission of Japanese stocks onto the New York Stock Exchange in 1961, as the country's automotive and technological champions powered a resurgent economy. These companies were now part of Western high finance, which came with more investor- and market-oriented accounting requirements. They would, for example, have to produce consolidated accounts for groups of companies and recognize a greater variety of assets and liabilities than they had under the old *zaibatsu* system of concentrated, opaque corporate ownership. In the absence of a strong local profession or tradition – Japan had adopted double-entry bookkeeping only a few decades before – the major firms of the US and UK were the only ones equipped for this task. They would quickly dominate the profession in Japan.

Elsewhere, the global takeover was slower. Germany had a profession built on its own strong accounting tradition (in 1795, one of Goethe's characters had described 'bookkeeping by double entry' as 'among the finest inventions of the human mind').[5] And when the big Anglo-American firms were expelled in the war, the profession came under the control of a group of auditing companies owned by the country's banks. As the Brits and Americans reappeared, the largest German accountancy businesses came together to provide a viable national alternative in Deutsche Treuhand-Gesellschaft. Under pioneering chairman Reinhard Goerdeler, in 1979 the firm then merged with Dutch firm Klynveld Kraayenhof to create a European accounting giant, KMG, to rival the Big Eight US and British outfits. But, as the premium on size increased in the financial frenzy of the 1980s, even this could not stay out of the clutches of the acquisitive world accountancy establishment for long. In 1987, KMG merged with Peat Marwick to create what was soon rebranded as today's KPMG.

Within a couple of years, the Big Eight became a Big Six and then, through three more mergers and a bankruptcy, in 2002 the Big Four of today. Although each national arm of these firms is legally independent, all are uniformly branded in order to win contracts with international clients under a global offer. PwC, for example, boasts of being 'both a local and global partner, sharing knowledge, skills and resources'. In return for using the Big Four name, slogans and branding, national firms pay a share of central marketing costs to special companies that own this 'intellectual property' in Switzerland (in the case of Deloitte and KPMG), Delaware (PwC) and the Bahamas (Ernst & Young). Commercially, the Big Four are indisputably global businesses. If anything goes wrong in one location, however, the centres of their empires in London, New York and elsewhere wash their hands of the affair by pointing to each national partnership's separate legal identity. The arrangement brings all the benefits of globalization to the Big Four without commensurate accountability. The top bean counters can slide into any market with few fears for the consequences.

RUSSIAN FUDGE

The fall of the Soviet Union presented the unmissable commercial opportunity to advise on, and audit, the legendarily corrupt privatizations of the era. In March 2002, a *New York Times* reporter interviewed current and former employees of the major firms and concluded that 'in their rush for a foothold, the Big Six (now Big Five) auditors lent their reputations to practices that in the West would be regarded as unethical if not illegal'. Often this would involve looking away from dubious deals that, in one former Price Waterhouse employee's words, in reality amounted to 'organized robbery'.[6] One banker exposed certain deals by Russia's largest energy company Gazprom with 'related parties', i.e., directors and other companies linked to them, which should be reported because of the obvious opportunities for manipulation. He compared them with the company's subsequent accounts, commenting wryly: 'If you believe their [auditor PwC's] assessment, you would conclude we found 100% of the related-party deals. I doubt that is true.'[7] More junior bean counters were left with little choice but to play along. 'A big client is God,' remarked one ex-Ernst & Young employee. 'You do what they want and tell you to do . . . If you lose that account, no matter how justified you are, that's the end of a career.'

Adverse auditing findings came only when they suited powerful interests. In 2007, PwC withdrew ten years' worth of clean audit certificates that it had given for oil company Yukos's accounts. The company and its politically ambitious chief executive Mikhail Khodorkovsky were on the receiving end of a fierce campaign by the government of Vladimir Putin that would be greatly assisted if Yukos could be shown to have produced false accounts. PwC's Moscow boss, Mike Kubena, initially objected in high-minded terms to any state interference: 'This case challenges the basic role of the auditor, which represents a key element in the development of a normal, functioning economy.' The Russian tax authorities then raided PwC's office, alleging tax evasion and collusion with Yukos to suppress profits. A few weeks later, PwC withdrew its audit certificates for all years from 1995 to 2004, ostensibly on the grounds of new information provided by prosecutors. Most observers sensed what was going on. 'I don't think anyone is going to believe this is anything other than bowing to pressure from the Kremlin,' was the reaction of one of the company's main overseas shareholders. 'I'm astonished to see such a complete lack of backbone in an organization like that.'[8] The exact truth behind the story – whether PwC's clean audit certificates should not have been issued in the first place, or whether they were improperly withdrawn – never fully emerged. The later Wikileaks episode would, however, reveal a diplomatic cable stating that the evidence 'may show that PwC received [Russian government] pressure to disavow its prior Yukos audits'.[9]

The one certainty is that PwC continued to prosper in Russia, auditing such state-controlled monoliths as Gazprom and Sberbank. As another cable estimated, 'it is the auditor of firms comprising more than 50% of Russian GDP'.[10] Its income from the

Russian and Eastern Europe region was already more than $500m a year and growing at around 25% annually.[11] The cost of losing a licence in one of the important 'BRIC' (Brazil, Russia, India and China) emerging economies, for which there were high economic hopes at the time, would have been serious. Against that, there was little downside to failing to stand up to corrupt regimes. In the words of *The Economist* magazine at the time, 'PwC's volte-face [on the Yukos audits] seems unlikely to hurt it elsewhere in the world because of its federated structure . . . Instead, the likeliest victim of the saga is that normal, functioning economy of which Mr Kubena used to speak.'[12]

A decade later, that depressing view of the region would remain true. In 2017, PwC was removed as auditor of Ukraine's largest privately owned bank, Privatbank, after it was nationalized following accusations that its leaders had been siphoning billions from it. The country's central bank would find a $5bn hole in the accounts and conclude that 'PwC failed to become the third line of defence [after the bankers themselves and its internal checks and balances]' as cash was 'drained from the bank through related-party lending'.[13] The former Soviet republics would be stuck with the same corrupt economies and businesses, rubber-stamped by the same Big Four bean counters.

MILKING IT

When the culture at the top of the accountancy profession was exposed by the great American accounting failures at the turn of the twentieth century, a host of similar scandals proved how far and wide it had soured. They also showed the enduring effectiveness of the bean counters' arrangements to dodge responsibility.

'Europe's Enron', as some called it, was Dutch supermarket group Royal Ahold, the world's third largest retailer, which overstated its revenues by around €1bn before auditor Deloitte finally cottoned on in 2003. Arguably more extreme, though, were the same accountancy firm's lapses at Italian dairy company Parmalat, which concocted billions of euros' worth of profits by writing two invoices for each sale of milk to supermarkets. When the expensive private interests of the company's owner Calisto Tanzi, including local football club Parma FC, demanded even more than this scam could provide, the firm simply invented business. Parmalat began reporting sales of enough milk to the Cuban government, supposedly through a Cayman Islands company, for the island's inhabitants to enjoy 60 gallons each every year. None of it was delivered.[14] It shouldn't have been difficult for a half-competent audit firm to spot.

The wrangling about compensation at least offered a glimpse of how the big firms worked. Although Deloitte argued that only its Italian partnership was liable over the affair, it emerged that the lead partner there had told those who had raised objections to the fraud that 'we are an integrated firm worldwide'. Parmalat, he'd said, was 'a crown jewel for our organization worldwide' and they should keep quiet about their star client.[15] When an accountant from Deloitte's Brazilian arm threatened to withhold a clean audit certificate for the Parmalat subsidiary company in his country, Deloitte's Italian lead partner appealed to the international co-ordinating company, Deloitte Touche Tohmatsu. This firm, Swiss-registered but run by Deloitte's worldwide boss, Jim Copeland from the US, took the diligent Brazilian bean counter off the case. Because of this explicit, proven interference from the headquarters firm, in 2009 Deloitte's US arm was forced by a New York judge to cough up $149m compensation to shareholders.[16] But this was the exception, of a Big Four firm being held accountable at home for its operations abroad, that proved the rule that they generally wouldn't be. 'It is very rare that worldwide co-ordinating audit networks enter into settlements like what we have,' said the investors' lawyer.[17] The bean counters' liability-dodging international structures ensured that, in the absence of arduous and inordinately expensive litigation, the bill didn't land on HQ's doorstep.

In any case, direct intervention from the top of a firm wasn't needed for accountancy to go wrong. The unhealthy culture of late-twentieth-century American accountancy now suffused the Big Four's international operations, which were capable of false accounting all by themselves. 'Australia's Enron' was the country's largest insurance company HIH, which went down in 2001 with a previously concealed deficit of several billion dollars. As at Enron, over-mighty executives were jailed, while auditors from Arthur Andersen were found by a royal commission to have been 'insufficiently rigorous'.[18] In Japan, PwC's local arm achieved the rare distinction of being banned for a couple of months, with three of its executives being found guilty of conspiracy, over a fraud at cosmetics company Kanebo.[19] Even in Germany, thought to have relatively upstanding auditors, the Big Four turn blind eyes. In 2002, KPMG had to admit it had cleared the accounts of an early sat-nav software company, Comroad, when 97% of its sales were fake ones that had supposedly been made to a non-existent Hong Kong company.[20] More shockingly still, the firm diligently built up by Reinhard Goerdeler over decades had to be replaced as auditor of engineering giant Siemens after it failed to spot more than 4,000 illicit payments over a decade from the mid 1990s, including some under the Iraq oil-for-food programme. 'This pattern of bribery by Siemens was unprecedented in scale and geographic reach,' said a US prosecutor. 'The corruption involved more than $1.4 billion in bribes to government officials in Asia, Africa, Europe, the Middle East and the Americas.'[21] Lawyers brought in to investigate unsurprisingly found that the sleepy bean counters could have done more to alert the company's supervisory board to the corruption.[22]

Soon, major accounting scandals were erupting in Japan, with Ernst & Young's network firm proving unable to stand up to the country's fierce corporate culture while accounting fraud ran wild at national giants Olympus and Toshiba. After the latter overstated its income by $1.3bn over seven years to mask its declining business fortunes, Ernst & Young ShinNihon was fined $17m for a 'grave breach of duty', having 'built a misplaced sense of confidence that Toshiba would not do such things'.[23]

The procession of false accounting sanctioned by the bean counters away from home was not halted by what should have been the corrective of a world financial crisis. Spain's Bankia was formed in 2010 when several troubled regional savings banks were brought together. It appeared to be weathering the storm and in 2011 raised almost €2bn from shareholders in a rights issue based on a reasonably healthy outlook. But this would later turn out to have been based on false figures. What was initially reported as a small profit for the year would be assessed more accurately as a €3.3bn loss thanks to previously ignored falls in value of property loans. The parallels with Royal Bank of Scotland in the UK were striking. And once again, a chunk of the blame lay with auditors from Deloitte. The firm had advised Bankia on its accounting and then, marking its own homework, given the fund-raising prospectus the all-clear. The extent of its conflicts of interest was obvious from the numbers: it had received 50% more for consultancy than it had for auditing the bank. According to the Spanish financial regulator, Deloitte 'showed a more than reproachable lack of attention and care' and 'absolute non-observance of the rules of independence'.[24] The firm was fined €12m over the affair, and in 2017, a judge would charge the partner who signed off the accounts with criminal offences.[25]

CONDUCT UNBECOMING

The Big Four's habit of professing high standards in their main centres such as New York and London while flouting them in distant lands became more visible as companies growing in emerging markets were wooed by Western capital markets and their stock exchanges. In the US in particular this occasionally brought the overseas bean counters into the sights of aggrieved investors and regulators.

In 2011, PwC's Indian firm was fined $7.5m by the US Securities and Exchange Commission – and forced to pay even more in compensation – over deficient audits that had emerged a couple of years earlier at New York-listed Indian IT company Satyam. At the heart of the case was $1bn in cash and revenues, based on fake bank confirmations created in the (later jailed) chairman's office, which appeared on the company's books under its auditor's nose. PwC's response to the affair said much about the Big Four's self-interested view of shoddy auditing performed in their name. When the scandal broke, the firm's worldwide chief executive Sam DiPiazza cut short his stay at the 2009 World Economic Forum in Davos and jetted to Mumbai. A couple of auditors were suspended and DiPiazza was soon making the requisite noises about conducting 'an extensive review of our processes globally'. He claimed to one interviewer, however, that 'we are as much a victim as anyone'. His audit partners 'were clearly misled'.[26] The notion that PwC's auditors should not have been hoodwinked to the tune of $1bn appeared to have escaped DiPiazza. And it was clear from what he presumably thought a reassuring remark, that 'India will be one of the key engines of our future growth', where the priorities of PwC's world leader really lay. Even in the face of a scandal over which the bean counters would subsequently be found seriously wanting, they remained preoccupied by their own fortunes.

Such cases began to draw increasing amounts of regulatory fire. Deloitte's Brazilian arm was found to have been covering up fraud at low-cost airline Gol, and in 2016 was fined a record $8m by the US's Public Company Accounting and Oversight Board for 'materially false audit reports and attempting to cover up audit violations by improperly altering documents and providing false testimony'.[27] The regulator's director of enforcement described the case as 'the most serious misconduct we've uncovered'. It was 'cover-up after cover-up after cover-up'. One sad footnote to the affair was that the 'national professional practice director' of the firm, Wanderley Olivetti, received a five-year ban for misleading investigators.[28] He was the same accountant who, a decade and a half earlier, had spoken out in the Parmalat affair. Higher up in a Big Four firm, it appeared, commercial pressures became harder to resist. The affair wasn't exceptional. According to the US accountancy regulator, Deloitte's member firms had not obtained 'reasonable assurances' about the figures it had signed off for 67% of its non-US audit clients that had listings in the States. The average for the other three firms, 45%, wasn't much more reassuring.[29]

Far from harming their worldwide business, however, lax standards abroad appear to have helped the Big Four dominate the accountancy professions outside their home markets. In the decade up to 2016, their Asia-Pacific fees more than doubled, from $9bn to $19.3bn.[30] A bit of bad publicity is a price worth paying for building a large client base. If that means giving companies what they want, not what their investors and the public need, so be it.

BREAKING CHINA

Nowhere was the aggressively expansive strategy more evident, or effective, than in the country that by 2010 had grown to be the world's second-largest economy. The Big Four firms had been given the right to audit Chinese companies in 1992 under Deng Xiaoping's market reforms. In the twenty-first century, as the country's financial borders opened wider, they began to dominate accounting in what was now a highly lucrative market.

In its 2009 annual report, Deloitte could boast of 28% growth in China on the back of its 'strategic interest in that country'. It soon became apparent, however, that this growth came at a price. Short-sellers exposed a string of blatant accounting frauds: in 2013, one researcher linked Deloitte's China arm to 17 major known cases. The firm had already been forced to resign from two important clients after signing off vastly inflated profit figures for years.[31]

By this time, the Big Four firms had a litany of suspect Chinese audits to their names. But they were shielded from too much exposure by the refusal of their local arms to release papers to overseas regulators, citing prohibitive domestic laws. It was left to the short-sellers to discover cases such as China Integrated Energy, a biodiesel producer whose healthy financial results belied its near-dormancy. The company had just raised funds on the US markets thanks to accounts signed off by KPMG reflecting production that would have demanded a dozen trucks' worth of raw material every day entering its plant. A short-seller put the company under surveillance and saw just six in four months, five of them on the day of a visit by investors. Basic auditing checks would have exposed the scam, and KPMG duly had to resign as auditor.[32] Ernst & Young was equally embarrassed by its approval of figures for Sino-Forest, a timber company that claimed swathes of forest that it didn't actually own. And so it went on, as more than a hundred Chinese companies, the larger ones mainly audited by the Big Four, were forced to de-list from the US markets in 2011 and 2012.[33]

A charitable view would be that in China the bean counters had bitten off more than they could chew. One accounting professor in Beijing thought they were 'guilty of taking bad clients', and that 'given the Big Four's pace of expansion, it's no surprise that they have a shortage of what you can call gray-hair or no-hair partners'.[34] But behind the incompetence was the reality that, as multinational enterprises, the Big Four had put fees and global expansion above their capability to shoulder the responsibilities they had taken on. In its 2009 worldwide report, KPMG boasted how it had grown fivefold in China since the turn of the century, and planned to continue to do so. It would 'proactively identify potential ... targets for clients and work with KPMG member firms in other countries, leveraging the global M&A network to help clients target new markets'. Given the extent of fraud and misrepresentation in corporate China, decent auditing would have scuppered quite a number of such mergers and acquisitions. The conflict between KPMG's aggressively fee-generating objectives and sound auditing was therefore obvious. But the overriding aim was to claim territory, not to ensure that the world's most rapidly expanding economy had the accounting it needed.

The strategy that has been deployed in the West for decades is now being rolled out across the emerging economies: control the audit market, build tax and consultancy services around it, and inveigle into the political establishment (KPMG, for example, advises the Chinese government on its tax policy). The firms are even managing to limit accountability in the way they have in the West. In the aftermath of all the accounting scandals, the Big Four's Chinese outposts converted to the local equivalent of limited liability partnerships, replicating the structure that allows them to relinquish responsibility back home.

FULL SERVICE

Failed accounting isn't all that the Big Four bean counters have been exporting for some time. Almost all the services developed in the main offices in the UK and US to capitalize on their status and access as auditors to large companies have been adapted for a wider market.

When dozens of countries' journalists went to work on the LuxLeaks files in 2014, the story became sensational precisely because the industrial-scale tax avoidance organized by PwC was clearly a global phenomenon. Along with schemes for the US and UK corporations were tax-avoidance plans for a couple of the largest companies in Finland, a care hospital operator in Sweden, a federal agency from Canada, two of Brazil's largest banks plus similar set-ups in twenty other countries.[35] And these were just glimpses of the tax avoidance made possible by the Big Four firms' omnipresence. Offices in all real economies, plus more than twenty recognized tax havens such as the Cayman Islands and the British Virgin Islands, enable them to orchestrate the great cross-border tax-dodging game.[36] They are expert in each place's tax laws, as well as the overarching international rules, and can easily spot the loopholes and gaps in this patchwork.

Tax scheming designed by the Big Four now stretches as far as the wholesale reorganization of multinational business, usually under the euphemism of 'tax-efficient supply-chain management'. This involves carefully carving it up into profitable and less profitable parts, parking the former somewhere tax-friendly. At a 2008 International Fiscal Association conference in New Delhi, an Ernst & Young partner set out the plan. 'Centralization of management, control and business risks' (the profitable part) would be 'located in low tax jurisdiction'. Elsewhere, in the countries where the multinational really did business, its operations would 'perform routine functions and bear subordinate risk' and thus make smaller profits.[37] A couple of years later, PwC pitched similar ideas to brewer Heineken, recommending that such 'tax arbitrage' was incorporated into its supply chain. PwC's anticipated fee was a handy £21m.[38] In this way the Big Four firms routinely help multinationals dance around the international tax system. According to the United Nations, such international tax avoidance costs developing countries as much as £100bn a year – around the same amount as they receive in aid – and makes a 'significant negative impact on their prospects for sustainable development'.[39]

The richest individuals get a similar tax-saving service thanks to the Big Four's global coverage. Expertise in the laws of a client's home country and those of the world's tax havens, with a permanent physical presence in each, enables their accountants to find just the right tax structure. The Big Four are particularly well qualified for the task because they help the tax havens frame their tax- and regulation-dodging laws in the first place. The Cayman Islands government's private sector consultative committee, for example, includes representatives from every Big Four firm.[40] As Nicholas Shaxson, author of the acclaimed tax haven exposé *Treasure Islands* told me: 'The Big Four have done more than any other group to sustain the global system of offshore tax havens.'

The Panama Papers leak of documents from inside law firm Mossack Fonseca in 2016 revealed thousands of examples of the Big Four's offices around the world advising clients on using offshore companies and trusts to own private and business assets. When the scandal broke, the same bean counters were naturally on hand to calm fears. 'Responding to the Panama Papers' was the title of one pamphlet used by Ernst & Young to drum up business. It didn't mention the firm's own extensive presence in the leak, setting up offshore structures for clients from South America to Russia.

The following year, when the same team from Germany's *Süddeutsche Zeitung* and the International Consortium of Investigative Journalism released the Paradise Papers, leaked from inside more upmarket offshore law firm Appleby, the Big Four's role at the centre of the offshore web became clearer still. EY's Isle of Man operation was merrily selling VAT avoidance schemes to Russian oligarchs bringing private jets into Europe. PwC were mining a similarly rich seam. 'Appleby are good friends of ours,' wrote one of the firm's Isle of Man tax directors to a colleague in its Moscow office in 2013 in a comment that betrayed the importance of the offshore world to the Big Four.[41]

KPMG's tax advisers on the Irish Sea island remained shameless about the services they could offer tax avoiders on the British mainland. Two years after Chancellor of the Exchequer George Osborne had brought in a 'general anti-abuse rule', the firm was informing clients on a number of ways still to dodge their dues. In an October 2014 presentation headed *UK Tax Planning Post-GAAR: What's Left?*, one tax manager explained techniques to avoid inheritance tax on valuable property, and how to escape a new tax on property held through offshore shell companies. Even more controversial, given the UK government's long-running battle against the avoidance of employment taxes, was a suggested ruse to get round the latest legislative clampdown. Under the heading 'Employment structures', KPMG noted extensive 'legislation aimed at "false" self-employment and offshore employers generally'. It had 'a possible solution' involving separate UK and Isle of Man employers for the same person – who was really working for another, real UK business. Fees for the individual's services would head to the offshore company before being lent back to him or her in the UK tax-free.[42]

In London and elsewhere, the Big Four firms were claiming to have retreated from tax avoidance. KPMG was even spearheading a 'responsible tax' initiative. Away from home, their colleagues had evidently not got the memo.

LOCAL COUNSEL

As 'independent' firms with expertise spanning any number of disciplines and sectors, the Big Four have become trusted advisers to governments around the world – even as they empty their coffers with tax avoidance schemes. This in turn enables them to ensure that policy promotes the manifold services they have to offer, further entrenching their positions close to power. The result is that some of the worst public policy failures in which they have been instrumental at home are adopted by other countries. The private finance initiative, for example, has been sold to an array of countries by the UK with the help of the Big Four. 'To secure the best advice for foreign governments,' an official City of London guide promoting PFI in India set out in 2008, 'the UK works closely with a range of accountancy and management consultancy firms, including KPMG and PwC.'[43] Studies conducted by the Big Four firms pointing out the advantages of PFI, but not its costs or unconvincing record, became persuasive evidence in the sales pitch. On the ground, however, what are known as public–private partnerships, worth $70bn by 2012, have not worked out so well in an economy even less suited to extended deals with large private companies than the UK's. Despite benefiting from the Big Four's expert counsel, contracts have proved uneconomical and service providers have pulled out. 'RIPPP', wrote an *Economist* headline-writer.[44] Now the Big Four are focusing on services across the board: PwC's Indian public sector practice promises advice on 'government process reengineering', 'government enterprise architecture design', and 'strategy and roadmap', among a dozen other euphemisms for the commercialization of services.[45] KPMG, meanwhile, advises the New Delhi government on 'robust fiscal management, including revenue enhancement, fiscal consolidation and expenditure rationalization', and claims to be 'at the helm of providing high-end investment promotion and regulatory advice'.[46] More of the small government, deregulatory, neo-liberal economic medicine, in other words. Whether or not it works for nation states, it has the happy consequence of opening up plenty of opportunities for the Big Four.

The urge to get close to power even turned part of a Big Four firm into a tool of a corrupt regime. In 2017, KPMG was forced to withdraw a report it had written a couple of years earlier on an alleged rogue unit within the South African Revenue Service (SARS). On the back of its investigation, former SARS boss and anti-corruption campaigner Pravin Gordhan – a leading critic of President Jacob Zuma – had been sacked as finance minister. KPMG's report had indicated, incorrectly, that Gordhan knew of the alleged rogue unit. The accountancy firm eventually admitted that its work 'fell considerably short of KPMG's standards', forcing its South African leader and five other partners to resign.[47] Other verdicts were even more damning. Save South Africa, a civil society group that exposed a mass of scandal swirling around Zuma, accused KPMG of 'a hatchet job, a weapon to create political division and deal with those fighting against state capture and the looting of state resources'. The accountants had 'provided ammunition for a purge of some of our finest and most honest leaders and government officials'.[48] Equally symptomatic of how KPMG saw its role in the country was its approach to Zuma crony and billionaire businessman Atul Gupta. The firm had allowed payments from his media and mining business empire, which should have been used for a dairy project under post-apartheid black empowerment laws, to fund his daughter's lavish 2013 wedding in Sun City and be treated as a business expense. A number of KPMG's partners had attended the $3m bash, its then Africa chairman Moses Kgosana writing to Gupta after the 'world-class wedding' that he and his wife 'enjoyed every moment . . . it was an event of the millennium'.[49] As elsewhere in the world, the bean counters preferred to cosy up to economic power rather than hold it to account.

The scandal's political dimensions brought the most adverse publicity to a Big Four firm for some time.[50] KPMG's worldwide chairman, American John Veihmeyer, tried the standard moral gymnastics when caught out: contrition and denial. 'I sincerely apologize for what went wrong in South Africa,' began his statement on the matter. 'It is not who we are.'[51] The nature of the affair, not to mention the role of no less a figure than KPMG's chairman for the whole of Africa, told otherwise.

PROFIT, NOT PEOPLE

Market economies are the modern bean counter's natural habitat. They provide the corporate profits from which to extract fees and often produce amenable governments to assist in doing so. Even their crises present more opportunity. The Big Four will accordingly go to great lengths to defend the market, as events in one of its main twenty-first-century centres graphically illustrated.

In June 2014, pro-democracy campaigners were planning a mass demonstration in downtown Hong Kong. They were demanding open elections after Beijing had ruled that voters would have to choose a new local leader from a selection of Communist Party-approved candidates. Outside the world's tyrannies, most would have agreed that here was, at the very least, a legitimate protest. But just as they had in Berlin seventy-six years earlier, the bean counters took a more myopic view.

'In Opposition to the Occupy Central Movement', ran the headline above official-looking notices in Hong Kong's newspapers on 27 June 2014. 'Acting lawfully and respecting the rights of others is the responsibility of every citizen,' they lectured. The area targeted for the protest was 'the heart of Hong Kong's financial and business activity', where 'financial and professional services companies conduct key large transactions and commercial activities'. The action 'would increase the instability and confusion on the market and cause inestimable losses in the economy', while 'multinational companies and investors would consider moving their regional headquarters from Hong Kong, or indeed leave the city entirely'. At the bottom of the notices were the names: 'EY KPMG Deloitte PwC')[52].

The protests went ahead and lasted until the end of the year. Hundreds of demonstrators were arrested and beaten. International condemnation came from the United Nations and governments around the world, who called for the right to peaceful demonstration: matters that the Big Four evidently thought should be subordinated to undisturbed commerce. The economic effects were in fact short-lived. Companies did not leave Hong Kong. Economic growth was not harmed, never mind 'inestimably'. The accountants were wrong. More remarkable, though, was that the world's leading custodians of financial probity, who had once prided themselves on prudence and objectivity, should have made such an alarmist and partisan intervention – whether on their own initiative or at the behest of the administration. The financial crisis and countless other sobering episodes had not, it appeared, dented either their misplaced loyalties or their self-belief.

11

UNREFORMED AND UNREPENTANT

THE BEAN COUNTERS' BLINDNESS TO THEIR OWN FAILINGS

If the 2008 financial crisis proved anything, it was that, contrary to the assertions of President George W. Bush six years earlier, the era of false profits was not over. While the world descended into a great recession, the accountants were not, as Dubya had promised, 'held to account'. Only a few questions were asked of them, and then with insufficient authority.

This in turn meant that when reforms to the accountancy profession were proposed, they could be blocked fairly easily by the Big Four firms' chequebooks. In the US, lobbying donations to senators and congressmen through political action committees made up of the Big Four's employees hit record levels. Leading beneficiaries included the chairman of the Senate committee overseeing accountancy regulation, and influential members of the banking committee.[1] Plans put forward by the US's Public Company Accounting Oversight Board to limit the time a firm could audit the same company were duly rejected. More serious changes, such as breaking the firms up or splitting off their consultancy services, didn't stand a chance.

Across the Atlantic, the accountants reacted ferociously to tough proposals from the European Commission's internal market commissioner (and now EU Brexit negotiator) Michel Barnier.

'Investor confidence in audit has been shaken by the crisis,' he said in 2011, undertaking to restore it by 'eliminating conflicts of interest, ensuring independence and robust supervision and by facilitating more diversity in what is an overly concentrated market, especially at the top end'.[2] He would split the firms' audit and consultancy arms entirely, require joint audits of the largest companies (including the major banks) and allow firms to audit the same company for just six years so that they would not become too close. With Barnier threatening to blow apart the commercial model that they had built over decades, the big firms dispatched armies of lobbyists to Brussels. The senior partner of an accountancy firm just below the Big Four, who agreed with the Commission that the plans would help loosen the major firms' stranglehold on the profession, blogged that one of the Big Four 'has no less than sixty – YES SIXTY – senior people in Europe engaged full-time in lobbying against the Barnier proposals'.[3] And that was without the corporate lobbying bodies, such as the One Hundred Group of the largest UK companies' finance directors, that the Big Four corralled into arguing that the proposals would damage auditing. Once again, the financial watchdogs and the managers of capital teamed up against the investors and other stakeholders in business on whose side they should have been.

A member of the European Parliament summed up the top bean counters' approach: 'The Big Four have done everything they can to stand in the way of further regulation. There is a lot of effort in maintaining the status quo.'[4] It paid off. In the absence of a proper post-mortem of the bean counters' role in the crisis – thanks largely to their capture of the regulators who ought to have performed one – a general loss of confidence in audit was not enough on which to hang serious reform. The accountants' gripes about extra costs and the alleged loss of understanding of their audit clients' businesses were allowed to prevail. Before long, the plan to separate the auditing and non-auditing arms of the firms was dropped. In its place came a hardly draconian limit on non-audit services for a client to 70% of the audit fees, plus an outright ban on certain services. The length for which a single firm could audit a company without its contract being re-tendered was extended from a planned six years to ten, after which the same firm could still carry on for another ten if it won the bid.

It seemed that the bean counters had, once again, got pretty much what they wanted. One Big Four partner told me that 'the conflict of interest [in providing both audit and non-audit services] has just moved along a time period', to when the auditor is preparing to surrender the audit contract and teeing up the client as a major consultancy client. A KPMG partner publicly celebrated the possibilities under the new system as a 'fantastic opportunity to work with clients as trusted advisers'.[5]

The watchdogs were to be trusted as if nothing had changed. I decided to see if this faith was justified.

MEETING THE BEAN COUNTERS ...

An interview request from a *Private Eye* journalist might not be the most welcome email to land in a businessman's inbox. But when I wrote to each senior UK partner of the Big Four firms in 2016 telling them I was taking a 'critical look' at their profession, I expected them to face the challenge. They all routinely pontificated about transparency and accountability and enjoyed their occasional uncritical appearances in the papers. If I'd been their PR adviser, I'd have told them they would come across as evasive and spineless if they refused to answer a sceptic on matters such as their roles in the financial crisis and their conflicts of interest.

I was wrong. Just one of Britain's top four bean counters, KPMG's senior partner at the time, Simon Collins, agreed to meet me. Deloitte's top man could not spare an hour due to 'diary commitments in the coming few months' and offered a deputy. Somehow, in those few months he did find time to hold forth in the *Evening Standard* under the flattering headline 'David Sproul: lifelong numbers man who's happy to be held to account for Deloitte's dramas'.[6] EY's senior partner, Steve Varley, a 48-year-old ex-Accenture management consultant and triathlete who boasts of his firm's connections at the heart of power, refused point-blank. His firm's mantra – 'The better the question, the better the answer, the better the world works' – was evidently of selective application. (It appeared further removed from reality a few months later when the firm blocked an entry to a business journalism award it was sponsoring in New Zealand because the reporting covered one of its failed audits.)[7]

PwC's UK senior partner, Kevin Ellis, also declined my request, 'after careful consideration'. This 'careful consideration' had not, however, included looking at the speech he had given just two weeks before at the firm's Building Public Trust Awards. 'There's a clear need, indeed a responsibility,' Ellis had said, 'for leaders to understand better how the public sees us, and engage more closely and openly to bridge the trust gap'. A few days after I sent the comments to his press team, I received a call admitting the point 'gave us food for thought' and agreeing that a couple of partners – although not Ellis himself – would meet me after all.

My first port of call was the Canary Wharf base of KPMG. Arriving at the firm's 15-storey glass-and-steel HQ – nestled symbolically between the taller HSBC and Barclays towers – I was particularly keen to learn how the accountancy profession had responded to the financial crisis. Simon Collins, an earnest 56-year-old who would fit most preconceptions of an accountant but with the management-speak of a thoroughly modern bean counter, had clearly given the point some thought. 'Like anyone responsible who played a role in it,' he told me, 'we were stung by it and we've been on a self-improvement and an imposed improvement drive since the financial crisis.' The outcome was that 'auditing [today] would prevent yesterday's financial crisis'. This struck me as quite an admission and a marked departure from the well-worn 'expectations gap' excuse for bean-counting failure, which said that the accountants shouldn't be relied on in the first place. Collins accepted that 'all around the world banks fell over, in some instances not very long after getting clean audit opinions'. It was therefore 'really hard to look back on that and go "yeah, but the audits were fine"'.

At this point I thought I'd encountered some overdue self-awareness on the part of the profession. But then it was time to pass the blame. It was the rules' fault, not ours. 'What I *can* defend is that the audits were done properly to the standards of the day,' he continued. 'What I can't defend is the societal outcome.' A number of legal cases in the United States, however, had shown that in many cases auditing had *not* met the standards of the day. When I rattled off several KPMG audit clients that demonstrated the point – Countrywide, Fannie Mae, New Century, Tier One, Wachovia – Collins replied that these were 'too far away' for him to comment. Nearer to home, he could not talk about HBOS because it was being investigated by the regulators at the time. I put it to him that, under a British worldwide chairman at the time in Mike Rake, these failures reflected a flawed global culture at his firm. 'I don't recognize an international or local culture of carelessness,' he replied. Audit failures were improbable events. 'It's a bit like a plane crash. It requires multiple failings. It requires a client who wants to essentially corrupt the auditor; it requires the auditor to go along with it and hold out the promise of something else; and it requires the other reviews and [the checks] we've put in place to go wrong.'

I found this view of the financial crisis troubling. Given the numbers of audits that had fallen out of the skies above Wall

Street and the City of London, the airline safety analogy didn't look exactly airworthy itself. Experience, I suggested, showed the converse was true. Audits are likely to fail in the absence of success at multiple levels. From bean counters on the ground ensuring, for example, that provisions for losses are sufficient, right up to lead partners being bold enough to confront a bank's directors with their uncomfortable findings, the auditors have to be on their mettle. A lapse at any level can lead to inadequate or fraudulent accounting being signed off. It seemed that Collins's initial, welcome introspection stopped at the point where it required an examination of his firm's actual record. He had become KPMG's senior UK partner in 2012 after many years running its corporate finance advisory arm. This gave him a personal alibi for the audit failures, but did not, I thought, excuse ignorance of his firm's record. On any analysis, including his own, there were important lessons to learn. But they would not be learned by looking away from the scene of the disaster. As he was now running an organization auditing major banks such as Barclays and sitting on the board of KPMG International – whose member firms audit dozens of other financial institutions, including Citigroup in the US and Deutsche Bank in Germany – it was not a reassuring conclusion. It does bear repeating, however, that in contrast to his counterparts, Steve Varley at Ernst & Young, David Sproul at Deloitte and Kevin Ellis at PwC, Collins at least had the guts to talk about it.

I was to find similarly reflective but ultimately self-serving reactions at the other firms. We learned from the financial crisis, they would say, but we didn't really do anything wrong. Deloitte's appointed representative was David Barnes, a dapper 53-year-old from Blackpool who doubles up as the firm's managing partner for public affairs and chairman of its Swiss member firm. More pertinently, he had been at the heart of auditing in the years leading up to the financial crisis as head of the firm's 'financial services audit division' between 2006 and 2011. This experience was not, alas, about to help my understanding of his firm's role. While Barnes made the ritual noises about being 'sure there are lessons we have learned', when it came to the audits themselves it seemed all was up to scratch. Of his firm's work at its largest, most controversial client, Royal Bank of Scotland – including vouching for the bank's finances as part of the contentious 2008 fund-raising – Barnes didn't 'know enough about the specifics'. He held the party line, nevertheless. 'I'm sure there were things we could have done better, but [after reviewing the audits] I think ultimately we concluded that our work was of the right quality to support the opinions we gave both on the financial statements and the rights issue.'

NEW ERA, NEW SCANDAL

Looking ahead, KPMG's Simon Collins insisted to me that 'auditing has changed materially since the financial crisis'. There was 'a huge amount of additional work, of additional professional scepticism, changed approaches to things', plus greater power for companies' audit committees and more detailed audit reports. That additional scepticism should be required seemed a serious indictment of pre-crisis accounting. Professional scepticism had always been part of the bean-counting job description. Nevertheless, some figures do attest to slight improvement in the UK. Over a five-year period up to 2015, the Financial Reporting Council's audit inspection unit reported an increase in the proportion of audits it examined (on FTSE350 clients) that were 'good or only requiring limited improvements', from 48% to 67%. These were, however, the findings of the same body that concluded from its 2007 inspections that UK auditing was 'fundamentally sound'. Its judgements need to be treated with a certain caution.[8] It might also be asked whether 33% of large audits needing more than limited improvements is much to cheer about anyway.

In the US, things looked less impressive, its accountancy regulator reporting rising levels of 'deficiencies' in audit inspections from 2009. By 2014, the figure had more than doubled, with around 40% of audits not properly conducted.[9] 'That means a high percentage of the audits we inspected had serious defects,' said Public Company Accounting Oversight Board (PCAOB) chairman James Doty in 2016. The profession's defenders claimed the figures reflected more rigour on the part of the inspectors post-crisis. Other indications of audit quality, such as the number of listed companies forced to 'restate' previously published accounts because of fiddles or errors, remained pretty consistent at around half their 2006 peak.[10]

Broad-brush statistics and checklist inspections of uncontroversial cases fail, however, to test the accountants' ability to perform when it really matters. A steady stream of accounting scandals suggested that, when faced with examinations of their resolve at the big moments, things had not changed much. In Britain, PwC was placed under the spotlight for its work on a totemic recession-era crisis: the collapse of the high street chain British Home Stores (BHS) with the loss of thousands of jobs. Six days before the 2015 sale of the company by perma-tanned retail tycoon Sir Philip Green to perma-tanned serial bankrupt Dominic Chappell, and with the company solvent only because of support from its owners, PwC had given BHS a clean audit certificate. There had been, the bean counters had testified, no 'material uncertainty' over its future – even with a sale to the unreliable Chappell in the offing. When the company went bust a year later, parliamentarians who examined the entrails of the business were 'surprised that PwC did not more deeply question whether BHS was genuinely being sold as a going concern'.[11] They noted pointedly that signing the clean audit certificate had been brought forward by a couple of months, apparently so the deal could go through. PwC's earnings from BHS, meanwhile, had the look of Enron-era America rather than a new age of supposed bean-counting probity. While auditing BHS and its holding companies for years, the firm had earned four times as much again – £9m between 2009 and 2014 – from consultancy services.[12]

By now, after accusations of inactivity following the financial crisis, regulators were seeking to show a glint of steel. In 2017, for example, PwC was fined £5.1m by Britain's Financial Reporting Council for 'extensive' misconduct in its 2011 audit of second-tier accountancy firm RSM Tenon.[13] US regulators weighed in with a $6m penalty for KPMG over its auditing of oil company Miller Energy for the same year. It had cleared 'grossly overstated' values of oil wells after failing to 'consider and address facts known to them that should have raised serious doubts about the company's valuation'. The result was 'investors being misinformed that [oil and gas interests] purchased for less than $5m were worth more than half a billion dollars'.[14] The nadir that year was perhaps reached when KPMG was forced to fire five partners, including the vice chair of its US audit practice, for keeping quiet about tip-offs ahead of inspections by the PCAOB regulator.[15]

NEW FRONTIERS, OLD CONFLICTS

The inadequacy of the Big Four's response to the financial crisis as auditors correlates directly with their renewed commercial success as consultants. In the seven years from 2009, the Big Four's worldwide consultancy income (excluding tax advice) nearly doubled from $26bn to $48bn, an annual growth rate of 9%. Their income from auditing and related 'assurance' work, by contrast, rose only by inflation over the period (see Figure 12).[16] Ominously, the Big Four now make 38% of their income from

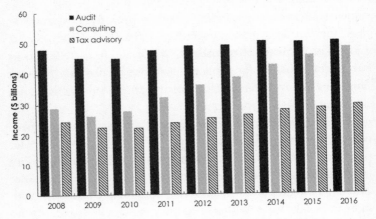

Figure 12: Since the financial crisis, the Big Four have prioritized advisory work, not auditing

non-tax consulting services. That's five percentage points *more* than in 2000, just before they were forced to sell off their main consultancy arms and with the 'numbers game' scandals like Enron about to blow.

Business and government addiction to consultancy is great for the bean counters' pay packets, but its social and economic usefulness is far less certain. While consultancy's shortcomings in the public sector have been exposed to a certain extent, companies have no requirement to test whether the consultants' prescriptions have improved performance – never mind provide any information to shareholders or workers on the matter. The overall picture, however, doesn't look great. In the countries in which the Big Four have embedded consultancy, the great splurge has coincided with historically low productivity growth of barely above 0%, compared with post-war averages of around 2% (see Figure 13).[17] As improving productivity has been the purpose of consulting ever since cost accounting spawned scientific management,

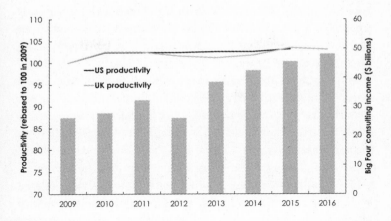

Figure 13: Rapid growth in consultancy services coincides with little or no growth in real economic productivity

whatever else the industry is achieving, it is certainly not meeting its founders' expectations.

It was less than a decade before this rapid post-crisis growth in non-audit work started that the same firms had hived off their dedicated consultancy arms as incompatible with the essential business of accounting. When economic historian John Kenneth Galbraith had said, 'There can be few fields of human endeavour in which history counts for so little as in the world of finance,' he could have been referring to accountancy just as well as to the stock markets.[18] The impatience of the consultancy resurgence has fed an acquisition spree by the Big Four firms. In just three years, from 2011 to 2013, they bought 66 independent consultancy outfits. Often the purpose was to forge ahead in the tech-enabled world by bolting on so-called 'digitally native' businesses. Sometimes it was simply to grab more of the market in services such as human resources consulting or the 'strategy' advice long provided by the likes of McKinsey and Bain & Co. In 2013, PwC swallowed hundred-year-old US firm Booz & Co. whole and immediately renamed it 'Strategy&'. When the world's largest accountancy firm brands a business to look like a typo, maybe fastidious accounting isn't uppermost in its leaders' minds.

The quality of accounting *was* on the mind of PCAOB board member Steven Harris in 2014 when he addressed an audience of New York lawyers on the rise of advisory services. 'People tend to forget the trillions of dollars of investor losses that resulted from the failures of Enron, WorldCom, Tyco, Adelphia Communications and a host of other major companies at the time,' he cautioned, before breathlessly listing a dozen consultancy services offered by the Big Four in everything from immigration to corporate finance and enterprise strategy, concluding, '. . . and the list goes on'. It all made 'investors wonder if we are returning to the era in which firms will focus more of their energies on building their consulting practices and revenues to the detriment of audit quality and auditor independence'.[19]

At my meeting with Simon Collins, I put it to him that the poor auditing of pre-crisis banking might be explained by such conflicts and the accountants' intimacy with an industry that they should have been holding to account. 'The personal integrity of individuals protects you against a closeness in the corrupt sense,' he responded. 'Closeness in terms of group-think is much more troubling.' But while he was at least aware of the dangers of accountants thinking too much like their clients, Collins was unwilling to see this as a cause of the financial crisis. On the contrary, he was evangelical for the accountancy firms' role as both advisers and auditors. 'You've got to be inside the industry and inside the thinking and inside the regulator's mind, otherwise you can't do the job,' he insisted. 'I feel really strongly about multi-disciplinary partnerships . . . Doing more than just audit [is] not just desirable but fundamental for audit quality because we might be auditing bank X but we might be doing risk returns or regulatory investigations for banks Y and Z. Without the ability to take an industry-wide view, to have the expertise in complex financial instruments and their accountancy treatment, our chances of auditing well and sceptically would be really low.' It seemed not to matter that when put to the test in the years leading up to the financial crisis, this optimistic theory had failed spectacularly. When, for example, it had become apparent even to the credit ratings agencies in 2007 that rising mortgage defaults threw the value of CDOs into doubt, the 'expertise' acquired by the Big Four in helping to create these instruments had not translated into the better, more sceptical auditing as Collins's analysis would have it.

The view of conflicting interests as actually being complement-ary went for the Big Four's growing influence over public services, too. I put it to Collins that his firm's advice to government might favour corporate clients also involved in the issue being considered rather than the public interest, if only because his consultants would come to think like their major clients. What about, for example, KPMG's role as 'strategic adviser' to the Ministry of Defence and the recent acquisition of Lockheed Martin as a consultancy client? 'If you are experts in the industry you are in demand for that expertise,' he replied. 'To pretend that has no danger of conflict is crass and inappropriate. To pretend equally that you could just be an MoD contractor without ever working for the private sector and having an understanding of the way it works is equally crass.' Everyone could still be a winner. 'I see it as business convening, I see it as expertise needing to work on both sides of the market and I see a real awareness of potential conflicts.' Again, I believed the 'awareness' of the conflict but I still suspected that the strategic advice KPMG gives the MoD is more to Lockheed Martin's liking than to Campaign Against the Arms Trade's.

Simon Collins's belief in the social value of his firm's public sector work was clear. He adamantly rejected my suggestion that the financial incentives in ensuring the contracts keep coming made it 'too eager to please', especially when advising on major projects. When I asked whether his firm had ever said 'don't go ahead with that project, don't go ahead with that PFI deal', he insisted it had – although he couldn't give examples 'off the top of my head'. But 'the idea that we would put our name to something we didn't believe in is total anathema', and 'we will not accept a piece of work where a client influences our opinion'. I respected Collins's view that his firm's advice would not be deliberately rigged to suit a client's wishes. But the evidence of cases like the HS2 project suggests this isn't enough. The accountants' integrity, plus the checks and balances within their firms, might generally prevent overt manipulation. But I doubted they could counter the natural tendency to side with the client, or a whole bunch of clients with broadly aligned interests.

The ascendancy of money over ethics appeared to be clear when I raised KPMG's consultancy contract with Imperial Tobacco:

RB: Do you not see any conflict advising Imperial Tobacco, essentially selling cigarettes, and making so much money from the National Health Service?

SC: That's a long and difficult one.

RB: And how does it fit with your values? You said in an interview with Radio 4: 'Healthcare's hugely important to us because it's hugely important to society.'[20] How can a chairman say that and then take Imperial Tobacco as a client?

SC: Well, we look at a number of things, and we're really working on this at the moment to try and codify for 180,000 people worldwide, what does it mean to be a purpose-led organization. But it is very complicated.

RB: It looks very simple to me, and to most people: they kill people through cancer and you care passionately about health. That doesn't look complicated.

SC: You can have some very badly run and dangerous, effect on society [*sic*], companies in some very fluffy sectors. Equally you can have things like natural resources and other areas and you can look at them and say don't they pollute, don't they do that . . . The question is, those activities are going to happen and you have to make a judgement about whether you are providing good governance, transparency, trust in the capital markets around it.

For all the firm's emphasis on values and integrity, internal contradictions count for little. Collins did say that 'what we wouldn't do for a tobacco company is advocacy around the product' (and, appearing uncomfortable, 'it's a journey, but we do think about it'). His own firm's annual report, however, cited the Imperial Tobacco contract as an example of 'how we're working with our clients to bring success in a rapidly changing world'. They were helping to sell fags. Whatever reasoning KPMG's leaders use to square this with their passion for health, it doesn't testify to superhuman levels of integrity. When it suits the firms to strike a moral pose, they do so. When it comes to the decisions that matter – whether or not to take the money – the approach is a harder-nosed commercial one.

STATE OF DENIAL

At PwC's offices on London's Embankment, I was to find an equally unconvincing response to the tax-avoidance scandal that had followed quickly on the heels of the financial crisis. It was now a couple of years since the firm had been forced to close its tax ruling factory in Luxembourg. The whistleblowers who had exposed it were appealing their convictions, the European Commission was investigating the Grand Duchy's deals, and the world's tax administrators were working out how to prevent similar scheming in future. I was intrigued to learn what the authors of the whole episode made of it.

Although PwC had initially declined my interview request, I was now privileged to be met by not one but two of its partners. Richard Sexton was the firm's 'global assurance partner', who in 2011 had been given a special role enhancing his firm's reputation following the unwelcome conclusions of the House of Lords post-financial-crisis inquiry. Alongside him sat PwC's head of 'corporate purpose', Gaenor Bagley, a Cambridge maths graduate who had moved on from number-crunching. Neither was in mistake-admitting mood.

Sexton insisted that his firm would advise on deals only where 'there's a business rationale'. Yet the Luxembourg tax schemes (not a word PwC itself is prepared to use) worked by inserting shell companies and arcane financial transactions into otherwise legitimate investments simply to pick up an extra tax break. When I asked if tax reduction on its own would count as a business rationale, Sexton said: 'No, that is not a business rationale.' So why, I wanted to know, if a UK multinational company wants to invest in the US, 'does it have to be dog-legged through Luxembourg if it's not to avoid tax?' As with questions on audits of the failed banks, that was the end of the analysis. 'I can't comment on specific client instances,' replied Sexton.

It seemed that, despite the worldwide debate and reform sparked by LuxLeaks, PwC remained in denial over the episode. One exchange with Ms Bagley summed up its position:

RB: Do you accept this [the Luxembourg operation] was tax avoidance?

GB: No, because it was within the law.

RB: I'm not accusing you of anything illegal. But I would say it would be tax avoidance if there were no real purpose other than tax. Do you accept that's the case?

GB: No, I don't accept that. There are different tax rules in different countries and countries compete and have different tax systems and there are beneficial ways of doing it and they [Luxembourg] were very open about that particularly ten years ago.

RB: Do you think what PwC was doing in Luxembourg was acceptable?

GB: At the time it was acceptable.

RB: Well, what's changed?

GB: What's changed is the public scrutiny.

RB: Are you saying that if the public aren't scrutinizing it, it's acceptable, but when the public look at it, it's not acceptable?

GB No, I am not saying that. I am saying that now when companies do things they need to think broader than the pure letter of the law and they need to think about the reputational impact and about how they're going to disclose it and what long-term impact there is going to be. That has changed over time.

RB: 'Are you going to get caught?' is what you mean.

GB: No, I don't mean that. My own experience is that you tell clients very clearly that this has to have a business purpose. If it is not within the intention of the law, we tell them very clearly that there is a risk that you will get caught, that you will have a nasty investigation and that it will damage your reputation. Faced with that, clients often don't do it.

RB: That's what you tell them now, but going back to 2008, 2009 ... or 2010 maybe [the period covered by the LuxLeaks papers]. Is that what you were telling clients then?

GB: Well, it has evolved over time. I wish we weren't part of the system that has created the sort of comments and the conversation you are having ... We need to do better about being open and disclosing and that has changed.

RB: Do you regret what PwC Luxembourg did?

GB: I don't think I can say that.

RB: [After describing Pearson's scheme in Luxembourg housed in a room containing twenty shell companies, including the supposed branch of an English one.] Are you saying you have no regrets over that?

GB: I have regrets about a tax system that clearly wasn't working.

RB: Well, there was a reason it wasn't working. It was because you were exploiting it. It would have worked if firms like yours had not decided to wheedle every possible advantage out of it.

GB: Our advice is to help companies pay the right amount of tax. You can quibble about the word 'right'. If the law allows them to do something, it is our duty to tell them, so that's what we were doing.

RB: But you're not doing it any more, so why have you stopped?

GB: The rules change over time.

RB: It would still be possible to do those things through Luxembourg; do you still do that?

GB: ... We still use Luxembourg as a territory sometimes for all sorts of reasons and you would still get a tax ruling. Most of those are done for efficiency reasons. So, you're right, it has changed. I can't put my finger on a watershed moment where we're suddenly doing things differently, but we are thinking about the broader intention of the rules. We are insisting clients put more substance and business purpose around what they're doing because we know that's what they should be doing. We know that's going to be expected.

RB: That seems a tacit admission that you weren't doing it properly, that what you were doing before wasn't acceptable.

GB: Well, the world has changed.

CASHING IN

However the world changes, the Big Four's guaranteed audit income streams give them a competitive advantage in adapting to and exploiting it. They constantly make new 'alliances', politically and economically, to entrench their dominance. From becoming strategic advisers to government departments to teaming up with tech companies, they are to be found at every cutting edge. PwC's tie-in with Google is typical. 'From strategy through execution,' it says, 'PwC's alliance with Google for Work takes a business-focused approach that brings together PwC's business transformation, process and organizational change capabilities and Google for Work's collaborative and innovative applications & technologies.'[21] KPMG boasts a similar 'Global Digital Solution Hub' tie-in with Microsoft. Deloitte attributed a 10% growth in consulting revenues in 2017 to 'artificial intelligence, robotics, cognitive, creative digital consulting, cloud computing, blockchain and [the] Internet of Things'. The Big Four are where management consultancy and information technology now meet.

They are perfectly placed to capitalize on the age of mass data, with troubling potential conflicts of interest. The firms offer firstly to use client companies' own data to improve their audits and, through that, their audit clients' performance. The promise, in effect, is to update the methods of cost accounting and 'scientific management' for the digital age. KPMG's Data & Analytics (D&A) division, for example, says it will 'turn data into value'. The firm's 'global network of D&A specialists works with leading organizations to . . . help them to confidently capture new customer segments, capitalize on emerging market trends and create new products and services'. Thus the same firms that advise governments and major companies in sectors affecting every part of life are positioned to exploit troves of personal information. While there are of course concerns over all organizations' use of data – for example in selling it on – the fact that a range of commercial uses are being developed within the same Big Four firms poses additional risks.

The Big Four also dominate the cyber-security business, notwithstanding the vulnerabilities in their own sprawling networks that a 2017 attack on Deloitte exposed. By 2015, the firms occupied all four top spots in cyber-security consulting, with 46% of the total market, pushing IT consulting firms like IBM and Accenture into the shadows.[22] Between them, they earned $7.6bn from the business. Although their operations are naturally secretive, PwC did give a glimpse into its methods in 2013. 'The kind of employees at PwC are the same kind of people you see at GCHQ [the UK's secret monitoring service] or the NCA [the National Crime Agency, charged with tackling organized crime],' said the firm's cyber adviser Stephen Page.[23] He also happens to be a director of the NCA itself. The Big Four firms and the government's key security agencies exchange staff in a manner familiar from other business areas, notably tax, in which a professional acquires government experience, then takes a job at a Big Four firm on a higher salary. The revolving door also spins at the top end: in 2010, the former head of the Secret Intelligence Services, John Scarlett, joined PwC as a consultant. When several major companies were paralysed by a concerted hacking attack from China in April 2017, PwC and the government's cyber-security centre teamed up to tackle it. 'Operating alone, none of us would have joined the dots to uncover this new campaign of indirect attacks,' said a PwC partner.[24]

The state and the Big Four have thus become entwined in cyber security, as in so much else. While this can lead to success against sometimes major cyber attacks, the long-term ramifications might not be so beneficial. Would any government dare threaten the licence, and therefore the survival, of an accountancy firm on which it was dependent in certain critical areas of cyber security (and thus perhaps even national security)? The prospect of such a firm being properly held to account over its accountancy, which is what it really exists for, diminishes further. The Big Four may become not just too big to fail and too few to fail, but also too critical to fail.

NEW ERA, NEW DANGER

The risks to which the accountants ought to be alive have certainly not receded in the way that their attention to them has. The sticking plasters applied to flawed economic and financial systems after the 2008 crash, such as relatively mild tightening of banking regulations, fail to address major systemic risks. As former Bank of England governor Sir Mervyn King wrote in 2016: 'The strange thing is that after arguably the biggest financial crisis in history, nothing has really changed in terms either of the fundamental structure of banking or the reliance on central banks to restore macroeconomic prosperity.'[25] With a crisis in the eurozone unresolved and political fragmentation throwing up new dangers, in 2017 the International Monetary Fund warned that 'threats to financial stability are emerging from elevated political and policy uncertainty around the globe'.[26]

At the same time, the Trump era (and perhaps post-Brexit Britain) is ushering in a new period of financial deregulation, with many of the post-2008-crash measures being repealed. Debt levels across the globe, including US household debt, are above their pre-crisis levels, and regulators are warning of possible bubbles in areas from the multi-trillion-dollar bond market to car loans and credit card debt. Troublingly, these are partly inflated by generous accounting of the sort seen in the subprime housing bubble.[27] The accounting standard-setters' response to the financial crisis, in the view of many commentators, was inadequate. Where likely future losses on some assets could be ignored under the old rules, the new ones require a mere twelve months' forward look and thus still allow substantial risks to be buried. For others they allow the same market-to-market manipulation as before. The vigilance of the financial watchdogs is certainly as necessary as it was leading up to the last crash. They aren't, alas, looking all that alert. In fact, repeating the familiar pattern, they see recent political upheavals as an opportunity to lessen their own responsibility. In May 2017, American accountancy commentator Francine McKenna revealed how 'the Big Four's congressional lobbying activity shows the auditors and their trade association taking advantage of the "Trump window" to roll back the 2002 post-Enron and WoldCom reforms that changed their business'. In the first quarter of 2017, Deloitte, for example, spent \$560,000 lobbying on 'modernization of auditor independence requirements'. Not long before, the firm had been fined by the Public Company Accounting Oversight Board for breaching precisely these rules.[28]

If the threats to rigorous auditing in the West are serious, the future in the East looks every bit as precarious. The heavily indebted Chinese economy is expected to be twice the size of that of the US in three decades or so. Its companies are acquiring swathes of Western and developing countries' industry and infrastructure, often employing the consultancy services of the same Big Four firms that audit them. The conflicts of interest are every bit as profound, and in this new economic and illiberal powerhouse the pressures may be even greater to acquiesce in false accounting.

Around the world, the accountancy establishment will before long be controlled by men and women who have been recruited to become not expert auditors but profit-driven 'professional services' providers. Its leaders will have no memory of a time when auditing was their main task. Already, as the Big Four's interests spread ever wider and their conflict-riddled business model becomes harder to justify, the only place they can find coherence is in mumbo-jumbo. KPMG has an 'anthem' to its 'One Firm' philosophy (an odd choice given its previous outing as Arthur Andersen's mantra). I've listened to it so you don't have to. 'What do we do at KPMG? We work in concert,' intones a narrator over a rousing orchestral piece. 'Every function, every skill, every background working in harmony. We can see ourselves as soloists or we can see the possibilities when we all perform as one. Our "One Firm" anthem, created as a symbol of our diversity and our unity, because when we all come together with a common purpose we achieve great things.'[29] At New Year 2016, Deloitte's worldwide chief executive, management consultant Punit Renjen, wrote to the firm's 220,000 staff resolving to 'deliver an exceptional, and consistent, talent experience across the Deloitte network'. They were invited to sign the 'Deloitte Journey Declaration'. The whole memo, wrote the *Financial Times*' scourge of management-speak Lucy Kellaway, was 'a forest of guff so thick and dark they are unlikely ever to get out again'.[30]

There is a serious side to this. These organizations have grave public responsibilities demanding intelligent, hard-headed thought. The corporate culture bred by such drivel kills the critical thinking that should define accountancy. And because only those who enthuse over it can hope to progress, the Big Four firms come to be managed more by vacuous cheerleaders than the intellectually rigorous sceptics that their core public-interest task requires.

CLUB MEN

When I met the bean counters, I wanted to see if the contemporary face of the profession could be reconciled with its heritage and its central purpose of getting the numbers right. Simon Collins certainly thought it could. 'I can honestly say I've never seen or had any feeling that auditors or the audit firms' leadership ever think they would do anything that would compromise the quality of an audit,' he told me. Deloitte's David Barnes voiced the same sentiment: 'I can tell you, every time I sign an account you are being judged. Is that a true and fair view of the company's historic position as at that balance sheet date? When you're the audit partner the worst thing you could ever do is sign off something you do not think is true and fair.' However dominant the consultancy parts of the Big Four's businesses are now, and however compromised auditing by the 'professional services' firms has become, there at least remains an awareness of the Hippocratic connection with the sound accounting for which the profession was established.

Collins waxed lyrical on the point: 'I draw pictures in my mind of audit being the trunk of the tree. Audit is what we're defined by; it's where virtually all of our risk is carried, where our reputation is carried. It's where our heritage and roots are. It's not all that we do now but it's that central and that core to us.' Clinging onto the arboreal analogy, he added: 'It is only by having the strength of the core of audit that we have licence to hang branches [of other services].' But since auditing is now a minority of the firms' business – in the UK it makes up just 28% of KPMG's income – is this core task safe? The numbers were less important to Collins. 'We care very passionately about [audit]; we are regulated by virtue of being an audit firm, there's an audit firm governance code . . . If you think about it in that trunk of the tree, the centrality and importance of it, then it's hard to imagine why we would do something that would harm it.' It's difficult, however, to square this confidence with the real world. Audits by the Big Four have gone wrong far too often. I wondered whether the resort to overworked analogies was a way of avoiding this unpalatable truth. Deloitte's David Barnes appeared more realistic when I raised the financial incentive not to be too tough on a client paying big fees. 'I think you've hit the nail on the head in terms of the challenges. [As] one of our non-execs says, the robbers are paying the police.' The answer to this unreassuring image? 'That is why you have your integrity, judgement, et cetera.' The prophylactic for all accountancy ills, my meetings with the bean counters were to prove, was 'integrity'.

The evidence shows that it isn't enough in the profit-driven multinational enterprises that the Big Four have become. Good intentions alone will never be able to counter the commercial forces that shape their thinking and actions. Most accountancy failings are less about dishonesty and more tales of insufficient courage, curiosity and independence of thought in the face of huge commercial incentives. A century ago, leading accountants understood this. Some, such as Price Waterhouse's George May, avoided conflicts of interest altogether. Arthur Andersen embraced them but almost belligerently enforced the most zealous auditing. Today's bean counters have a far more conflicted business model than Arthur Andersen ever had, but not his standards or character. They do, however, seem to have an unswerving belief in their unimpeachable integrity. This blinds them to many overwhelming, sometimes insidious, threats to their impartiality. And when things go wrong as a result, it prevents them acknowledging manifest shortcomings.

My final question to Simon Collins was to ask what he thought his firms' founders, William Peat and James Marwick, would have made of KPMG's new club in Mayfair, No. 20. 'I think they would burst with pride,' he said. 'I think they'd think the old firm's come a long way, but I think they'd still think it was true to what they set out to do.' PwC's Richard Sexton was equally confident of his firm's place in history. If it hadn't properly addressed issues like the LuxLeaks tax scandal and the financial crisis, 'we wouldn't have been around 165 years'.

I disagree with both. History shows that the Big Four accountancy firms have prospered by avoiding accountability for their part in false accounting, financial crises and the plundering of economies while paying more attention to ever-expanding commercial opportunities. What I've seen of the unremarkable men and women who made this remarkable result possible doesn't lead me to expect them to change that. The difficult question is: what will?

CONCLUSION: WHAT CAN BE DONE?

A NEW BEAN-COUNTING BLUEPRINT

Repeated accounting scandals and responses to them have shown that simply patching up the existing model does not work. Widespread failures are becoming more frequent and more harmful as accountancy's core weaknesses remain unaddressed. The subprime meltdown and financial crisis so soon after the post-WorldCom and Enron repair work made that clear enough.

When I interviewed KPMG's Simon Collins, I asked him whether he considered his organization to be an auditing firm, an accountancy firm or a professional services firm. He wanted to be all three but acknowledged that, if he had to choose one, it would be 'professional services'. I'd like to talk to his successor in a decade or so and hear the answer 'accountancy' or 'auditing'. Leaving the critical task of checking the finances of the banks and companies that occupy the commanding heights of capitalism to what are essentially all-purpose management consultancies is a recipe for further disaster. The firms that audit almost every major company must become accounting and auditing firms again, with corresponding priorities and responsibilities. Below is an outline of how I think this reform should take shape.

Separation of accounting and consulting

For the necessary change to happen, the critical accounting functions of the major accountancy firms have to be entirely separated from the rest of their business. They need to be carved out in the way that the European Commission's Michel Barnier proposed in 2010. Shorn of their consultancy business, accountancy firms would provide other services only to the extent that they were auxiliary to the core task of auditing. What remains, such as advice on accounting systems and routine tax compliance services, should be fully identified and not exceed a certain low level – perhaps 25% – of a firm's fees from a client. This and other changes will meet fierce resistance from the Big Four as the current model is what generates their partners' six- and seven-figure incomes. But it is time for their claims that what they call a 'multi-disciplinary' business model improves audit quality to be answered with the evidence that it does not. Policy-makers around the world must acquire the courage to withstand the lobbying onslaught that will inevitably come.

Public auditing of major institutions

Even a total separation of accounting and consulting would not address the fundamental flaw in auditing being performed for profit, with the auditee paying the auditor. Some have argued that this central contradiction is so fatal that the requirement for companies to be audited should simply be dropped. Investors could take their chances in the way that those buying the first nineteenth-century railway stocks did. To attract and appease shareholders, companies would then buy insurance against defective accounting and reduce their premiums through demonstrably thorough audits. The market would favour the well-audited and drive auditing standards upwards. In reality, it is likely that making auditing optional would leave too much room for the unscrupulous to inflate performance and make false promises. History shows that investors and markets look first at declared profits, even illusory ones, and worry about the veracity of them only later. Bubbles and mania result.

The last financial crisis proved that sound accounting for significant financial services companies is of economically existential importance. This demands ending the 'for profit' audit system for the largest, systemically important financial businesses that are already identified by financial regulators such as the Bank of England. Auditing these would become a public regulatory function funded by taxation and/or levies in the way that other financial services regulation is. It would be performed by new national bodies or within countries' main financial regulators such as the UK's Financial Conduct Authority and the US's Securities and Exchange Commission. The process also ought to be far more open, disclosing key features such as how valuations affect the institution's financial positions and what the results would show under alternative methods. Public-sector auditing in these cases would facilitate much closer working with financial regulators under strengthened requirements for the exchange of information between the two.

This system would also enable the most important accounting to be held democratically accountable itself, ensuring that it was conducted in the public rather than private interest. Financial incentives for the bean counters to appease the most powerful clients would disappear and an ethos of scrutiny and accountability would be restored. If the auditors began to underperform or became too close to the institutions they were auditing – in the way that tax authorities became too close to the large companies they should have been scrutinizing – Parliament could step in. Recent effective action to improve tax administration by the British Parliament's Public Accounts Committee shows that democratically empowered representatives are the best hope of keeping the bean counters' eyes on the ball.

Without exorbitant partner profits to pay, public auditing of systemically important institutions could also be performed less expensively and at a higher quality by more senior accountants than at present. The days of auditing as something for junior bean counters to slog through as billing fodder while their superiors look for more interesting and lucrative opportunities would be over.

Independent regulation

A unified, independent and well-resourced body would then regulate other accounting activities: the auditing of companies other than systemically important ones, insolvency work, and the provision of other services such as tax advice. The regulators' membership should be carefully circumscribed to limit the influence of the major firms. Professional bodies would continue to award qualifications and promote high standards among accountants, and administer disciplinary proceedings in relatively minor cases. But independent regulators – subject to democratic scrutiny themselves – would put an end to the self-regulation that has proven inadequate for too long. At the same time, national and international accounting rule-setting needs to be freed from the grip of the big firms and handed to more independent bodies adequately representing investor, worker, academic and other interests.

Accountability

The bean counters must also be made more financially accountable for their work. As supposedly professional firms, the Big Four (and others auditing any large company) should not be eligible for the limited liability status that has seen them relinquish responsibility for a decade and a half. The narrowing of those who can sue the major firms for substandard work should also be reversed so that the bean counters once again feel the threat of litigation from all the stakeholders – shareholders, customers, suppliers and employees – who pay the price when they fail to do their job properly. Particular accountability needs to be asked of the most senior accountants. Those running the major firms should have to demonstrate that they operate meaningful systems to uphold high auditing standards and prevent audit failure – in the same way that companies now have to demonstrate effective measures to prevent certain financial crime – with serious penalties for those who do not. There should also be a statutory mechanism for blowing the whistle on false accounting to the new public regulator, with substantial financial rewards. This would not only reveal more poor accounting, perhaps before it causes real damage over a number of years, but would also deter false accounting and blind-eye auditing in the first place.

When accounting does go wrong, investigation needs to be prompter and more searching. There is no reason why the accounting part of a corporate collapse or other scandal, which will often be at the heart of it anyway, cannot be investigated at the same time as other aspects. It may be that accountancy disciplinary measures have to remain confidential until criminal proceedings are concluded but there is no reason to wait until this point before beginning to look at the bean counting. The days of investigations into poor auditing starting a decade after the events, which have greatly held back accountability and reform, must end.

Ending the quadropoly

To overcome the dangers inherent in overfamiliarity between auditor and client, companies should have to change auditors more often, perhaps every seven years rather than the twenty still possible even after some progress on this point in Europe. This requires a greater number of major accountancy firms capable of taking on large audits without being conflicted by acting for too many competitors. At a minimum, therefore, the Big Four should be broken up into a not-quite-so-Big Eight. With auditors and audit teams already arranged by reference to clients, splitting up the Big Four would be relatively uncomplicated. It should ideally occur at the worldwide level, demanding co-operation among governments of major economies, but could helpfully be done nationally as well. The dominance of this new group would be more assailable by 'challenger' firms. But if greater distribution of auditing did not result within a few years, further breaking up of the Big Eight should be considered.

Transparency

For organizations that should be all about providing useful financial information, accountancy firms are remarkably opaque. All the Big Four register large parts of their operations and assets in jurisdictions where secrecy is the principal selling point. Their US partnerships are based in the tax haven of Delaware, allowing them not to publish accounts. Thus nobody knows, for example, how much profit the Big Four make in their largest single market. For firms with so many public privileges, such as a quadropoly of the audit market and limited liability, this has to end. Auditing licences should be conditional on registration in open jurisdictions, with the corresponding disclosure of information on matters such as profits, legal risks and related-party transactions. The same should apply to assets such as the brand names and other intellectual property used by the firms, making them subject to the laws of the more open democracies.

Consultancy

Separated from their accountancy arms, and thus without the special access provided by a guaranteed base of audit clients, the consultancy arms of the Big Four would have to compete more fairly with others. While this is not the place to discuss essential reforms to the consultancy industry, it is worth pointing out how the record of the Big Four in the UK demonstrates the need for far greater openness. The terms on which public bodies from government departments to hospital trusts and local authorities employ consultants should be radically opened up, identifying contract details such as fee levels and success criteria, personnel, and conflicts with the consultants' other activities.

Underpinning these recommendations is the need for accounting to be as independent as possible from those with incentives to account falsely. The story of the bean counters shows that when they are objective and brave, they protect and transform the world for the better. When they are biased or weak, catastrophe soon follows. It is time to reckon with the value of accounting and to count the beans properly.

EPILOGUE

Carillion's rise and spectacular fall was a story of recklessness, hubris and greed. Its business model was a relentless dash for cash, driven by acquisitions, rising debt, expansion into new markets and exploitation of suppliers. It presented accounts that misrepresented the reality of the business, and increased its dividend every year, come what may. Long-term obligations, such as adequately funding its pension schemes, were treated with contempt. Even as the company very publicly began to unravel, the board was concerned with increasing and protecting generous executive bonuses. Carillion was unsustainable. The mystery is not that it collapsed, but that it lasted so long.

House of Commons Business, Energy and Industrial
Strategy and Work and Pensions committees, May 2018.[1]

Soon after I finished writing *Bean Counters*, one of Britain's most important providers of public services, in every sector from healthcare to prisons, announced that it was insolvent. Hundreds of workers lost their jobs, pension savers and taxpayers took a major hit and half-built hospitals were left to decay.

The members of Parliament who trawled through this corporate dystopia found the 'triumph of the accountants' that I had set out to show. Every stage in Carillion's story had been facilitated by the bean counters. And in the process, they had broken this particular corner of capitalism.

Carillion began life in 1999 when it was spun out of construction company Tarmac to take advantage of the explosion in outsourcing and private finance initiative business which, as set out in Chapter 8, had itself come about partly on the advice of the major accountancy firms. (And which Chancellor of the Exchequer Philip Hammond would finally scrap in 2018, admitting it was a misuse of public money.) Long-term government contracts had served the purpose of getting commitments to spend taxpayers' money off the government's balance sheet but had also created the conditions for misleading accounting.

In the early 2000s, the market for outsourcing and private finance initiative deals became a crowded one. The easiest way to succeed in it was to bid low, overvalue the long-term contracts won, then seek more on the back of this apparently healthy position to bring in some much needed cash. But, just like the accounting scams of the 1990s and the financial markets built on subprime housing, it was unsustainable. In the summer of 2017, Carillion had to admit that its books were inflated by around £1bn. At the start of the next year, lacking further government support, it went under.

Just as in the lead up to the financial crisis, the accountants who'd had access to the company's books and ought to have highlighted the risks said nothing. Only when a senior Carillion director, Emma Mercer, returned from an overseas posting and alerted the board to some 'sloppy accounting' did auditors KPMG conduct the more thorough review that led to the overdue write-downs. As with the banks a decade earlier, the bean counters had failed to get to grips with a particular model of business. And as before, they were so invested in it through consultancy contracts and the development of the government policies that had produced it that they lacked the objectivity to question it.

Surveying the wreckage of Carillion and a new wave of accounting scandals emerging in the post-financial crisis economic downturn, the parliamentarians concluded that 'KPMG's long and complacent tenure auditing Carillion was not an isolated failure'. It was 'symptomatic of a market which works for the members of the oligopoly but fails the wider economy'.

The oligopoly of the Big Four firms certainly was doing well out of it, pocketing around £70m from Carillion alone in less than ten years. Along with the auditing, there was advice on everything from internal controls to directors' (lavish) pay and, for PwC, a heavily conflicted role providing pensions advice at various times to both the company and the trustees of its staff's pension schemes. Demonstrating how wide the bean counters' conflicts of interest spread, EY even advised high-speed rail company HS2 that it could safely sign a major contract with a Carillion-led consortium immediately after it had announced an £845m profit write-off. At the same time it was earning large fees as a restructuring adviser to Carillion (work which would continue only if the company stayed afloat by winning such contracts).

In the final twist, while workers were laid off, PwC would become 'special manager' in the administration for an anticipated £50m, with its partners and directors earning four-figure hourly rates on the job.

Carillion's wasn't the only woeful accounting hitting the headlines. In June 2018, PwC received a record £10m fine (reduced to £6.5m for co-operation) over its reckless auditing of British Home Stores discussed in Chapter 11. A senior partner had connived with executives at Sir Philip Green's company to get out the clean audit certificate required for a quick sale to serial bankrupt Dominic Chappell. Around the world the scandals were now coming thick and fast, perhaps most seriously in the United States when KPMG accountants conspired with inspectors from the auditing regulator to cheat on inspections of its work.

All the new failures reflected now long-standing flaws at the top end of the modern accountancy profession: conflicts of interest, skewed priorities and excessive profit motivation at the expense of a professional ethos. The retreat from audit by the 'professional services' firms continued even as the public interest in how they were performing their core job grew. The 39% of their worldwide income I reported at the start of this book as coming from auditing in 2016 fell to 34.5% by 2018, partly thanks to the expansion of tech-driven consultancy services.[2]

Even as the world woke up to their failings and demanded improvement, the Big Four remained the same schmoozing-at-Davos, interminably bullshitting outfits. In one post-Carillion interview, held at the No. 20 club where this book started, new KPMG UK boss Bill Michael promised 'we will collaborate more with clients and share problem solving . . . we have moved from what we do to clients to what we do with clients'.[3] The bean counters had decided that now was the time to get still cosier with the companies they should have been holding to account. Meanwhile, behind the rhetoric of reform in the wake of the great corporate tax scandals, it was business pretty much as usual. PwC, mastermind of the Luxembourg avoidance factory, can still be found offering to help corporates with 'tax-savvy restructuring', boasting how it could reduce tax on profits by 15% through the careful use of tax jurisdictions for profitable business.[4]

Calls for change became amplified in the wake of Carillion's collapse. They were led by the parliamentary committee, which recommended that the UK competition authorities launch a review that 'should explicitly include consideration of both breaking up the Big Four into more audit firms, and detaching audit arms from those providing other professional services'. The Competition and Markets Authority duly began an investigation, alongside a separate government inquiry into the regulation of the profession.

With a wearying inevitability, the Big Four accountancy firms circled their wagons. They acknowledged the case for a degree of change, but not so far as to restrain their fee-earning. Ideas such as opening up larger audits to smaller firms and an independent system for appointing auditors were entertained. But any notion of breaking up the firms, and making the major auditors become purely accountancy firms, was dismissed. The principal argument was a familiar one, updated for the modern age: auditing complex businesses required the expertise that their consultancy business gave them on tap. 'We audit Google, Amazon, Facebook, Salesforce and Oracle', EY's global boss Mark Weinberger told the *Financial Times*. 'You could not serve those clients without a multidisciplinary group of people to assess their risks going forward as a business, and [those employees] don't all sit in our audit practice'. This had also been the defence for advising banks on complex financial instruments while also auditing the banks that used them. Those audits had failed spectacularly – perhaps because the consultants are not just experts in the business being audited, they are *heavily conflicted* experts. The same problem will arise in the tech world. Asked to assess the risks associated with, say, a certain use of data, an auditor will turn to a consultant who is profiting from such business and likely to play down those risks.

As I hope has become clear in this book, auditing is strongest when it is questioning, objective and determined to get answers to difficult questions. On complex matters, experts might be consulted but it is essential that someone without the pre-conceived notions of a highly remunerated consultant should have to be satisfied of the correct accounting. This independent, demanding standard can be met only by audit firms that are just that: audit firms alone.

Bean Counters coincided roughly with the tenth anniversary of the financial crisis. This milestone, plus its legacy of damaged economies and political upheaval, prompted some serious consideration of the nature of capitalism. Strikingly, commentators from left and right identified the accountancy profession as a key point of failure in contemporary capitalism. In his book *The Finance Curse*, Nicholas Shaxson laid a chunk of the blame for the eponymous scourge – where excessive financialization causes social harm – at the door of the Big Four.[5] 'Why are the Big Four accounting firms not broken up, along the fault lines of their conflicts of interest?' he asked rhetorically. In a study of the renewed relevance of the 'father of modern capitalism' Adam Smith, Tory MP Jesse Norman railed against 'crony capitalism' and oligopolies.[6] 'Whether it is the banks, the Big Four accounting firms, the electricity markets, executive pay or the increasing dominance of electronic platforms', he wrote in the *Financial Times*, '21st-century capitalism offers plenty of targets to a modern Smithian reformer of energy and intent'.[7]

A chance for reform has arisen, in the UK at least. But we have been here before: after the Enron era and, more recently, after the financial crisis. On both occasions, despite plenty of noise, nothing much was done. Marginal changes demonstrably did not work. The danger of passing up the latest opportunity is all too real. In the UK (and elsewhere) the Big Four are again heavily lobbying, not just the government – which remains too close to the Big Four to be expected to confront them in any serious way – but also the City institutions. Representing shareholders, they are treated as having the primary interest in companies' accounting, but are easily enlisted into maintaining the status quo. These passive shareholders never want their auditors to be too thorough and will, as before, happily see the argument drift into technocratic backwaters where any energy for real reform will be dissipated, leaving the existing model essentially in tact.

The history *Bean Counters* sets out shows that the interests of wider society in sound accounting are far greater than those of corporate shareholders alone. Its needs must be the priority. And they demand the radical break up of the Big Four recommended here. With global debt rising to pre-crisis levels, do we want those responsible for vouching for the banks and other institutions that hold the loans and associated financial instruments also to be cashing in on this very growth? Do we want the auditors of the remarkably powerful and not always ethical tech companies commercially wrapped up in their businesses? The answer is surely a clear 'no'. Extricating the twenty-first century's accountants from such Faustian pacts is no less than a pressing democratic challenge.

APPENDIX

THE BIG FOUR FAMILY TREES

PricewaterhouseCoopers (PwC): Simplified Firm History

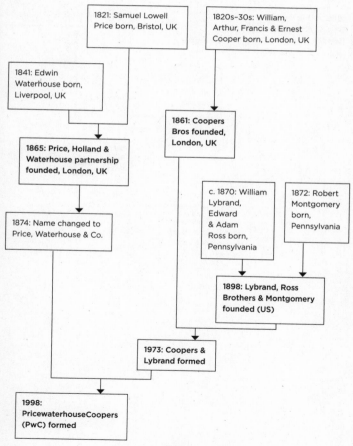

1821: Samuel Lowell Price born, Bristol, UK

1820s–30s: William, Arthur, Francis & Ernest Cooper born, London, UK

1841: Edwin Waterhouse born, Liverpool, UK

1861: Coopers Bros founded, London, UK

1865: Price, Holland & Waterhouse partnership founded, London, UK

c. 1870: William Lybrand, Edward & Adam Ross born, Pennsylvania

1872: Robert Montgomery born, Pennsylvania

1874: Name changed to Price, Waterhouse & Co.

1898: Lybrand, Ross Brothers & Montgomery founded (US)

1973: Coopers & Lybrand formed

1998: PricewaterhouseCoopers (PwC) formed

Ernst & Young: Simplified Firm History

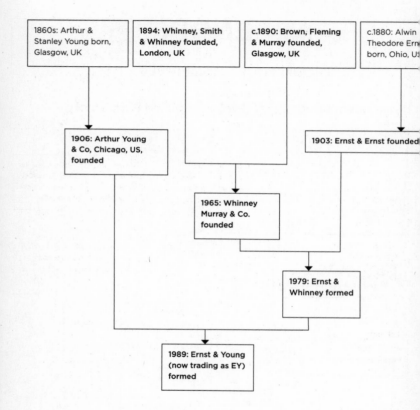

KPMG: Simplified Firm History

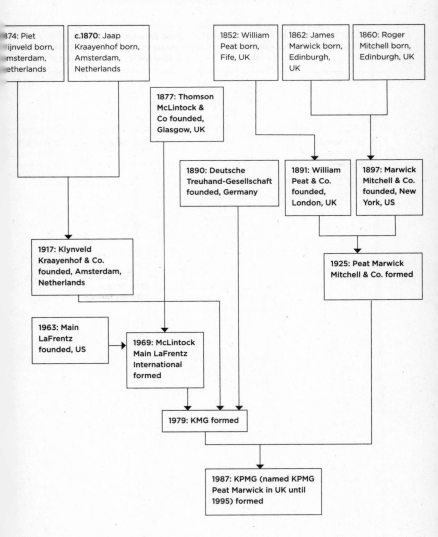

1874: Piet Klijnveld born, Amsterdam, Netherlands

c.1870: Jaap Kraayenhof born, Amsterdam, Netherlands

1852: William Peat born, Fife, UK

1862: James Marwick born, Edinburgh, UK

1860: Roger Mitchell born, Edinburgh, UK

1877: Thomson McLintock & Co founded, Glasgow, UK

1890: Deutsche Treuhand-Gesellschaft founded, Germany

1891: William Peat & Co. founded, London, UK

1897: Marwick Mitchell & Co. founded, New York, US

1917: Klynveld Kraayenhof & Co. founded, Amsterdam, Netherlands

1925: Peat Marwick Mitchell & Co. formed

1963: Main LaFrentz founded, US

1969: McLintock Main LaFrentz International formed

1979: KMG formed

1987: KPMG (named KPMG Peat Marwick in UK until 1995) formed

Deloitte: Simplified Firm History

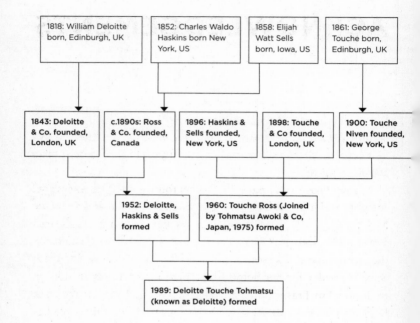

ACKNOWLEDGEMENTS

You meet plenty of interesting people researching a book on accountancy. Really. Many have been working on the subject and thanklessly campaigning for the importance of decent bean counting for years.

Among those who have been generous with their expertise, insights and information were Tim Bush in the UK and Francine McKenna in the United States. Discussions with Professors Prem Sikka and Atul Shah gave me useful food for thought, as did author Jane Gleeson-White, and I'm grateful to Professor Stella Fearnley for her helpful historical material. My thanks go to author Ian Fraser and journalist Christian Eriksson for their help with Scottish banking scandals and collating some statistics respectively.

Inevitably, several people who discussed today's accountancy profession with me cannot be named, but my appreciation is no less for that. One of those principled chartered accountants in particular was especially important to my understanding of the modern bean-counting world. No gaps or errors in this understanding, however, are his or anyone's fault other than mine.

I am especially grateful to those who were prepared to speak about some of the darker corners of bean counting, usually confidentially. Raphaël Halet, a brave whistleblower, spoke openly and candidly and has performed a great service in doing so.

I was helped along through some of the slog by motivating and thought-provoking discussions with friends and colleagues including Andrew Bousfield, Solomon Hughes, Nick Shaxson and John Neighbour.

On particular stories two other journalists were especially helpful. One was the man without whom world football would still be operating under the corrupt old regime, Andrew Jennings. The other was bilingual American tax journalist Teri Sprackland, who helped me to follow the LuxLeaks trial in 2016 despite my very ropey French.

Once again, I am grateful to my agent Karolina Sutton and editor at Atlantic Books, Mike Harpley, for helping me tell a story in a way that I hope informs and entertains, to Jane Selley for expert copy-editing and Kate Ballard for work on images.

Finally, as ever my deepest thanks go to my family and partner Brigitte for immeasurable support throughout my preoccupation with the bean counters.

BIBLIOGRAPHY

BOOKS

Pre twentieth century

Balen, M., *The Secret History of the South Sea Bubble* (Fourth Estate, US, 2002)

Chatfield, R., and Vangermeersch, R. (eds), *The History of Accounting: An International Encyclopedia* (Routledge, UK, 1996)

de Roover, R., *The Medici Bank: Its Organization, Management, Operations and Decline* (New York University Press, US, 1948)

Galbraith, J. K., *A Short History of Financial Euphoria* (Penguin Business, US, 1994)

Gleeson-White, J., *Double-Entry: How the Merchants of Venice Created Modern Finance* (Allen & Unwin, Australia, 2011)

Micklethwaite, J., and Woolridge, A., *The Company: A Short History of a Revolutionary Idea* (Weidenfeld & Nicolson, UK, 2003)

Pacioli, L., *The Rules of Double-Entry Bookkeeping [Particularis de Computis et Scripturis*, originally published Venice 1494]. Version used by author edited by Michael Schemmann (IICPA Publications, US, 2010)

Parker, R., and Yamey, B. (eds), *Accounting History – Some British Contributions* (Clarendon Press, UK, 1994)

Parks, T., *Medici Money: Banking, Metaphysics and Art in Fifteenth Century Florence* (Profile, UK, 2005)

Reilly, R., *Josiah Wedgwood* (Macmillan, UK, 1992)

Soll, J., *The Reckoning: Financial Accountability and the Making and Breaking of Nations* (Penguin, US, 2014)

Twentieth century

Allen, D. G., and McDermott, K., *Accounting for Success – a History of Price Waterhouse in America, 1890–1990* (Harvard Business Review, US, 1993)

Brewster, M., *Unaccountable: How the Accounting Profession Forfeited a Public Trust* (John Wiley & Sons, US, 2003)

Brooks, J., *The Go-Go Years: The Drama and Crashing Finale of Wall Street's Bullish 60s* (John Wiley & Sons, US, 1973)

Clikeman, P., *Called to Account: Financial Frauds that Shaped the Accounting Profession* (Routledge, US, 2013)

Feinstein, A., *The Shadow World – Inside the Global Arms Trade* (Hamish Hamilton, UK, 2011)

Galbraith, J. K., *The Great Crash* (Penguin, US, 1954)

Gilby, N., *Deception in High Places: A History of Bribery in Britain's Arms Trade* (Pluto Press, UK, 2014)

Higgins, J. A., *The First Sixty Years – Arthur Andersen & Co, 1913–1973* (Arthur Andersen, US, 1974)

Levitt, A., with Dwyer, P., *Take on the Street: How to Fight for Your Financial Future* (Vintage, US, 2003)

McLean, B., and Elkind, P., *The Smartest Guys in the Room: The Rise and Scandalous Fall of Enron* (Penguin, US, 2004)

MacDonald, D., *The Firm – the Inside Story of McKinsey* (Simon & Schuster, US, 2013)

Shaxson, N., *Treasure Islands: Tax Havens and the Men Who Stole the World* (Bodley Head, UK, 2010)

Squires, S., and Smith, C., *Inside Arthur Andersen: Shifting Values, Unexpected Consequences* (Financial Times Prentice Hall, US, 2003)

Stevens, M., *The Big Six: The Selling Out of America's Top Accounting Firms* (Pocket Books, US, 1992)

Toffler, B. L., with Reingold, J., *Final Accounting: Ambition, Greed and the Fall of Arthur Andersen* (Crown Business, US, 2004)

Wise, T. A., *Peat, Marwick, Mitchell & Co – 85 Years* (Peat Marwick Mitchell & Co., US, 1982)

Twenty-first century

Brooks, R., *The Great Tax Robbery – How Britain Became a Tax Haven for Fat Cats and Big Business* (Oneworld, UK, 2013)

Davies, H., *The Financial Crisis – Who is to Blame?* (Polity, UK, 2010)

Fraser, I., *Shredded: Inside RBS, the Bank that Broke Britain* (Birlinn, UK, 2014)

Gill, M., *Accountants' Truth – Knowledge and Ethics in the Financial World* (Oxford University Press, UK, 2009)

Jennings, A., *Foul! The Secret World of FIFA: Bribes, Vote-Rigging and Ticket Scandals* (Harper Sport, UK, 2006)

Jennings, A., *The Dirty Game: Uncovering the Scandal at FIFA* (Penguin Random House, UK, 2015)

Kay, J., *Other People's Money: Masters of the Universe or Servants of the People?* (Profile Books, UK, 2015)

Lewis, M., *The Big Short – Inside the Doomsday Machine* (Norton & Co., US, 2010)

McLean, B., and Nocera, J., *All the Devils Are Here: The Hidden History of the Financial Crisis* (Penguin, US, 2010)

Zucman, G., *The Hidden Wealth of Nations – the Scourge of Tax Havens* (University of Chicago Press, US, 2015)

ACADEMIC AND PROFESSIONAL PAPERS

Beattie, Vivien; Fearnley, Stella; and Hines, Tony, 'Does IFRS Undermine UK Reporting Integrity?' (*Accountancy*, December 2008)

Bush, T., *Divided by Common Language – Where Economics Meets the Law: US versus non-US financial reporting models* (ICAEW, UK, June 2005), http://www.icaew.com/-/media/corporate/files/technical/corporate-governance/dialogue-in-corporate-governance/divided-by-common-language-publication.ashx?la=en

Matthews, D., and Pirie, J., *Auditors Talk: An Oral History of the Profession from the 1920s to the Present Day* (Taylor & Francis, UK, 2001)

Napier, C. J., 'Intersections of Law and Accountancy: Unlimited Auditor Liability in the United Kingdom' (*Accounting, Organisations and Society*, UK, Vol. 23, No. 1, pp.105–28, 1998)

Shah, A., *Systemic Regulatory Arbitrage: A Case Study of KPMG* (Suffolk Business School, UK, 2015)

Sikka, Professor P., and Mitchell, A., *The Pinstripe Mafia: How Accountancy Firms Destroy Societies* (Association of Accountancy & Business Affairs, UK, 2011)

Wootton, C. W., and Wolk, C. M., 'The Development of "The Big Eight" Accounting Firms in the United States, 1900 to 1990' (*Accounting Historians Journal*, US, June 1992)

Zeff, Professor Stephen, 'How the US Accounting Profession Got Where It Is Today', Parts I and II (*Accounting Horizons*, US, Vol. 17, No. 3, September 2003, and No. 4, December 2003)

Zucman, Gabriel, 'Taxing Across Borders: Tracking Personal Wealth and Corporate Profits' (*Journal of Economic Perspectives*, US, Vol. 28, No. 4, Fall 2014), http://gabriel-zucman.eu/files/Zucman2014JEP.pdf

NEWSPAPER REPORTS

Agnew, Harriet, 'Professional Services: Accounting for Change', *Financial Times*, 28 August 2015

Alexander, Delroy; Burns, Greg; Manor, Robert; McRoberts, Flynn; and Torriero, E.A., 'Ties to Enron Blinded Andersen', *Chicago Tribune*, 3 September 2002

Bajaj, Vikas, and Creswell, Julie, 'A Lender Failed. Did Its Auditor?', *New York Times*, 13 April 2008

Berg, Eric, 'Losing $2 billion – an Accounting Quagmire; the Lapses by Lincoln's Auditors', *New York Times*, 28 December 1989

Brooks, R., 'Tax, Lies and Videotape', *Private Eye*, issue 1349, 20 September 2013

Brooks, R., 'Shady Arabia and the Desert Fix', *Private Eye*, issue 1375, 19 September 2014

Brown, Ken, and Duggan, Ianthe Jeanne, 'Arthur Andersen's Fall from Grace is a Sad Tale of Greed and Miscues', *Wall Street Journal*, 7 June 2002

Drucker, Jesse, 'Man Making Ireland Tax Avoidance Hub Proves Local Hero', *Bloomberg*, 28 October 2013

Tavernise, Sabrina, 'US Auditors Find Things Are Different in Russia', *New York Times*, 12 March 2002

'The Big Five?', *Economist*, 18 September 1997

BROADCASTS

Cox, Simon, and Proctor, Lucy, 'The Accountant Kings' (BBC Radio 4 *File on 4*, broadcast 4 March 2014), available at http://www.bbc.co.uk/programmes/b03wpjjq

Jenkins, J., 'A Brief History of Double-Entry Bookkeeping' (BBC Radio 4, broadcast 2010)

NOTES AND REFERENCES

PREFACE

1. Harriet Agnew, 'KPMG to Open Mayfair Members' Club', *Financial Times*, 31 August 2015.

INTRODUCTION: MEET THE BEAN COUNTERS

1. Fernando Pessoa, *The Book of Disquiet*, trans. Margaret Jull Costa, Serpent's Tail, 2010.
2. Research by *CA* magazine, 14 November 2016, based on 2016 results.
3. From Max Weber, *The Protestant Ethic and the Spirit of Capitalism*, 1905, cited in Gleeson-White, *Double Entry*.
4. From Werner Sombart, *Der Moderne Kapitalismus*, 1902, cited in Gleeson-White.
5. Edward Thomas Jones, *'Jones's 'English System of Book-keeping by Single or Double Entry. . . .'*, 1796, cited in Gleeson-White.
6. PwC UK's income of £3.1bn in 2015 translated into profit of £818m. Applying the same ratio gives an estimated worldwide profit figure of $9.2bn.
7. Quoted in Agnew, 'Professional Services'.
8. Brooks, *The Go-Go Years*.
9. Figures from Big Four firms' annual reports, available on their websites.
10. Interview by author with David Barnes, Deloitte partner and global managing director for public policy, 16 December 2016.
11. Figures from annual international reports of the Big Four firms, available on their websites.
12. The figures are for the year ended in the calendar year given, as reported in the firms' worldwide and UK annual reports. PwC's year end is June, Deloitte's May, EY's June and KPMG's September. The firms' United States partnerships do not publish accounts. The figures used in the second graph are those given in their worldwide reviews for all of the Americas, converted

into US dollars. The vast majority of the income is from the US. GDP Data is from the UK's Office of National Statistics and the World Bank.

13. At the time of writing in 2017, latest figures were: Apple, 116,000; Alphabet (Google), 75,000; Microsoft, 114,000; Amazon, 341,000; Johnson & Johnson, 127,000. Source: *Financial Times* Global 500 ranking, second quarter 2017.

14. KPMG LLP 2014 annual report, p.37. It would work on '71 of the 130 banks stress-tested by the ECB . . .'

15. Annual reports for the firms worldwide and in the UK. Percentages of audit work in the UK firms are: Deloitte, 16%; KPMG, 24%; EY, 20%; PwC 22%.

16. For Deloitte, 'audit and assurance' also includes 'risk advisory' ($4.1bn in 2016). This was not separated from auditing for years before 2014 so is included in all years for consistency and more accurately showing trends. Auditing numbers are therefore slightly overstated for 2014, 2015 and 2016. 'Non-audit' includes categories variously described as 'consulting', 'advisory', 'transactional advice services', 'financial advisory', 'tax' and 'tax and legal'.

17. Agnew 'Professional Services'.

18. KPMG Thought Leadership, https://home.kpmg.com/xx/en/home/insights/2015/01/strategy.html; accessed 26 August 2017.

19. See https://www.pwc.com/us/en/cfodirect/issues/strategy-operations.html.

20. Interview by author with David Barnes, Deloitte partner and global managing director for public policy, 16 December 2016.

21. The part played by the change of the major investment, or merchant, banks from partnerships to companies is explained more in Kay, *Other People's Money*.

22. Evidence of Lord Stevenson to Parliamentary Commission on Banking Standards, 4 December 2012.

23. Figures from Ian Fraser, 'KPMG and the HBOS Whistleblower', *Sunday Herald*, 18 December 2011.

24. Galbraith, *The Great Crash*.

25. From Upton Sinclair, *I, Candidate for Governor: And how I got Licked*, Upton Sinclair, 1934.

26. Robert Half, CEO tracker survey, April 2016, https://www.roberthalf.co.uk/news-insights/reports-guides/cfo-insights/robert-half-ftse-100-ceo-tracker; accessed 5 March 2017.

27. Stuart Pfeifer, 'Former KPMG Partner Sentenced for Insider Trading', *Los Angeles Times*, 24 April 2014.

28. Gill, *Accountants' Truth*.

29. Only PwC and Deloitte reported figures globally. In 2016, their female partners were 18.1% (1,963 out of 10,830) and 18.4% (2,068 out of 11,262) respectively. See *Economia*, magazine of the ICAEW, 4 August 2017, http://economia.icaew.com/en/news/august-2017/accountancy-firms-revenues-grow-3-per-cent-globally.

30. Worldwide chairman and chief executive of EY, Mark Weinberger, is a lawyer who made his career as a White House adviser and tax counsel. Worldwide chief executive of Deloitte is Punit Renjen, a management consultant. All

the worldwide firm leaders were men, as were all the UK leaders, although since 2015 KPMG's and Deloitte's US arms have been run by women. Lynne Doughtie was elected senior partner of KPMG US; Cathy Engelbert of Deloitte's US partnership.

31. The EY Tate Arts Partnership, EY website: http://www.ey.com/gl/en/about-us/our-sponsorships-and-programs/our-partnership-with-tate; accessed 10 August 2017.
32. Short video interview with Varley: ibid.
33. EY Global, interview with John Rudaizky, YouTube, 12 March 2016; accessed 7 January 2017.
34. Deloitte Global Impact Report 2016.
35. From Edward Luce, *The Retreat of Western Liberalism*, Little, Brown, London, 2017. See Part I, 'Fusion', p.19.
36. Remark made at a talk to Philanthropy Round Table, California, November 2000. Charlie Munger is the 93-year-old vice chairman of Warren Buffet's Berkshire Hathaway group.
37. http://integratedreporting.org/the-iirc-2/structure-of-the-iirc/council/; accessed 25 August 2017.

1 MERCHANTS AND MAYHEM

1. Fibonacci's *Liber Abaci*, trans. L. E. Sigler, Springer, New York, 2002.
2. Michael Chatfield, in Chatfield and Vangermeersch, *The History of Accoiunting*.
3. Answers are MCMLIII and XXV or 1,953 and 25 respectively.
4. While it is clear that the rise of mathematical methods and demand from growing trade lay behind the adoption and refinement of double-entry bookkeeping in early Renaissance Italy, its genesis is a matter of doubt. The first recorded use, not long after Fibonacci's work, by a thirteenth-century moneylender in the Champagne region, fits with the theory that his advance of mathematical method and Arabic numerals was the precursor. But far earlier origins are also possible. In her history *Double Entry: How the Merchants of Venice Created Modern Finance*, Jane Gleeson-White suggests that some form of double-entry was used in the earlier Hindu or Arab worlds, and that elements might have been imported directly from India to Venice during the Middle Ages when the city on the Adriatic was 'the emporium of Indian commerce'. A system bearing some resemblance to double-entry, known as *bahi-khata*, appears to have been used in India before the Roman period and its principles might well have informed the Italian pioneers.
5. Werner Sombart, *Der moderne Kapitalismus*. Historisch-systematische Darstellung des gesamteuropäischen Wirtschaftslebens von seinen Anfängen bis zur Gegenwart, final edn, 1928.
6. Lance Elliott LaGroue, 'Accounting and Auditing in Roman Society', dissertation under direction of Richard Talbert, University of North Carolina, 2014, https://cdr.lib.unc.edu/indexablecontent/

uuid:4aa259f4-2bbb-4e93-b2ef-9876b0c771b3; accessed 7 January 2014.

7. Iris Origo, *Merchant of Prato*, Jonathan Cape, 1957, cited by Soll, *The Reckoning*.

8. Ibid. Datini's records and account books are kept at the Prato Museum near Florence.

9. Soll, p.30.

10. Raymond de Roover, *The Rise and Decline of the Medici Bank 1397–1494*, the President and Fellows of Harvard College, 1963.

11. The Acciaioli, Bardi and Peruzzi banks were the main ones.

12. Drawing on Parks, *Medici Money*.

13. The Sassetti chapel is in the basilica of Santa Trinita in Florence. The frescoes are by leading Renaissance artist Ghirlandaio.

14. Detail from fresco by Ghirlandaio in Sassetti Chapel, basilica of Santa Trinita, Florence.

15. De Roover, *The Medici Bank*.

16. Parks.

17. Attributed to Jacopo de' Barbari, 1495–1500, now at Capodimonte Museum, Naples.

18. Vahé Baladouni, *Accounting in the Early Years of the East India Company*, 1925, Academy of Accounting Historians, published digitally in 2005 by University of Mississippi Library.

19. Stephanie E. Smallwood, *Saltwater Slavery: A Middle Passage from Africa to American Diaspora*, Harvard University Press, 2007.

20. From Mary Poovey, *The History of the Modern Fact – Problems of Knowledge in the Sciences of Wealth and Society*, University of Chicago Press, 1998.

21. Daniel Defoe, *A Tour through England and Wales: Divided into Circuits or Journeys, 1724–7*, quoted in Natalie Roxburgh, *Representing Public Credit: Credible Commitment, Fiction and the Rise of the Financial Subject*, Routledge, 2016.

22. Roxburgh, *Representing Public Credit*.

23. Histories of the South Sea Bubble used include that by J. Bruce Tabb in Chatfield and Vangermeersch, and Balen.

24. Benjamin Wardhaught, *Poor Robin's Prophecies: A Curious Almanac and the Everyday Mathematics of Georgian Britain*, Oxford University Press, 2012.

25. It took the economy around seven years to return to its pre-bubble-level GDP. In the wake of the 2008 crash, the same point was reached after six years. See David Blanchflower, 'Britain has taken longer to recover from recession than at any time since the South Sea Bubble', *Independent*, 3 August 2014, citing research by Spectator editor Fraser Nelson. See also Bank of England figures for 'total GDP in the UK since 1270'.

2 FULL STEAM AHEAD

1. Mair's 1727 textbook was called *Book-keeping Methodiz'd*.

2. H. W. Dickinson, *Matthew Boulton*, Cambridge University Press, 1937, cited

in S. Toms, *Accounting and Labour Control at Boulton and Watt*, University of York Management School, 2010, https://www.york.ac.uk/media/tyms/documents/research/workingpaper/52%20Accounting%20and%20Labour%20Control%20at%20Boulton%20and%20Watt1c.pdf; accessed 1 March 2016.

3. Reilly, *Josiah Wedgwood*.

4. Ibid.

5. 'Second Report of the Committee of Investigation to be laid before the meeting of the shareholders on the 6th day of September 1849', Henry Sotheran, York, 1849.

6. Andrew MacEwan, of MacEwan & Auld.

7. The value of British railway company securities rose from £246m in 1850 to £1,176m in 1900: figures given in R. C. Michie, *The Global Securities Market, A History*, Oxford University Press, 2006. GDP was £1,854m: Bank of England, *Three Centuries of Data*.

8. George Robb, *White Collar Crime in Modern England: Financial Fraud and Business Morality 1845–1929*, Cambridge University Press, 1992.

9. James Hutton, practising Glasgow accountant from 1847, quoted in Chatfield and Vangermeersch.

10. In 1854 and 1855 respectively.

11. Wise, *Peat, Marwick, Mitchell & Co.* and Roger White, *Peats to KPMG: Gracious Family to Global Firm*, 1974, published independently and cited in KPMG 2013 alumni newsletter.

12. House of Commons debate, 1 February 1856, Vol. 140. By 'parties interested', Lowe meant the directors and shareholders, not the employees or anybody else dealing with the company. This was laissez-faire applied to accounting and raised a question that still troubles accountancy: for whom does a company account? http://hansard.millbanksystems.com/commons/1856/feb/01/law-of-partnership-and-joint-stock.

13. Micklethwaite and Woolridge, *The Company*.

14. ICAEW statistics, provided in email to author, 16 March 2016.

15. E. Cooper, 'Chartered Accountants as Auditors of Companies', *The Accountant* magazine, 13 November 1886, pp.644–9, cited by P. Sikka, et al., 'The Impossibility of Eliminating the Expectations Gap: Some Theory and Evidence', *Critical Perspectives on Accounting*, 1998, No. 9.

16. Discussed in Soll.

17. Micklethwaite and Wooldridge, citing Alfred Chandler, *The Dawn of Industrial Capitalism*, Harvard University Press, 1990.

18. Allen and McDermott, *Accounting for Success*.

19. Ibid.

20. C. W. DeMond, *Price Waterhouse & Co. in America: A History of a Public Accounting Firm*, Price Waterhouse, cited in *Accounting Historians Journal*, Vol. 12, No. 1, 1985.

21. Haskins biography on Deloitte website: https://www2.deloitte.com/us/en/pages/about-deloitte/articles/about-deloitte-history-leader-charles-waldo-haskins.html.

22. Cited in Brewster, *Unaccountable*.
23. Account of 1902 industrial commission by Barbara D. Merino in Chatfield and Vangermeersch.
24. William Z. Ripley, *From Main Street to Wall Street*, Atlantic Monthly, 1926, cited in Bush, *Divided by Common Language*.
25. Galbraith, *The Great Crash*.
26. Strictly, the Securities Act 1933.
27. House of Representatives Report No. 85, 1933, cited in Bush.

3 ACCOUNTANCY GOES WRONG

1. National Bureau of Economic Research, *Mergers and Acquisitions in the US Economy: An Aggregate and Historical Overview*, University of Chicago Press, 1987. Their value rose from $10bn to around $250bn in today's prices. http://www.nber.org/chapters/c5820; accessed 15 May 2016.
2. Research cited in Frank R. Rayburn and Ollie S. Powers, 'A History of Pooling of Interests Accounting for Business Combinations in the United States', University of Alabama at Birmingham, published in *Accounting Historians Journal*, Vol. 18, No. 2, 1991.
3. Wise.
4. Zeff, Part I, citing Leonard M. Savoie.
5. Allen and McDermott.
6. Figures cited in Wootton and Wolk, 'Development of "The Big Eight"'.
7. A. J. Briloff, 'Dirty Pooling', *Accounting Review*, July 1967, cited in Chatfield and Vangermeersch.
8. It had been established for thirty years that auditors needed to do more than accept a company's numbers at face value when approving accounts and that they could be sued if they were grossly negligent. In the famous 1931 case of Ultramares Corporation v. Touche, Niven & Co., a lender (Ultramares) funded a rubber importer (Fred Stern & Co.) on the strength of falsified balance sheets. Touche could be held liable as its audits had been so grossly negligent as to constitute fraud. In 1938, the case of US v. McKesson & Robbins, involving falsified ledgers and theft by the company's proprietors, overlooked by auditors Price Waterhouse, established that auditors had to make some effort to establish the veracity of information presented to them. But the bean counters continued to use 'generally accepted accounting principles' (GAAP) – essentially a concept of their own making – as a shield against civil and criminal action. They claimed that if they followed these principles they had done their job. In 1967, the chairman of the Continental Vending Machine Corporation, Harold Roth, was found to have been squirrelling millions of dollars out of the company by lending money to a shell company he controlled. Auditors from Lybrand, Ross Bros & Montgomery certified the amounts as regular loans. When three of its accountants were prosecuted over the affair, Continental employees testified in court that the auditors had been told year after year that the money was being taken by Roth. Despite the evidence

of blatant deception, and fearing the implications for the whole profession, senior accountants from Lybrand and other firms lined up to say that there was nothing wrong with the accounts; they still met the GAAP standards required. The jury was unimpressed and convicted (though the auditors later received pardons from none other than President Richard Nixon). An appeal judge agreed with the jury: accounting standards were fine when all was above board, but once an auditor had reason to suspect dishonesty, 'an entirely different situation confronts him'.

9. Rush Loving Jr, *The Men Who Loved Trains: The Story of the Men who Battled Greed to Save an Ailing Industry*, Indiana University Press, 2008, and Daniel Guttman and Barry Willner, *The Shadow Government: the Government's Multi-Billion Dollar Giveaway of its Decision-Making Powers to Private Management Consultants, 'Experts' and Think Tanks*, Pantheon Books, 1973.

10. 'The Financial Collapse of the Penn Central Company', Staff Report of the Securities and Exchange Commission, report to the Special Sub-committee on Investigations, 1972.

11. Figures cited in Squires and Smith, *Inside Arthur Andersen*.

12. The more official Federal Accounting Standards Board, under the aegis of the SEC, was set up to succeed the failed Auditing Practices Board in 1973.

13. The Continental Vending Machine Corporation case, see note 8 above.

14. A. M. C. Morison, cited in Clikeman, *Called to Account*.

15. Henry Gunders, in Price Waterhouse Oral History, cited by Brewster.

16. For an illuminating history of the divergence of US and UK accounting standards, see Bush.

17. Securities and Exchange Commission Oral History project, interview with former Price Waterhouse partner Shaun O'Malley, 1 April 2011.

18. In *Financial Reporting in the UK: A History of the Accounting Standards Committee 1969–70*, Routledge, 2007, B. A. Rutherford cites an ICAEW survey finding that in 1969/70, the height of this period of M&A activity, just six cases of merger accounting were found.

19. *Economist*, 10 September 1966.

20. Current Keeper of the Privy Purse is Sir Alan Reid, a senior partner in KPMG until 2002.

21. The Chief Secretary to the Treasury was grammar school boy and Labour MP John Diamond. Figures from Lee J. Seidler, 'A Comparison of the Economic and Social Status of the Accountancy Profession in Great Britain and the United States of America', *The Accountants' Magazine*, September 1969.

22. Ibid.

23. Matthews and Pirie, *Auditors' Talk*.

24. Seidler, 'A Comparison'.

4 TRUST ME, I'M A CONSULTANT

1. Figure from consultancy.co.uk for 2016. This breaks down into: £31bn strategy consulting; $71bn operational consulting; $70bn financial consulting; $31bn HR consulting; $48bn technology consulting.
2. Cited in Trevor Boyns, John R. Edwards and Marc Nitiken, *The Birth of Industrial Accounting in Britain and France*, Routledge, 2013.
3. *On the Economy of Machinery and Manufactures*, 1832, cited in Chatfield and Vangermeersch.
4. MacDonald, *The Firm*.
5. Higgins, *The First Sixty Years*.
6. Ibid.
7. Brewster.
8. Ibid.
9. MacDonald. The term 'contractor state' was coined by Christopher McKenna in *The World's Newest Profession*, Cambridge University Press, New York, 2006.
10. Higgins.
11. Toffler, *First Accountancy*.
12. Manya A. Brachear, obituary of Joseph Glickauf Jr, *Chicago Tribune*, 28 July 2005.
13. Toffler, and Squires and Smith.
14. Allen and McDermott.
15. Ibid, citing Price Waterhouse US 1966 annual report.
16. *The Accounting Establishment*, a staff study prepared by the Subcommittee on Reports, Accounting and Management for the Senate Committee on Government Operations, 1976.
17. Data from Zeff, Part II, citing G. J. Previts, *The Scope of CPA Services*, John Wiley & Sons, New York, 1985.
18. Allen and McDermott, p.233.
19. Wootton and Wolk, citing Public Accounting Report, 15 November 1989.
20. Stevens, cited by Zeff.
21. Stevens, *The Big Six*.
22. The firm was founded by Scotsman George Touche in the late nineteenth century. He was in fact born George Touch, but as the word – when incorrectly pronounced 'tutch' – also meant to get money out of someone illicitly, he later added the 'e'.
23. Touche Ross partner Ralph Waters, writing to Stephen Zeff, cited in Zeff, Part II, pp. 267–86.
24. Stevens.

5 FREE FOR ALL

1. Berg, 'Losing $2 billion'.
2. Public Accounting Report, 15 November 1989, cited in Wootton and Wolk.

3. Comment of Ronald Rus, lawyer for bondholders of Lincoln's parent company American Continental. Reported in Berg.

4. Figures for compensation payments cited in Clikeman.

5. Congressman Henry Gonzalez at congressional hearing, quoted in Clikeman.

6. See for example official report on Mirror Group Newspapers plc, 2001, http://webarchive.nationalarchives.gov.uk/+/http://www.dti.gov.uk/cld/mirrorgroup/summary.htm.

7. Joint Disciplinary Scheme Report, 1999, and DTI report, 2001.

8. Joint Disciplinary Scheme report, 7 July 1995, seen by author.

9. Interview by Chris Quick in *CCH Daily*, 1 August 2003, https://www.cchdaily.co.uk/analysis-hotseat-rise-and-rise-deloitte-touche; accessed 9 July 2016.

10. For example, the late Professor Stewart Hamilton, interviewed by Ian Fraser for his book on the collapse of RBS, *Shredded*.

11. Shaxson, *Treasure Islands*.

12. For a discussion of the effects of the change in structure of the investment banks, see Kay. Of historical interest is that Overend & Gurney's collapse in 1866 followed soon after the bank's conversion from partnership to limited company.

13. The legislation was the Private Securities Litigation Reform Act, 1995.

14. The case was Caparo Industries v. Dickman, 1990, UKHL 2.

15. Financial Reporting Council chair Sir Ron Dearing, deputy chair Philip Couse, ex-Coopers, plus Stock Exchange chairman Andrew Hugh Smith and CBI president Sir Trevor Holdsworth were among those concerned.

16. Prem Sikka, Jim Cousins and Austin Mitchell, *Race to the Bottom: the Case of the Accountancy Firms*, Association for Accountancy and Business Affairs, 2004.

17. ICAEW Council, quoted in *Accountancy* magazine, April 1994, cited in Napier, 'Intersections of Law and Accountancy'.

18. Sikka, Cousins and Mitchell, Race to the Bottom.

19. *Financial Times*, 11 June 1998.

20. Written parliamentary answer, 7 November 1996. Hansard, Col. 618.

21. House of Commons Trade and Industry Select Committee, 16 February 1999.

22. Levitt's 'Numbers Game' speech, New York University Centre for Law and Business, 28 September 1998.

23. For a full account of the Sunbeam case, see Clikeman.

24. Levitt, *Take on the Street*.

25. 'The Big Five?', *Economist*, 18 September 1997, http://www.economist.com/node/157334; accessed 10 August 2017.

26. Discussed in Sikka and Mitchell, *The Pinstripe Mafia*. Re PwC 'kickbacks', see US Department of Justice press release, 16 August 2007.

27. Levitt.

28. Levitt speech to American Institute of Certified Public Accountants, 10 December 1996, cited by Brewster. The speech was made a few days after Federal Reserve chairman Alan Greenspan's famously unheeded 'irrational exuberance' warning.

29. Stephen Labaton, 'Enron's Collapse: The Lobbying – Auditing Firms Exercise Power In Washington', *New York Times*, 19 January 2002.

30. Levitt.

31. Ibid., note 22.

32. Shown in the film of *The Smartest Guys in the Room*, directed by Alex Gibney, produced by 2929 Entertainment and HDNet Films, 2005.

33. McLean and Elkind, *The Smartest Guys in the Room*.

34. Ibid.

35. Brown and Duggan, 'Arthur Andersen's Fall from Grace'.

36. Senior Andersen auditor Leigh Anne Dear, quoted in Alexander et al., 'Ties to Enron Blinded Andersen'.

37. *Wall Street Journal*, 15 May 2002.

38. Levitt.

39. McLean and Elkind.

40. Dan Ackman, 'Enron Documents Indicate Possible Cover-Up', *Forbes*, 3 April 2002.

41. Based on interviews reported in Squires and Smith.

42. McLean and Elkind.

43. 'KPMG Pays $22m to Settle SEC Litigation Relating to Xerox Audits', SEC press notice, 19 April 2005.

6 CRASH!

1. Letter from British Academy to HM Queen Elizabeth II, 22 July 2009, signed by Professors Tim Besley, Patrick Hennessey and thirty-one other academics, politicians, civil servants, bankers and others.

2. Lewis, *The Big Short*.

3. Ibid., pp.13–14

4. Based on Big Four worldwide annual reports. Fees from auditing as percentage of total income were: KPMG 47%, Deloitte 45%, PwC 49.5%. Ernst & Young did not disclose figures.

5. Joseph Stiglitz, *The Roaring Nineties: Seeds of Destruction*, Penguin, 2003.

6. Financial Stability Board, Global Shadow Banking Monitoring Report 2012, pp.8–9, http://www.fsb.org/wp-content/uploads/r_121118c.pdf; accessed 20 November 2016.

7. Ibid.

8. Final Report of Michael J. Missal, Bankruptcy Examiner in New Century TRS Holdings Inc., Case No. 07-10416 (KJC), US Bankruptcy Court for the District of Delaware.

9. The New Century Liquidating Trust and Reorganized New Century Warehouse Corporation, by and through Alan M. Jacobs, Liquidating Trustee and Plan Administrator, Plaintiff v. KPMG International, Defendant. Complaint and Jury Demand, 1 April 2009, http://online.wsj.com/public/resources/documents/KPMGIntl0401.pdf; accessed 9 March 2017.

10. Final Report of Michael J. Missal, Bankruptcy Examiner; see note 8 above.
11. Bajaj and Creswell 'A Lender Failed'.
12. Ibid.
13. KPMG paid part of a $153m settlement with Fannie Mae to pension funds for misleading figures produced between 2001 and 2004; see, for example, http://www.reuters.com/article/us-kpmg-settlement/fannie-mae-kpmg-agree-to-pay-153-million-to-end-shareholder-lawsuit-idUSBRE94617S20130507.
14. Wise. The $350,000 would be about $10m at current prices, but was more economically significant than this number suggests.
15. Final Report of Michael J. Missal, Bankruptcy Examiner; see note 8 above.
16. University of North Carolina research note, 2012, http://www.stat.unc.edu/faculty/cji/fys/2012/Subprime%20mortgage%20crisis.pdf; accessed 29 December 2016.
17. Issuers' and Investors' Summit on CDOs/Credit Derivatives 2006, conference programme, https://www.imn.org/structured-finance/conference/The-10th-Annual-Issuers-And-Investors-Summit-On-CDOsCredit-Derivatives-US/Sponsors.html; accessed 9 March 2017.
18. Worldwide reports. In 2006, KPMG and PwC in UK were earning 25% and 30% of their fees respectively from the financial services sector.
19. Speaking at Conference on Bank Structure and Competition, Chicago, Illinois, 8 May 2003.
20. In 1965, President Lyndon Johnson criticized him for raising interest rates to address inflation caused by the Vietnam War. The 'punchbowl' comment was Martin's response.
21. *How Fair is Fair Value?*, Ernst & Young, May 2005. No longer publicly available.
22. The US accounting standard was Federal Accounting Standard 5. It required a provision to be made when it was probable that an asset such as a debt was impaired and the amount of the loss could be reasonably estimated.
23. *Joining the Dots: IFRS-Global Reporting Revolution*, PwC, March 2004. No longer publicly available.
24. Reported by the chairman of the Accounting Standards Board, Ian Mackintosh, in a letter to the *Financial Times*, 24 August 2006, http://www.ft.com/cms/s/0/ea4d0718-330c-11db-87ac-0000779e2340.html?ft_site=falcon&desktop=true#axzz4WP25aY9z; accessed 21 January 2017.
25. Research by Vivien Beattie, accounting professor at Glasgow University, Stella Fearnley, accounting professor at Bournemouth University, and Toby Hines, principal lecturer in accounting at the University of Portsmouth, published in *The Finance Director*, 23 April 2009.
26. See annual reports and, for example, 13 May 2005 announcement of restatements because of using IAS39, https://www.investegate.co.uk/Article.aspx?id=200505130900012438M; accessed 14 July 2017.
27. House of Commons Library Standard Note SN/SG/0263, Appendix C1, 15 February 2011.
28. House of Lords Economic Affairs Committee inquiry into 'Auditors: market

concentration and their role', memo submitted by Timothy Bush, 25 January 2011.

29. Stephen Seawright, 'Northern Rock Boosts Loan Book', *Daily Telegraph*, 29 July 2005.

30. Lord Turner, speech to ICAEW, 21 January 2010, http://www.iasplus.com/en/binary/uk/1001turnerspeech.pdf.

31. Written evidence to Parliamentary Commission on Banking Standards from Timothy Bush, 21 August 2012.

32. Chirac's comments were in a letter to EC president Romano Prodi; see for example *Advances in International Accounting*, Vol. 17, ed. J. Timothy Sale, Elsevier, 2004.

33. Louise Armistead, 'British Bank Accounting Standards Not "Fit for Purpose"', *Daily Telegraph*, 13 March 2011, reporting interview with Peter Wyman.

34. Report of House of Lords Economic Affairs Committee on 'Auditors: market concentration and their role', 30 March 2011.

35. Statutory Instrument No. 2587, 17 July 2001, made under S.342 Financial Services and Markets Act 2000.

36. FSA evidence to Lords Economic Affairs Committee, 14 Deember 2010.

37. Northern Rock's 2007 annual report, for example, showed that it earned £0.8m from auditing the bank and its subsidiaries and £1m from other services, £0.7m from 'services provided in respect of securitisation transactions and the raising of wholesale funding'.

38. Interview with author, 28 November 2016.

39. Quoted in Andrew Ross Sorkin, *Too Big to Fail: Inside the Battle to Save Wall Street*, Penguin, 2009. The financial controller was Michael McGarvey; the senior banker was head of equities Bart McDade.

40. Bankruptcy examiner's report *in re* Lehman Brothers Holdings Inc. Report of Anton R. Valukas, Chapter 11, Case No. 08-13555 (JMP), US Bankruptcy Court, Southern District New York, 11 March 2010, p. 959.

41. District Judge Lewis A. Kaplan *in re* Lehman Brothers Securities & ERISA litigation, New York District Court, 18 September 2015.

42. http://www.ag.ny.gov/press-release/ag-schneiderman-announces-settlement-ernst-young-over-auditor's-involvement-alleged.

43. Final Report of the National Commission on the Causes of the Financial and Economic Crisis in the United States, January 2011, p.273

44. Interview with Stanford University professor Joseph A. Grundfest, 2009. Available on the website of Ian Fraser, http://www.ianfraser.org/charlie-munger-getting-accounting-integrity-right-has-enormous-implications-for-future-of-mankind/.

45. Final Report of the National Commission on the Causes of the Financial and Economic Crisis in the United States, January 2011, p.273.

46. PwC worldwide annual report, 2007. Income includes banking and capital markets, investment management and insurance.

47. Figures from RBS annual reports. In 2005, fees were: £9.9m audit, £7m 'audit-related' (e.g. due diligence on acquisitions) and £7.4m non-audit.

48. *The Times*, 16 August 2008, http://www.thetimes.co.uk/tto/business/moversshakers/article1891060.ece.

49. Interview conducted with senior RBS official by Ian Fraser, author of *Shredded: Inside RBS, the Bank that Broke Britain*.

50. FSA report, *The Failure of the Royal Bank of Scotland*, December 2011, Part 3, paragraph 183.

51. Details given in Amended Consolidated Particulars of Claim of the Claimants amended by Order of Chief Master Marsh dated 15 September 2016, High Court of Justice, Chancery Division, in Greenwood & Others v. Goodwin & others.

52. Defence served in High Court in Greenwood & Others v. Goodwin & Others.

53. Emma Dunkley, 'RBS and Retail Investors Reach £200m Rights Issue Settlement', *Financial Times*, 6 June 2017.

54. Parliamentary Commission on Banking Standards – Fourth Report, *'An Accident Waiting to Happen': The Failure of HBOS*, 7 March 2013.

55. The Failure of HBOS plc (HBOS): a report by the Financial Conduct Authority and the Prudential Regulatory Authority, November 2015.

56. Paul Moore's story is colourfully told in his book *Crash Bank Wallop*, New Wilberforce Media Ltd, 2015.

57. http://www.ianfraser.org/kpmg-and-the-hbos-whisteblower/.

58. Evidence of Lord Stevenson to Lords Economic Affairs Committee, 4 December 2012.

59. Disciplinary case relating to PwC's audits of Cattles plc and Welcome Financial Services Limited, FRC press release, 31 August 2016.

60. Correspondence between Andrew Tyrie MP, then chairman of the Commons Treasury Select Committee, and Stephen Haddrill, 10 December 2015, 21 January 2016 and 3 February 2016. Available from TSC website: https://www.parliament.uk/business/committees/committees-a-z/commons-select/treasury-committee/news-parliament-2015/financial-reporting-council-correspondence-15-16/; accessed 9 March 2017.

61. Minutes of meeting of Company Reporting and Auditing Group, 11 December 2007, comprising representatives of all the Big Four and a number of institutional investors, seen by author and reported by Patrick Hosking in 'Accounting Watchdog "was aware of bank problems in 2007"', *The Times*, 22 September 2017.

62. House of Lords Economic Affairs Committee, 9 November 2010, http://www.publications.parliament.uk/pa/cm200708/cmselect/cmtreasy/56/56i.pdf.

63. Discussion between author and Stephen Haddrill following FRC annual open meeting, 21 September 2017.

64. Donal O'Donovan, 'Ernst & Young "Should have Known about Massive Scam"', *Irish Independent*, 20 July 2016, http://www.independent.ie/irish-news/ernst-young-should-have-known-about-massive-scam-34924439.html.

65. Cited in letter from Senator Elizabeth Warren to DoJ Inspector General Michael Horowitz, 15 September 2016, http://www.warren.senate.gov/files/documents/2016-9-15_Referral_DOJ_IG_letter.pdf; accessed 29 December 2016.

66. Speech on signing into law the Sarbanes–Oxley Act, 30 July 2002.

67. http://retheauditors.com/2010/11/28/ big-4-bombshell-we-didnt-fail-banks-because-they-were-getting-a-bailout/.

68. Report of House of Lords Economic Affairs Committee on 'Auditors: market concentration and their role'.

69. Parliamentary Commission on Banking Standards, Fourth Report, 12 June 2013, http://www.publications.parliament.uk/pa/jt201314/jtselect/ jtpcbs/27/2704.htm.

70. Evidence to House of Lords Economic Affairs Committee on 'Auditors: market concentration and their role'.

71. Interview with Joseph A. Grundfest, 2009; see note 44 above.

72. See EY website: http://www.ey.com/uk/en/industries/financial-services/ banking---capital-markets/banking-capital-market_contact_us; accessed 9 March 2017.

73. Bill Michael's LinkedIn page shows he was head of Financial Services Audit 2005–9 and head of Financial Services UK 2009–14, https://www.linkedin. com/in/billmichaelkpmg/?ppe=1; accessed 14 July 2017

7 DUTY FREE

1. Allen and McDermott.

2. Zeff. The proportion ranged from 15% (Haskins & Sells) to 24% (Touche Ross). The largest firm, Peat Marwick Mitchell, was at 21%.

3. David Kocieniewski, 'GE's Strategies Let it Avoid Tax Altogether', New York Times, 24 March 2011, citing Donald T. Regan (Reagan's chief of staff), From Wall Street to Washington, Harcourt Brace Jovanovich, 1988.

4. Report of the Special Committee of the Board of Directors of Hollinger Inc., prepared by Richard Breedon, 30 August 2004, https://www.sec.gov/ Archives/edgar/data/868512/000095012304010413/y01437exv99w2.htm; accessed 9 March 2017.

5. Zucman, 'Taxing Across Borders'.

6. Lee J. Seidler, 'A Comparison of the Economic and Social Status of the Accountancy Profession in Great Britain and the United States of America', The Accountants' Magazine, September 1969.

7. Prudential plc v. Revenue & Customs [2007] UKSPC SPC00626.

8. A. Parker, 'Tax Probe to Centre on 30 Top Companies', Financial Times, 4 May 2004.

9. Nick Davies, 'Cosy Relationship Keeps Corporates Happy but Could Cost £20bn in Taxes', Guardian, 1 July 2002.

10. Estimation of Tax Gap for Direct Taxes, HMRC, 1 April 2005, available at:https://www.gov.uk/government/uploads/system/uploads/attachment_ data/file/329278/direct-tax-gaps.pdf; accessed 9 March 2017.

11. Information obtained by author under Freedom of Information Act, August 2007.

12. DB Group Services UK Ltd v. HMRC [2016] UKSC 13.

13. HMRC v. Smallwood & Anor [2010] EWCA Civ 778.

14. Drummond v. HMRC [2009] EWCA Civ 608, and Astall and Edwards v. HMRC [2009] EWCA Civ 1010.

15. 'KPMG to Pay $456 Million for Criminal Violations', IRS press notice, 29 August 2005.

16. Bond-linked issue premium structure; foreign leveraged investment programme; offshore portfolio investment strategy; short option strategies.

17. IRS press notice; see note 15 above.

18. Details of internal correspondence reproduced in report of US Senate Permanent Subcommittee on Investigations report, November 2003, *US Tax Shelter Industry: the Role of Accountants, Lawyers, and Financial Professionals. Four KPMG Case Studies: FLIP, OPIS, BLIPS, AND SC2.*

19. Ibid.

20. Ibid.

21. Lynnley Browning, 'Documents Show KPMG Secretly Met Prosecutors', *New York Times*, 6 July 2007.

22. Tax Shelters: Who's buying, who's selling and what's the government doing about it? Hearing of Senate Finance Committee, 21 October 2003.

23. Lynnley Browning, 'How an Accounting Firm Went From Resistance to Resignation', *New York Times*, 28 August 2005.

24. US Senate Permanent Subcommittee on Investigations report, November 2003; see note 18 above.

25. Edward Simpkins, 'Don't Play Fast and Loose with the IRS', *Sunday Telegraph*, 6 September 2005.

26. *Sunday Times*, 4 September 2005.

27. $1.2bn out of $3.2bn. US Senate Permanent Subcommittee on Investigations report, November 2003.

28. Lynnley Browning, 'Defendants File a Flurry of Motions Challenging the KPMG Tax Shelter Case', *New York Times*, 13 January 2006.

29. Nick Shaxson, 'How Ireland Became an Offshore Financial Centre', Tax Justice Network, 11 November 2015, http://www.taxjustice.net/2015/11/11/how-ireland-became-an-offshore-financial-centre/.

30. Fiona Reddan, 'Scion of a Prominent Political Dynasty who Gave his Vote to Accountancy', *Irish Times*, 8 May 2015.

31. O'Rourke's role in Ireland's tax avoidance activities was first exposed by Bloomberg reporter Jesse Drucker in a 28 October 2013 article, 'Man Making Ireland Tax Avoidance Hub Proves Local Hero'.

32. Based on Google Inc.'s annual accounts for y/e 31/12/2015.

33. Zucman, 'Taxing Across Borders'.

34. Public Accounts Committee, 9th report, 2012/13 session, *Tax Avoidance – Google*, 10 June 2013.

35. Vodafone investor presentation, 23 July 2010, recorded by Thomson Street Events.

36. Information on meetings provided in parliamentary answer to Rt Hon. David Davis MP, Hansard, 28 April 2011, Col. 517W. Re position with Deloitte, see

letter from Advisory Committee on Business Appointments, 4 March 2013, https://www.gov.uk/government/uploads/system/uploads/attachment_data/file/369294/approval_2oletter_20-_2owebsite.pdf.

37. BBC Panorama's *The Truth About Tax* was broadcast on 21 May 2012. *Private Eye* reported the story as 'Grand Duchy Originals' in issue 1314, published 22 May 2012.

38. *Aggressive Corporate Tax Planning Under Scrutiny*, European Parliamentary Research Service, 19 November 2015, http://www.europarl.europa.eu/RegData/etudes/ATAG/2015/571345/EPRS_ATA(2015)571345_EN.pdf.

39. Evidence from German Green MEP Sven Giegold at trial in Luxembourg, 29 April 2016.

40. 'PwC Luxembourg Crystal Park Offices Inaugurated', *Chronicle.lu*, 24 November 2014.

41. IMF figures for 2015, to nearest $1,000, show Luxembourg GDP per capita as $102,000. Its nearest EU rival was Ireland on $61,000. Others: UK $44,000, Germany $41,000, France $38,000.

42. 'Stone Laying Ceremony for Dramatic New PwC Offices', *Luxembourg Wort*, 10 June 2013.

43. Much of the information and commentary in this account of the affair was covered in a 2016 French TV film produced by Premières Lignes, the same company for which Edouard Perrin originally exposed the tax rulings in 2012. The later film, *Being a Whistleblower*, looked at the story of Raphaël Halet. It was broadcast on France 2 but has not appeared in the UK. Benoit Bringer was reporter and director. All documents referred to have been seen by the author, who also discussed the events at length with Raphaël Halet. He also asked PwC if they disagreed with any facts in the film. The firm disputed only minor points, none of which are included here.

44. Submission to Metz Cour d'Appel dated 29 December 2017, seen by author. Reported in *Le Quotidien*, Luxembourg, 8 January 2018: https://translate.google.co.uk/translate?hl=en&sl=fr&u=http://www.lequotidien.lu/a-la-une/perrin-contre-pwc-la-protection-des-sources-des-journalistes-au-coeur-des-debats/&prev=search

45. LuxLeaks Whistleblower has Conviction Quashed, BBC News, 11 January 2018. http://www.bbc.co.uk/news/world-europe-42652161

46. Public Accounts Committee, 38th report, 2014/15 session, *Tax Avoidance: the Role of Large Accountancy Firms (Follow-Up)*, 28 January 2015.

47. US Senate Permanent Subcommittee on Investigations, majority staff report on Caterpillar's Offshore Tax Strategy, released 1 April 2014. Senator Levin's comments made in his opening statement at hearings on the report.

48. Service outlined on Ernst & Young's website, http://www.ey.com/UK/en/Services/Tax/Tax-Policy-and-Controversy/Tax---TPD---About; accessed 2 September 2016.

49. Reported in *Private Eye* magazine, issue 1349, 20 September 2013.

50. Big Four firms' annual reports 2010–16.

51. PwC Luxembourg Annual Review 2016.

52. Jeremy Zabatta, 'Promise, PwC Luxembourg ne fera plus (beaucoup) de planification fiscale' ('Promise, PwC Luxembourg will not do (much) tax planning'), *Le Quotidien*, Luxembourg, 27 October 2016.

8 GREAT BRITAIN, LLP

1. Hansard, 20 January 1994, Col. 1119.
2. The consultants on the PFI task force were Ben Prynn and David Goldstone from Price Waterhouse and Tony Whitehead from Coopers & Lybrand.
3. Hansard, 2 April 2003, Col. 285WH.
4. From PFI summary data published annually by HM Treasury.
5. Comments from Professor David Heald, Aberdeen University, in Radio 4 *File on 4* programme 'The Accountant Kings', broadcast 4 March 2014.
6. Public Accounts Committee report, HM Treasury: *Tendering and Benchmarking in PFI*, 27 November 2007.
7. Treasury Taskforce Technical Note 3: How to Appoint and Manage Advisers to PFI Projects, https://ppp.worldbank.org/public-private-partnership/sites/ppp.worldbank.org/files/documents/How%20to%20Appoint 2017%20 and%20Manage%20Advisers%20to%20PFI%20Projects_TechNote3.pdf; accessed 9 March 2017.
8. The PFI Contract for the Redevelopment of West Middlesex University Hospital, National Audit Office, 21 November 2002.
9. Professor Allyson Pollock, then of the Centre for International Public Health Policy at the University of Edinburgh, produced a number of papers taking apart the 'evidence' of those linked to PFI schemes. A good summary of the flaws of the Arthur Andersen report can be found in her evidence to Parliament's Health Select Committee on 14 April 2000, available at http://www.publications.parliament.uk/pa/cm200102/cmselect/cmhealth/308/308ap30.htm; accessed on 16 September 2016.
10. Hansard, 30 January 2002, Col. 286.
11. Evidence of Dr Timothy Stone to House of Lords Economic Affairs Committee inquiry into Private Finance Projects and Off Balance Sheet Debts, 13 October 2009.
12. Based on 47 deals signed in 2004/5 and 61 signed in 2007/8, data from HM Treasury 'current projects' dataset.
13. Evidence to House of Commons Treasury Select Committee on Private Finance Initiative, 14 June 2011.
14. 'Delivering the Multi-role Tanker Aircraft Capability', National Audit Office, 30 March 2010.
15. BBC report, 30 March 2010, http://news.bbc.co.uk/1/hi/uk/8593788.stm.
16. Nick Prior, LinkedIn profile, accessed 16 September 2016.
17. Reported in Andrew Hankinson, 'NHS Boss Dubs PFI "Alice in Wonderland stuff"', *Construction News*, 22 September 2005, and in *Private Eye* magazine, issue 1200, December 2007.
18. https://www.mca.org.uk/library/documents/

PI_Pub_-_PwC_with_Barts_NHS.pdf.

19. Public Accounts Committee report, Hinchingbrooke Health Care NHS Trust, Peterborough and Stamford Hospitals NHS Foundation Trust, 7 February 2013. The background to the 2007 signing of the contract given in report by Caroline Molloy on Open Democracy website, 19 September 2013, https://www.opendemocracy.net/ournhs/caroline-molloy/peterborough-hospital-nhs-and-britains-privatisation-racket; accessed 18 September 2016.

20. Gill Plumber and Sarah Neville, 'NHS Trust Becomes First to Buy out its PFI Contract', *Financial Times*, 1 October 2014.

21. *Central Government's Use of Consultants*, report by National Audit Office, 15 December 2006. A further £125m was paid to them by the Department of Health centrally.

22. House of Commons Health Select Committee, 4th report, 2009/10 session, *Commissioning*.

23. Tamasin Cave, 'The NHS will be Shown no Mercy Says Cameron Health Adviser', *Spinwatch*, 9 May 2011, http://www.spinwatch.org/index.php/issues/lobbying/item/5343-the-nhs-will-be-shown-no-mercy-says-cameron-health-adviser.

24. *Mapping the Market: Commissioning Support Services*, NHS England and Cogora, 2013.

25. From NHS Leadership Academy prospectus, http://www.mbs.ac.uk/executive-education/_assets/pdf/nhs-leadership-academy-prospectus.pdf; accessed 9 March 2017.

26. Public Accounts Committee Report, Hinchingbrooke Health Care NHS Trust, Peterborough and Stamford Hospitals NHS Foundation Trust, 7 February 2013.

27. Public Accounts Committee Report, Unitingcare Partnership Contract, 16 November 2016.

28. NHS England review of Uniting Care contract, April 2016.

29. David Oliver, 'Stop Wasting Taxpayers' Money on Management Consultancy for the NHS', *British Medical Journal*, 10 December 2014.

30. Ibid.

31. *Redrawing the Health and Social Care Architecture*, PwC, 3 November 2016. See also 'Health structures complex and confused', BBC News, 3 November 2016, http://www.bbc.co.uk/news/health-37846112.

32. Public Accounts Committee report, 15 April 2013, *Tax Avoidance: the Role of the Large Accountancy Firms*. In 2011/12, PwC earned £162m; Deloitte £159m; KPMG £94.5m and EY £72.6m. In 2013/14, the figures for the three firms that gave data were: PwC £333m; Deloitte £179m; KPMG £140m.

33. Quoted in Mike Lee, *The Race for the 2012 Olympics: the Inside Story of How We Won the Bid*, Virgin Books Ltd, 2006.

34. National Audit office report, *The Budget for the 2012 Olympic and Paralympic Games*, 20 July 2007, and Guardian datablog: 'London Olympics 2012 – where does the money come from and where is it being

spent', https://www.theguardian.com/sport/datablog/2012/jul/26/london-2012-olympics-money#data.

35. Robert Peston, 'What KPMG Ignored When Arguing for HS2', 11 September 2013, http://www.bbc.co.uk/news/business-24047047; accessed 27 September 2016.

36. House of Commons Treasury Select Committee hearing, 5 November 2013.

37. Ibid.

38. Andrew Tyrie letter to Transport Secretary Chris Grayling, 14 September 2016. Stuart Westgate joined High Speed Two (HS2) Ltd from KPMG in February 2015; government announcment at https://www.gov.uk/government/news/stuart-westgate-joins-hs2-delivery-team.

39. Sue Kershaw was appointed November 2016. Her LinkedIn profile says: 'Responsible to the DfT Secretary of State for assuring HS2, the UK's new north–south high-speed rail line, is delivered to time and budget and of the quality the end user will expect, and most importantly that value is evidenced for expenditure of the public purse. This role is effectively the eyes and ears of government within the project. I lead a diverse team of talented, "best in class" specialists that provides insight and assurance across all aspects of the project, and works in genuine collaboration with the project's teams, the Department and Network Rail.' See https://www.linkedin.com/in/sue-kershaw-0249262/?ppe=1; accessed 21 July 2017.

40. EY International Trade, Economics and Policy Unit, biography of tax specialist Chris Sanger, http://www.ey.com/uk/en/issues/business-environment/ey-international-trade-economics-and-policy-unit#section4; accessed 18 October 2017.

41. Full data for 2007 available at https://www.gov.uk/government/uploads/system/uploads/attachment_data/file/61353/guide-hospitality-received-by-deptal-board-members.pdf; accessed 27 September 2016.

42. 'EY Partner Stories', an Ernst & Young video available on YouTube, https://www.youtube.com/watch?v=feTrncnAVEc; accessed 2 October 2016.

43. Described in KPMG 'Client Stories', https://www.kpmgcareers.co.uk/graduates/client-stories/civil-service-learning-csl; accessed 26 August 2017.

44. 'Who Really Runs This Place?', *Spinwatch*, April 2013.

45. Capita press release, 4 July 2016, http://www.capita.com/news/news/2016/capita-plc-appoints-ian-powell-as-chairman-designate/.

46. KPMG LLP annual report 2014, p.39.

47. EY International Trade, Economics and Policy Unit, section policy, http://www.ey.com/uk/en/issues/business-environment/ey-international-trade-economics-and-policy-unit#section4; accessed 18 October 2017.

48. *PFI: The STEPS Deal*, House of Commons Public Accounts Committee report, 6 April 2005.

49. *The Long View – How Will the Global Economic Order Change by 2050?*, PwC, 7 February 2017. An example of its use by Brexit supporters was on Radio 4 *Any Questions* on 24 June 2017. Darren Grimes, campaigner and deputy editor of BrexitCentral website, said: 'PwC put forward a report. It's all in . . .

Brexit Central's "reasons to be upbeat about Brexit". Until 2050 we will be the fastest-growing economy in the G7 according to PwC. The entire Project Fear argument has come crashing down . . .'

50. 'Entrepreneurship, technology and economic openness could help offset Brexit vulnerabilities', comments by KPMG head of Brexit Karen Briggs, 19 July 2017.

51. Harriet Agnew, 'Consultants and Lawyers Brace for Brexit Boom', *Financial Times*, 26 June 2016.

52. See, for example, 'When the Facts Change . . . Hinkley Point Would Tie Britain into an Energy System that is Already out of Date', *Economist*, 6 April 2016, quoting Professor Michael Grubb of University College London describing Hinkley as 'big and based on last-century technology, which is not what the UK's power system needs for the future'.

53. 'KPMG Strengthens Energy Practice with the Appointment of Simon Virley from DECC', KPMG press notice, 2 February 2015.

54. *Hinkley Point C*, report by the National Audit Office, 23 June 2017.

55. Sir Win Bischoff is former chief executive of Citigroup Europe and Lloyds Banking Group. In 2011, when chair of lobbying group CityUK, he wrote to the government protesting against EU plans to prevent auditors from performing consultancy work. Stephen Haddrill is formerly of the Department of Trade and Industry. The FRC directors from KPMG and PwC are Paul George and Melanie McLaren.

56. FRC annual report 2016/17.

57. Information supplied by FRC to author, October 2017. The 30 staff were: 13 lawyers, 11 forensic accountants, 5 support staff, 1 PA. The FRC's budget in 2017, for all its work going beyond investigations into standard-setting and similar duties covering the actuarial profession, was £36m. The Big Four's total fees were around £10bn.

58. Details of board members and figures available from FRC website, https://www.frc.org.uk/Home.aspx.

59. Explained to author by FRC in email, 18 September 2017.

60. Independent Review of Financial Reporting Council Sanctions, 21 November 2017.

9 CRIME AND VERY LITTLE PUNISHMENT

1. *In re* Kingston Cotton Mills Co. (1896), Lord Justice Lopes defined an auditor's duty of care:

'It is the duty of an auditor to bring to bear on the work he has to perform that skill, care and caution which a reasonably careful, cautious auditor would use. What is reasonable skill, care and caution must depend on the particular circumstances of each case. An auditor is not bound to be a detective, or, as was said to approach his work with suspicion, or with a forgone conclusion that there is something wrong. He is a watchdog, not a bloodhound. He is justified in believing tried servants of the company in whom confidence is placed by the company. He is entitled to assume that they are honest and rely upon their representations, provided he takes reasonable care. If there is anything calculated to excite suspicion he should probe it to the bottom; but in the absence of anything of that kind he is only bound to be reasonably cautious and careful.'

Since the 1970s, in reaching a 'true and fair view', UK accounting has followed a series of 'statements of standard accounting practice' (SSAPs) and 'financial reporting standards' (FRSs). These impose a general requirement that covers identifying 'material' fraud such as bribery. There are also duties to report criminal conduct and, since 2002, a specific reporting requirement under the Proceeds of Crime Act 2002. This requires reports to be made to the authorities where a regulated entity such an accountancy firm has 'reasonable grounds for knowing or suspecting that another person is engaged in money laundering'. Transferring funds connected to what would be criminal conduct in the UK, such as bribery, constitutes money laundering, so where an auditor should have had reasonable suspicion of bribery, a report should have been made to the authorities. On 17 March 2005, the OCED reported on the application of the 1997 anti-bribery convention in the UK. Parts B 2.c and 2.d cover the role of accounting and auditing.The review is available at http://www.oecd. org/investment/anti-bribery/anti-briberyconvention/34599062.pdf; accessed 17 October 2016. In addition, from 2001, International Standard on Auditing 240 has required auditors to assess the risks of fraud, of which bribery is a form, in financial statements. Auditors are 'responsible for obtaining reasonable assurance that the financial statements taken as a whole are free from material misstatement, whether caused by fraud or error'.

In the United States, Statement of Auditing Standards 82 (1997) and 99 (2002) make similar requirements. There are also extensive reporting requirements under the landmark anti-corruption legislation, the Foreign Corrupt Practices Act, enacted in 1977.

2. Press release by Congressman Les Aplin, 'US Companies pay $306 million for questionable business practices', 17 November 1975, based on Library of Congress Analysis.

3. Sir Donald Stokes, Ministry of Defence minute, 7 July 1965, available in the *Guardian*'s BAE files, http://image.guardian.co.uk/sys-files/Guardian/ documents/2007/05/28/cho1doco1.pdf; accessed 9 March 2017.

4. The so-called 'Cooper Directive', cited in Feinstein, *The Shadow World*.

5. Feinstein.

6. Interview with *Guardian* reporters David Leigh and Rob Evans in Feinstein.

7. BAE Systems was fined $400m in the United States (very small beer next to the value of the business) for failing to disclose its commissions. In the UK, the company's only penalty was a £500,000 fine and a requirement to make a £30m donation to Tanzanian charities for failing to keep accurate records of 'commissions' made on a deal for a military radar system for which the country had no use.

8. 'Profession scepticism and other key audit issues', ICAEW, 30 January 2012.

9. Ian Foxley's personal written record of the affair, shared with the author.

10. Information obtained by author, reported in *Private Eye*, issues 1331, January 2013, and 1375, September 2014.

11. Draft memo from the head of the Defence Sales Organisation, Sir Lester Suffield, to MoD permanent secretary Frank Cooper, 1976, cited in Gilby, *Deception in High Places*.

12. In the course of investigating the story the author spoke to a GPT employee from the 1980s, who gave details of a group of Saudis, largely from one family, who were the beneficiaries of the 'bought-in services'. The episode was reported at length in *Private Eye* in 2013 and 2014, including in a special report, 'Shady Arabia and the Desert Fix', issue 1375, September 2014.

13. International Standard on Auditing 240, 2010.

14. http://www.pwc.com/gx/en/services/advisory/consulting/forensics.html; accessed 25 November 2016.

15. http://www.pwc.com/m1/en/about-us/saudi-arabia.html.

16. Discussion between author and lawyer from City law firm.

17. 'Update on SFO Investigation and Board Change', Petrofac news release, 25 May 2017.

18. David Bond, 'The £66m "Bribe" Shadow Hanging over Fifa', *Daily Telegraph*, 13 March 2008.

19. Jennings, *The Dirty Game*.

20. Jens Weinreich, 'Funktionare im Zwielicht; Der Korruptionsprozess in Zug' ('Officials in spotlight; the corruption trial in Zug'), *Stuttgarter Zeitung*, 13 May 2008. The former ISL chief executive was Christoph Malms.

21. KPMG management letter regarding interim audit 1999, Zurich, 20 April 2000, seen by author.

22. Jennings, *Foul!*, p.198.

23. Photographs of Fredy Luthiger at the 59th FIFA Congress, Nassau, 3 June 2009, http://www.pressefotoulmer.de/CMDB/?action=301;sid= 478a735919fd1209188612a802ec2aab;query=+nassau%20dat:%20 25.5.2009%7C22.6.2009; http://sportfotos.photoshelter.com/image/ I0000SUrCAK245B8; accessed 2 Feb 2017.

24. Jennings, *Foul!*.

25. Andrew Jennings, 'Warner Asked Me to Make a Cheque out to his Personal Account. I Said we Don't do That', *Sunday Herald*, 24 December 2007.

26. FIFA 2009 annual report, p.11, comments of Franco Carraro, chairman of the internal audit committee.

27. FIFA 2008 annual report, p.18.

28. Quoted in Francine McKenna, 'FIFA Auditor KPMG Totally Missed the Soccer Scandal', *MarketWatch*, 5 June 2015.

29. FIFA press release, 3 June 2016, and linked document, http://www.fifa.com/ governance/news/y=2016/m=6/news=attorneys-for-fifa-provide-update-on-internal-investigation-and-detail-2799851.html; accessed 9 November 2016.

30. Federal Audit Oversight Authority Media Release, 2 October 2017.

31. Deferred Prosecution Agreement between HSBC Bank USA, NA, HSBC Holdings plc and United States Department of Justice, Agreed Statement of Facts, 10 December 2012.

32. Public Accounts Committee hearing, 9 March 2009. Transcript at http://data. parliament.uk/writtenevidence/committeeevidence.svc/evidencedocument/ public-accounts-committee/tax-avoidance-and-evasion-hsbc/oral/18507. html. Rona Fairhead's comments are not fully transcribed but are audible on Parliamentlive.tv recording at http://www.parliamentlive.tv/Event/Index/ a960faa6-db40-4b38-8fd4-707e4ed3d3a5.

33. Agreement between New York State Department of Financial Services and Deloitte Financial Advisory LLP, 18 June 2013, http://www.dfs.ny.gov/about/ ea/ea130618.pdf.

34. Agreement between New York State Department of Financial Services and PricewaterhouseCoopers LLP, 14 August 2014, http://www.dfs.ny.gov/about/ ea/ea140818.pdf; accessed 9 March 2017.

35. Ibid.

36. *Illicit Money: How Much is Out There?*, United Nations Office on Drugs and Crime, 25 October 2011, http://www.unodc.org/unodc/en/frontpage/2011/ October/illicit-money_-how-much-is-out-there.html; accessed 12 November 2016.

37. Agreement between New York State Department of Financial Services and PricewaterhouseCoopers LLP, 14 August 2014.

10 FAR FROM HOME

1. Rathia Dattin, *A History of Price Waterhouse, Lovelock & Lewes and PricewaterhouseCoopers Pvt Ltd in India*, https://www.pwc.in/assets/pdfs/ aboutus/history.pdf.

2. Stephen P. Walker, 'Encounters with Nazism: British Accountants and the Fifth International Congress on Accounting', *Critical Perspectives on Accounting* (2000) 11, 215–45.

3. Allen and McDermott.

4. Interview with John Biegler conducted by David Allen and Kathleen McDermott in 1987.

5. From *Willhelm Meinster's Apprenticeship*, 1795: 'What a thing it is to see the order which prevails throughout [a merchant's] business! By means of this he can at any time survey the general whole, without needing to perplex himself in the details. What advantages does he derive from the system of book-keeping by double entry! It is among the finest inventions of the human mind; every prudent master of a house should introduce it into his economy.'

6. Tavernise 'US Auditors Find Things Are Different in Russia'.

7. Charles E. Ryan, chairman United Financial Group, quoted in ibid.

8. Tim Osborne, managing director of GML, Yukos's main shareholder at the time, quoted in Catherine Belton, 'PwC Withdraws Yukos Audits', *Financial Times*, 24 June 2007.

9. US Moscow bureau cable dated 30 December 2009, https://wikileaks.org/ plusd/cables/09MOSCOW3144_a.html.

10. US Moscow bureau cable dated 27 December 2006, https://wikileaks.org/plusd/cables/06MOSCOW13123_a.html.

11. PwC annual worldwide report. Income from Russia and Eastern Europe: 2006 $474m; 2007 $659m; 2008 $861m.

12. *Economist*, 28 June 2007.

13. National Bank of Ukraine press release, 12 July 2017, https://bank.gov.ua/control/en/publish/article?art_id=51836146. Comments reported in Roman Olearchyk, 'PwC at Risk of Losing Bank Audit Rights in Ukraine', *Financial Times*, 6 July 2017.

14. *In re* Parmalat Securities Litigation, second amended consolidated class action complaint for violation of the Federal Securities Laws 04 Civ. 0030 (LAK) ECF Case, District Court of Southern District of New York, 22 August 2005, http://securities.stanford.edu/filings-documents/1029/PARAF-01/2005822_r01c_0430.pdf; accessed 9 March 2017.

15. David Reilly and Alessandra Galloni, 'Facing Lawsuits, Parmalat Auditor Stresses Its Disunity; Deloitte Presented Global Face, But Says Arms Acted Alone', *Wall Street Journal*, 28 April 2005.

16. Reasoning given by District Judge Kaplan, *in re* Parmalat Securities Litigation, US District Court, Southern District of New York, No. 04-1653, 27 January 2009, and related cases, https://www.nasba.org/app/uploads/2011/03/MASTER_DOCKET_3-27Jan09.pdf; accessed 8 July 2017.

17. Jonathan Stempel, 'Ex-Parmalat Auditors Settle US Investor Lawsuit', Reuters, 19 November 2009.

18. Reported in *The Age*, 16 April 2003.

19. 'Former PwC Accountants Guilty of Conspiracy', *Daily Telegraph*, 9 August 2006.

20. Duncan Hughes, 'KPMG Frustrated in Push on Europe', *The Business*, New York, 19 May 2002.

21. US Department of Justice press release, 15 December 2008.

22. David Crawford and Mike Esterl, 'KPMG Germany is Faulted in Siemens Probe', *Wall Street Journal*, 4 May 2007.

23. 'Japan Fines Ernst & Young Affiliate $17.4 million over Toshiba Audit', Reuters, 22 December 2015.

24. Carlos Segovia, 'Deloitte Construyó el Balance de Bankia en 2011 y Luego lo Auditó' ('Deloitte Built Bankia's Balance Sheet in 2001 and then Audited it'), *El Mundo*, 7 October 2014.

25. Tobias Buck, 'Spanish Judge Seeks Trial of 32 ex-Bankia Managers and Advisers', *Financial Times*, 11 May 2017.

26. Namrata Singh, 'We Are As Much a Victim As Anyone: PwC CEO', *Times of India*, 18 March 2009.

27. 'PCAOB Announces $8 Million Settlement with Deloitte Brazil for Violations Including Issuing Materially False Audit Reports and 12 Individuals Also Sanctioned for Various Violations', PCAOB press notice, 5 December 2016.

28. PCAOB release No. 105-2016-034, in the matter of Wanderley Olivetti, https://pcaobus.org/Enforcement/Decisions/Documents/105-2016-034-Olivetti.pdf.

29. Lewis H. Ferguson, 'Big Four Audit Quality Can Differ Widely – Even at the Same Firm', *MarketWatch*, 17 November 2015. Figure is for 2013, the latest available.

30. Figures are: Deloitte $2.1bn in 2006, $5.2bn in 2016; PwC $2.8bn and $5.8bn; KPMG $2.1bn and $4.1bn; EY $2.0bn and $4.1bn. Annual reports of the Big Four, plus *Business Wire* report, 1 December 2007, on EY's results: http://www.businesswire.com/news/home/20071101005128/en/Ernst-Young-Fiscal-Year-2007-Global-Revenues.

31. 'Updated data on auditors linked with issues', *China Finance*, 29 May 2013, https://www.tradingfloor.com/posts/china-finance-updated-data-auditors-linked-issues-606252080.

32. The case was China Integrated Energy; see Robert Cookson, 'Here Be Dragons: Anthony Bolton', *Financial Times*, 12 May 2012, for summary.

33. *How They Fell: The Collapse of Chinese Cross-border Listings*, McKinsey & Co. Strategy & Corporate Finance publication, December 2013.

34. Paul Gillis, visiting professor of accounting at Peking University's Guanghua School of Management, quoted in Dinny McMahon and Michael Rapoport, 'Challenges Auditing Chinese Firms', *Wall Street Journal*, 12 July 2011.

35. Luxembourg Leaks: Global Companies' Secrets Exposed, https://www.icij.org/project/luxembourg-leaks.

36. Lawrie Holmes and Alex Hawkes, 'Big Four Auditors "Embedded in Offshore World"', *Financial Mail*, 29 January 2011.

37. Tax Efficient Supply Chain Management and Transfer Pricing, presentation by Srinivasa Rao, partner, Ernst & Young, International Fiscal Association conference, 13 December 2008.

38. Proposal to work with Heineken on the design and implementation of a new group purchasing company, September 2010, PriceWaterhouse Coopers LLP, https://docs.google.com/viewer?a=v&pid=explorer&chrome=true&srcid=0B-YK4zVc_KuCODFjZjk2NDAtM2IzNy00NGE4LThmOGUtNGIzMjRmNzM1NmFj&hl=en; accessed 23 October 2011.

39. World Investment report 2015, United Nations Conference on Trade and Development, http://unctad.org/en/PublicationsLibrary/wir2015_en.pdf; accessed 7 July 2017.

40. http://www.gov.ky/portal/page/portal/cighome/find/organisations/azpublic bodies/pscc; accessed 9 July 2017.

41. The Paradise Papers, accessed by author and reported in *Private Eye* magzine, issue 1457, 17 November 2017.

42. Ibid.

43. *Developing India's Infrastructure Through Public Private Partnerships – a Resource Guide*, City of London, January 2008, https://www.cityoflondon.gov.uk/business/support-promotion-and-advice/promoting-the-city-internationally/india/Documents/PPPResourceGuideIndia.pdf; accessed 7 July 2017.

44. 'RIPPP: India's love affair with Public-Private Partnerships faces a Stern Test', *Economist*, 15 December 2012.

45. https://www.pwc.in/assets/pdfs/industries/government/government-and-public-sector.pdf.
46. https://home.kpmg.com/in/en/home/services/infrastructure-and-government-services/government-advisory.html.
47. KPMG media statement, 15 September 2017, https://home.kpmg.com/za/en/home/home/press-releases/2017/09/kpmg-international-media-statement.html.
48. Save South Africa media statement, 15 September 2017, http://www.savesouthafrica.org/component/jdownloads/send/13-2017/156-many-lessons-for-kpmg-and-other-state-capture-collaborators.
49. '#GuptaLeaks: The Dubai Laundromat – How KPMG Saw on Evil at the Sun City Wedding', amaBhungane Centre for Investigative Journalism, 30 June 2017, http://amabhungane.co.za/article/2017-06-30-guptaleaks-the-dubai-laundromat-how-kpmg-saw-no-evil-at-the-sun-city-wedding-1; accessed 23 August 2017.
50. For example, it was discussed in parliament by Lord Hain: Speech in debate on Anti-Money Laundering and Sanctions Bill, 1 November 2017, Hansard Cols 1387–1393.
51. KPMG International Statement on South African investigation, 22 September 2017.
52. 'Big Four Accountancy Firms Warn Hong Kong Over Democracy Push', *Financial Times*, 27 June 2014.

11 UNREFORMED AND UNREPENTANT

1. David Ingram and Dena Aubin, 'Insight: Big Four Auditors Spend More than Ever on US Lobbying', Reuters, 13 August 2012.
2. 'Restoring confidence in financial statements: the European Commission aims at a higher quality, dynamic and open audit market', Michel Barnier speaking at European Commission, Brussels, 30 November 2011, http://europa.eu/rapid/press-release_IP-11-1480_en.htm?locale=en.
3. Martin van Roekel, chief executive of BDO LLP, blogging under the headline 'Stand Tall, Commissioner Barnier!', 24 October 2011, http://webcache.googleusercontent.com/search?q=cache:11IVTbm_fioJ:www.bdoblog.com/ceoblog/Pages/Stand-tall,-Commissioner-Barnier.aspx+&cd=6&hl=en&ct=clnk&gl=uk&client=safari; accessed 22 January 2017.
4. Antonio Masip Hidalgo, Spanish MEP, quoted in Huw Jones, 'EU Says Auditors "Over Lobbying" against Eu Reform', Reuters, 27 March 2012, http://uk.reuters.com/article/uk-eu-auditing-idUKBRE82QoXN20120327.
5. KPMG LLP annual report 2014, p.39.
6. Jim Armitage, *Evening Standard*, 6 January 1917.
7. 'Media Withdraw from EY Journalism Awards', *New Zealand Herald*, 28 July 2017, http://www.nzherald.co.nz/business/news/article.cfm?c_id=3&objectid=11896377.

8. FRC's audit inspection reports for 2007 and 2014/15, available from https://www.frc.org.uk/Our-Work/Audit-and-Actuarial-Regulation/Audit-Quality-Review/Audit-Quality-Review-annual-reports.aspx.

9. See Mike Walworth, 'Insights from PCAOB Inspection Reports: Are Audits Getting Worse?', *GAAP Dynamics*, 17 May 2016, http://www.gaapdynamics.com/insights/blog/2016/05/17/insights-from-pcaob-inspection-reports-are-audits-getting-worse/.

10. See for example *2014 Financial Restatements – a 14 Year Comparison*, Audit Analytics, p.10. Restatements in 2014 were 831, in 2015 they were 683; in 2006 they were 1,842. In 2001 the figure was 625; in 2002 it was 701: https://www.complianceweek.com/sites/default/files/AuditAnalytics_RestatementRpt_4-15.pdf.

11. Commons Work & Pensions and Business, Innovation & Skills Select Committee report on BHS, House of Commons, 20 July 2016.

12. Prem Sikka, 'Comment: The UK Financial Reporting Council can't Investigate BHS Audits', *The Accountant*, 8 July 2016.

13. 'Sanctions Against Senior Auditor and PwC in Relation to RSM Tenon Group plc', FRC press release, 16 August 2017.

14. Securities and Exchange Commission press release, 15 August 2017.

15. 'KPMG Removes Audit Personnel, Including Head of Audit Practice', KPMG press release, 11 April 2017.

16. Big Four worldwide annual reports. A rise from $45.1bn to $50.2bn equates very closely to compounded US inflation over the period of 11% and is less than compounded inflation around the world (for example in the UK of 23%).

17. Gross value added per hour worked, from OECD Compendium of Productivity Indicators 2017, re-based to 100 for 2009 by author. Consulting income excludes tax advice services.

18. Galbraith, *A Short History of Financial Euphoria*.

19. 'The Rise of Advisory Services in Audit Firms', speech by Steven B. Harris, PCAOB, 24 November 2014, at Practising Law Institute, New York, https://pcaobus.org/News/Speech/Pages/11242014_Harris.aspx. In relation to the range of services offered by the Big Four, Harris said: 'A few examples of the many advisory and consulting services some of the largest firms now provide their non-audit clients include, but are certainly not limited to, enterprise strategy, marketing and sales, corporate finance, mergers and acquisitions, government consulting, legal services, immigration, and a wide variety of risk management services, including financial, insurance, and IT risk management, cybersecurity, human resources transformations . . . and the list goes on. In fact, a Big Four firm's foreign affiliate announced in March its ambitions to become a global top-20 legal services player within the next five years.'

20. The Radio 4 programme was *File on 4*, 'The Accountant Kings', 4 March 2014.

21. PwC and Google for Work: Reinventing Business, from PwC website, http://www.pwc.com/us/en/increasing-it-effectiveness/google-for-work.html; accessed 24 January 2017.

22. Deloitte had 15.7%, EY 11.4%, PwC 10%, KPMG 9.2%: *Market Share Analysis: Information Security Consulting, Worldwide, 2015*, Gartner, 5 July 2016, ID: G00291998; analysts: Jacqueline Heng, Elizabeth Kim.
23. Caroline Binham, 'The Hacker Hunters', *Financial Times*, 21 November 2013.
24. '"Serious" Hack Attacks from China Targeting UK Firms', BBC News website, 3 April 2017.
25. Mervyn King, *The End of Alchemy: Money, Banking and the Future of the Global Economy*, Little, Brown, 2016.
26. IMF Global Financial Stability report, April 2017.
27. Paul Davidson, 'Household Debt Tops 2008 Peak Ahead of Financial Crisis', *USA Today*, 17 May 2017, citing Federal Reserve Bank of New York figures. Re bubbles in personal finance markets, see for example Bank of England Financial Policy Committee meeting 22 March 2017, paragraph 17: 'The Committee also noted potential vulnerabilities stemming from interest-free offers on credit cards, including their accounting treatment which allowed lenders to record interest income during the period of the interest-free offer based on estimates of future interest payments. These estimates were highly dependent on assumptions around the future behaviour of borrowers at the end of the interest-free period, which was uncertain.'
28. Francine McKenna, 'How the Global Audit Firms, Led by Deloitte, Are Using Their Lobbying Clout to Dilute Sarbanes–Oxley Reforms', Pro-Market (blog of the Stigler Center at the University of Chicago Booth School of Business), 12 May 2017.
29. YouTube, https://www.youtube.com/watch?v=44We3OlEQMo; published 2015, accessed 9 March 2017.
30. Lucy Kellaway, 'Deloitte Chief's New Year Memo is a Classic in Demotivation', *Financial Times*, 17 January 2017.

EPILOGUE

1. House of Commons, *Carillion*, Second Joint report from the Business, Energy and Industrial Strategy and Work and Pensions Committees of Session 2017–19, 9 May 2018.
2. Figures from Big Four worldwide annual reports for years ended during 2018, except KPMG, where figures are for y/e 30 September 2017.
3. *Economia*, 8 February 2018, interview by Richard Cree.
4. The Tax-Savvy Company Restructuring, by Strategy&/PwC, 19 February 2018 https://www.pwc.com/us/en/cfodirect/issues/strategy-operations/restructuring-tax-implications.html.
5. Nicholas Shaxson, *The Finance Curse: How Global Finance Is Making Us All Poorer*, Bodley Head, 2018.
6. Jesse Norman, *Adam Smith: What He Thought and Why It Matters*, Allen Lane, 2018.
7. Jesse Norman, 'How Adam Smith Would Fix Capitalism', *Financial Times*, 22 June 2018.

INDEX

Abadie, Richard, 189
Aberdeen, Scotland, 48, 70
ABN Amro, 138
Accenture, 71, 256, 272
Accounting Establishment, The, 80
accounting standards, 73, 123–5
aconter, 2
Adelphia, 109, 264
Adidas, 220
Airbus, 214–19
Aislabie, John, 40
algebra, 21, 33, 38
Almond, Steve, 139–40, 148
alumni system, 17
Amazon, 170, 171, 178
American Institute of Certified
    Public Accountants, 61
American International Group
    (AIG), 133–5, 144, 145, 148
American Steel and Wire Company,
    55
Andersen, Arthur Edward, 72–4,
    75, 77, 78
Anglo Irish Bank, 144
Anne, queen of Great Britain and
    Ireland, 39
antitrust laws, 59, 61, 75
Antwerp, 36
Appleby, 247
Applegarth, Adam, 126
Appleton, Robert, 225
Arabic mathematics, 3, 21–2
ArcelorMittal, 171
Arthur Andersen & Co., 72–4, 75,
    77–8, 81, 97, 102–8, 112–13, 188

auditing, 4, 72–4, 85, 97, 102–8,
    109, 117
  collapse (2002), 5, 7, 11, 90, 108,
    110, 121
  and computing, 77–8
  consultancy, 77–8, 79, 81, 103
  and Enron, 4, 7, 11, 74, 102–8,
    113, 117
  global operations, 234
  and HIH, 240
  and Labour Party, 184, 188
  and Lincoln Savings and Loan,
    85
  'One Firm' philosophy, 74, 275
  and subprime mortgages, 112–13,
    116
  and Sunbeam, 97
  and United States Steel, 62
  and WorldCom, 109, 110
Arthur Young & Co., 63, 71, 85–7
asset-backed securities (ABS), 121
Associated Electrical Industries, 66
Aston Martin, 2
AT&T, 109
Atchison, Jack, 85–6
Atlantic Ocean, 39
Atter, Lewis, 197–8
Audit Company of Illinois, 72
auditing, 2, 5, 6, 10–16, 68–9,
    79–80, 259–61, 276, 280–84,
    289, 290–2
  1960s 'Go-Go' era, 63–5, 67
  1980s deregulation era, 85–91
  1990s/2000s 'numbers game'
    era, 95–110, 114

2007–8 financial crisis, 4, 13–14, 17, 18, 90, 111–50, 210, 241, 256–9, 265
2010s post-crisis era, 259–61
Barnier proposals (2010), 253–5, 280
Davey committee (1894), 52
and class action, 92
Companies Act (1900), 52
competing on price, 79
compulsory rotation, 5
and consultancy, 82, 97–8
and corruption, 211–32
and deregulation, 85–7
expectations gap', 65, 257
global operations, 235–46
and Joint Stock Companies Acts (1844, 1856), 47, 50
and Levitt, 96–8, 104
limited companies, 13
limited liability, 91–5, 114
Lincoln Savings and Loan, 85–6
Maxwell, 87–8
Medici system, 27
New York Stock Exchange, 55
public, 280–82
and Railway Regulation Act (1844), 45–7
Australia, 48, 51, 127, 170, 240
Avignon, France, 29
Avis Rent-a-Car, 59
Ayrshire, Scotland, 42

Babbage, Charles, 70
BAE Systems, 213–14, 219
Bagley, Gaenor, 268–71
Bahamas, 222, 236
Bain & Co., 263
Bainbridge, Guy, 141
Bank of America, 118
Bank of Credit and Commerce International, 91

Bank of England, 38, 91, 126, 273
Bank of Scotland, 140
Bank of Tokyo-Mitsubishi, 230–31
Bankia, 241
Banking Act (1879), 51
bankruptcy, 30, 45, 46, 49, 50–51
Barclays, 6, 121, 149, 256, 258
Baring Brothers, 92
Barkley, Alben, 58
Barlow, Ian, 181, 182
Barlow Clowes, 89–90, 136, 209
Barnes, David, 258–9, 276, 277
Barnier, Michel, 253–5, 280
Bass, Carl, 105–7
BCCI, 136
Bear Stearns, 121, 139, 145
Belfield, Gary, 192, 193
Benci, Giovanni, 27, 28, 29, 31
Bennett, Robert, 161
Berkshire Hathaway, 135
Bettel, Xavier, 170
Bevis, Herman, 62
Big Bang (1986), 156
Big Eight, 62, 80, 81, 82, 86, 87, 89, 136, 235, 283–4
Big Five, 95, 97, 236
Big Four, 2, 5–21, 110, 114, 283–4, 289, 290, 292
alumni system, 17
auditing, see under auditing
business advisory, 114
charity, 16–17
client relationship partners, 12
compulsory rotation, 5
consultancy, 6, 10–12, 114, 183–210, 261–7
and corruption, 211–32
cyber-security, 272–3
export earnings, 6
federal structure, 7–8
and financial crisis (2008), 111–50
global operations, 235–52

governments, advice to, 6, 180, 183–210, 248–50
growth, 9, 10
integrated reporting, 18
key performance indicators, 12
mark-to-model, 124
and media, 7
partners, 8, 11, 14, 15, 16
professional services, 11
recruits, 14–15
revolving door, 206–8, 272
and scandals, 7–8
and securitization, 121–3
tax avoidance, 156–82, 246–8
thought leadership, 12
Big Short, 112
Big Six, 81, 91–3, 95, 235, 236
Big Three, 110, 161
bills of exchange, 25, 26
Birmingham, West Midlands, 43
Bischoff, Winfried, 209
Black, Conrad, 154–5
Black, William, 60–62
Blackbeard (Edward Teach), 39
Blair, Anthony 'Tony', 184, 188, 191, 213
Blatter, Joseph 'Sepp', 221, 222, 225–8
BLIPS (Bond Linked Issue Premium Structures), 159–62, 181
Blockbuster, 106
Blunt, John, 39, 44
Board of Trade, 45
Book of Disquiet (Pessoa), 1
Book-keeping Methodiz'd (Mair), 53
Booz & Co., 264
Boston Consulting, 191
Boulton, Matthew, 43
Bower, Marvin, 75
Boy Scouts of America, 149
Bradford & Bingley, 141–2, 149

Brazil, 220, 238, 239, 242–3, 246
Breedon, Richard, 154
Brexit, 195, 203–4, 273
bribery, 211–28, 240
BRIC (Brazil, Russia, India and China), 238
Bristol, England, 49
Britannia Building Society, 142
British Academy, 111–12
British Aerospace, 212–14, 219
British Airways, 148
British American Tobacco, 148
British Broadcasting Corporation (BBC), 169, 197, 220
British Empire, 233
British Home Stores (BHS), 260–61, 289
British Virgin Islands, 213, 220, 246
Britnell, Mark, 192–3, 208
Brown, Gordon, 157, 184, 185, 186, 196
Bruges, 31
BT, 149
Bubble Act (1720), 44
Budgetary Control (McKinsey), 74–5
Buffett, Warren, 63, 135
Building Public Trust Awards, 256
Bureau d'Imposition Sociétés VI, 168
Bureau of Supplies and Accounts, US Navy, 77
Burgundy, Duchy of (1032–1477), 31
Bush, George Walker, 98, 114, 145, 253
Bush, Tim, 126, 127, 147
Butler, Stephen, 181
Byrne, Liam, 184
Byzantine Empire (285–1453), 21

Cabinet Office, 200, 201
Cable & Wireless, 215

Caesar, John, 54, 55, 56
Calcutta, India, 233
Cambridge, Cambridgeshire, 194
Cambridge University, 55, 268
Cameron, David, 192, 195, 203
Campaign Against the Arms Trade, 265
Canada, 246
Canary Wharf, London, 256
Cape Coast Castle, Gold Coast, 37
Capita, 201–2
capital, 3
Carell, Steve, 112
Caribbean Football Union, 221, 223, 224, 225
Carillion, 287–90
Carnegie, Andrew, 55, 71
Carter, Arthur, 58
Cash Investigation, 168, 171
Caterpillar, 178
Catholic Church, 3, 24–5, 26, 29, 34, 38
Cattles plc., 142
Causey, Rick, 104
Cayman Islands, 104, 164, 214, 239, 246, 247
Celanese, 60
Celler–Kefauver Act (1950), 59, 61
Celluloid Corporation, 60
certified public accountants, 53
CFO, 101, 109
Chaplin, Charlie, 71
Chappell, Dominic, 260, 289
Charles the Bold, Duke of Burgundy, 31
chartered accountancy, 14, 16, 45, 47–8, 49, 53
Chelsea Flower Show, 200
Chicago School, 84–5, 183
Chicago Sun-Times, 154
Chicago, Illinois, 54, 72–4, 101, 105
child labour, 44

China, 17, 111, 204, 238, 243–5, 251–2, 272, 274
China Integrated Energy, 244
Chirac, Jacques, 127
Christianity, 3, 24–5, 26, 34, 35, 38
    Catholicism, 3, 24–5, 26, 29, 34, 38
    Protestantism, 3, 42, 43
Christoffels, Jan Ympyn, 36
Churchill, John, 1st Duke of Marlborough, 41
Circle Health, 194
Citigroup, 149, 258
City of Glasgow Bank, 51, 147
City of London, 46, 49, 156, 249
Civil Rights Movement, 64
Claridges, London, 122
Clarke, Charles, 207
class-action lawsuits, 64–5, 92
Cleese, John, 15
climate change, 18
CloseMore University, 115
Clowes, Peter, 88–90, 91, 136, 209
Co-operative Bank, 142, 149, 150
Cohen, Manuel 'Manny', 80
Cold War, 95
Cole, Margaret, 208
Colin, Bernard, 173
collateralized debt obligations (CDOs), 120–21, 129–30, 133, 136–40, 265
Collier-Keywood, Richard, 182
Collins, Simon, ix, 11, 204, 218, 255–9, 264–7, 276, 277–8, 279
Colombia, 229
colonialism, 37
Comey, James, 161
commercial-mortgage-backed security (CMBS), 121
common accounting standards, 73, 123–5
common law, 39

Companies Act
  1862: 51
  1900: 52
  1929: 58
  1948: 66
  1989: 93
compulsory rotation, 5
computing, 77–8
Comroad, 240
conflicts of interest, 18, 60, 82, 91,
    98, 187, 254–5, 289, 292
  Arthur Andersen & Co., 73–4, 78,
    105, 277
  and Barnier proposals, 254–5
  in China, 274
  and data, 271
  Deloitte, 241
  KPMG, 202, 228
  Price Waterhouse & Co., 73, 277
  PricewaterhouseCoopers (PwC),
    143
  and Sarbanes–Oxley Act (2002),
    122
Connolly, John, 89–90, 136, 137,
    139, 146, 148, 150, 201
Conservative Party, 95, 185, 186
consultancy, 6, 10–12, 69, 70–83,
    97, 114, 183–210, 261–7,
    284–5, 291
Continental Baking, 59
Continental Bank, 101
convergence, 123
Cook, Martin, 16
'cooking the books', 36
Cooper, Cynthia, 109
Cooper, William and Arthur, 49
Coopers & Lybrand, 49, 56, 65,
    87–8, 95, 185, 216
Coopers Brothers, 87
Copeland, James, 239
Corbyn, Jeremy, 201
Cornwall, England, 43

corruption, 211–32, 240
cost accounting, 42–4, 70–71, 76
cost–profit calculus, 3
Cotswolds, England, 26
Countrywide Financial Corporation,
    48, 118, 257
Court of Appeal, 211
credit default swaps (CDSs), 120,
    122, 134–5
credit rating agencies, 130, 149
Cruickshank, David, 166
Crystal Park, Luxembourg, 170
Cuba, 239
Cuomo, Andrew, 133
currency swaps, 156–7
cyber-security, 272–3

Daily Mirror, 88
Daniel, Vincent, 112–13
Dante, 33
Dassler, Horst, 220
Datini, Francesco di Marco, 25
Davey, Horace, Baron Davey, 52
Davos, see World Economic Forum
Defoe, Daniel, 38
DeLany, Clarence Martin, 72
Delaware, United States, 8, 57, 92,
    236, 284
Deloitte, 2, 5, 8, 12–13, 82, 90, 98,
    276, 277
  and Adelphia, 109
  and bankers' bonuses, 158
  and Bankia, 241
  in Brazil, 242–3
  Brexit memo (2017), 195, 203
  charity, 16–17
  in China, 244, 251–2
  client relationship partners, 12–13
  cyber-security, 272
  and Deutsche Bank, 158
  dot after name, 12
  and Duke Energy, 109

and Financial Crisis Inquiry
Commission, 145
Global Impact Report, 17
global operations, 236
and GoI, 242–3
government, advice to, 187, 189,
190, 191, 193, 194
and GPT, 216
and Hong Kong protests (2014),
251–2
and House of Lords committee
(2010), 146
integrated reporting, 18
Journey Declaration, 275
and National Health Service
(NHS), 193, 194
and Parmalat, 239, 243
and private finance initiative
(PFI), 187, 189, 190, 191, 203
and Public Company Accounting
Oversight Board (PCAOB), 145
revolving door, 207, 208
and Royal Ahold, 238–9
and Royal Bank of Scotland, 47,
90, 136–40, 142, 147, 241, 259
and securitization, 121
and Standard Chartered Bank, 230
and tax avoidance, 157, 158, 166,
203
and technology, 271
and thrifts, 87
and World Economic Forum, 18
Deloitte, Haskins & Sells, 89
Deloitte, William Welch, 46–7, 49,
158
Deloitte & Touche, 89, 91, 136–40
Deloitte Touche Tohmatsu, 239
Deltour, Antoine, 166–8, 171,
173–4, 175, 175
Democratic Party, 58, 80, 159
Deng Xiaoping, 243
Department for Business, UK, 201

Department for Exiting the EU, 204
Department of Health, UK, 188,
191, 192
Department of Justice, US, 144,
161, 223
deregulation, 84, 85, 95, 112, 163,
273–4
derivatives, 117, 119–23, 125, 129–31,
133–40, 148, 265
Desmond, Dermot, 163
Deutsche Bank, 158, 166, 258
Deutsche Treuhand-Gesellschaft,
235
Devon, England, 73
Dickinson, Arthur, 55, 62, 73, 82
DiPiazza, Sam, 242
dirty pooling, 63
discrezione, 26, 29
Disney, 171
Dissenters, 43
dividends, 31, 39, 45
Donovan, John, 116–17
Doty, James, 260
'Double Irish' scheme, 164
double-entry bookkeeping, 3–4, 6,
18, 22–41, 42–4, 96
Bank of England, 38
and Catholicism, 24–5, 26, 29, 34
Christoffels, 36
East India Company, 37
Goethe, 235
Japan, 235
Medicis, 26–32, 36
Pacioli, 32–6, 100, 124
and Protestantism, 42
Royal African Company, 37
South Sea Company, 39–41, 42
Washington, 53
Watt, 42–3, 44
Wedgwood, 43, 44
Dow Jones, 5, 95
Drucker, Jesse, 164, 165

drug trafficking, 229, 231
Dublin, Ireland, 163
Duke Energy, 109
Duncan, David, 103–4, 105, *106*, 107, 108
Duranton International Ltd, 214

EADS, 216
East India Company, 37
Economist, The, 67, 238
EDF (*Électricité de France*), 205
Edinburgh, Scotland, 54
Edinburgh Society of Accountants, 47
Edison, Thomas, 55
Edward IV, king of England, 30
Edward VII, king of the United Kingdom, 68
Egypt, 21
Einzelunterschrift, 221
Eisenhower, Dwight, 76
Eisman, Steve, 112
Electronic Data Systems, 82
Elizabeth II, queen of the United Kingdom, 111–12
Elkind, Peter, 101
Ellis, Kevin, 256, 258
Enfield rifles, 71
England
  Bank of England, 38
  East India Company, 37
  Royal African Company, 37
  slave trade, 37
  Wars of the Roses (1455–1487), 30
  woollen industry, 26, 30
  see also United Kingdom
Ennis, Jessica, 196
Enron, 16, 40, 99–108, 110, 130, 186, 190, 209, 221, 240, 261, 264, 292
  and Arthur Andersen & Co., 4, 7, 11, 74, 102–8, 113, 117

and consultancy arms, sale of, 262
and mark-to-market, 99–102, 113
and regulation, 6, 10, 122, 162, 222, 274, 279
Ernst & Ernst, 63, 71, 87
Ernst & Whinney, 86, 87
Ernst & Young, 2, 56, 91, 97, 132–3, 148–9, 289, 291
  alumni system, 17
  and Anglo Irish Bank, 144
  Arthur Andersen structured finance purchase (2002), 121
  'Building a Better Working World', 12
  and Civil Service Awards, 200
  and Financial Crisis Inquiry Commission, 145
  global operations, 236
  government, advice to, 180, 187, 199, 202
  and HealthSouth, 109
  and Hong Kong protests (2014), 251–2
  integrated reporting, 18
  in Japan, 240–41
  and Lehman Brothers, 12, 13, 132–3, 145, 148–9
  and limited liability partnerships, 94, 95
  and Lincoln Savings and Loan, 86–7
  mark-to-model, 124
  Panama Papers scandal (2016), 247
  and private finance initiative (PFI), 187
  and Public Company Accounting Oversight Board (PCAOB), 144–5
  'Quality in Everything We Do', 12
  revolving door, 206, 207, 208
  and securitization, 121

and Sino-Forest, 244
Tate sponsorship, 16
and tax avoidance, 7, 156–7, 162, 180, 182, 246, 247
tax policy development team, 180, 199
thought leadership, 12
and VAT avoidance, 7
and Warner, 224
Weinberger's leadership, 17–18
and World Economic Forum, 17
European Central Bank, 10
European Commission, 170, 253–5, 268, 280
European Union (EU), 168, 170, 203, 253–5
eurozone, 273
Evans, Jonathan, 207
Evening Standard, 256
Everson, Mark, 159
executive pay, 76
'expectations gap', 65, 257
'Eye of the Tiger' (Survivor), 103

Facebook, 164
fair value, 123–5, 126
Fairhead, Rona, 230
Faisaliah Tower, Riyadh, 217
Falcon 900 jets, 100–101
Farah, Mohamed 'Mo', 196
Farrar, Michael, 208
Fastow, Andrew, 101–3, 104–5, 108, 109
Federal National Mortgage Association ('Fannie Mae'), 118–19, 145, 257
Federal Reserve, 122, 133
Federal Trade Commission, 79
Fiat, 170
Fibonacci, Leonardo, 21–2, 32
FIFA (Fédération Internationale de Football Association), 219–28

Fife, Scotland, 48
Financial Conduct Authority, 140, 149, 281
financial crisis (2007–8), x, 4, 7, 10, 13–14, 18, 111–50, 210, 253, 256–9, 265, 288, 291, 292
American International Group bailout, 133–5, 144, 145, 148
Anglo Irish Bank bailout, 144
Bear Stearns bailout, 139, 145
and China, 111
Fannie Mae crisis, 118–19, 145, 257
HBOS bailout, x, 140–41, 142–3, 149, 257
Lehman Brothers collapse, 12, 13, 92, 131–3, 138, 144, 145, 148–9
and IAS39 rules, 123–5, 126, 127, 147
and mark-to-market, 129–31
New Century Financial Corporation collapse, 115–18, 257
Northern Rock collapse, 125–9, 142–3, 148
Royal Bank of Scotland bailout, 47, 136–40, 142, 241
and securitization, 119–23, 129–31, 133–40, 265
and subprime mortgages, x, 10, 36, 48, 111–22, 126, 130, 133, 136, 142, 274
Washington Mutual collapse, 145
Financial Crisis Inquiry Commission, 134, 135, 144, 145
Financial Reporting Council, 138, 142, 144, 149, 182, 209–10, 213–14, 259, 261
Financial Services Authority, 127, 128, 137, 138, 140
Financial Times, 17, 94, 169, 275, 291, 292

Finland, 246
First World War (1914–18), 71
Flint, Douglas, 229
FLIP (Foreign Leveraged
    Investment Program), 159,
    162, 181
Florence, Republic of (1115–1532),
    16, 21, 25, 26–32
Flynn, Timothy, 149
Ford, 71, 181
Ford, Henry, 71
Fortune, 62
fossil fuels, 18
Foul! (Jennings), 224
Foxley, Ian, 214, 216
France, 31, 46, 89, 127, 171–7, 204,
    205
Franklin, Benjamin, 53
Friedman, Milton, 84
FTSE100 Index, 5, 14, 90, 125
FTSE350 Index, 259
Fuld, Richard 'Dick', 132
Future Strategic Tanker Aircraft, 189

G4S, 148, 201
Galbraith, John Kenneth, 14, 57,
    263
Galbraith, Thomas, 2nd Baron
    Strathclyde, 208
Galilei, Galileo, 22
Gap, 163
Gauke, David, 179
Gazprom, 236, 237
GCHQ (Government
    Communications
    Headquarters), 272
General Electric, 5–6, 55, 78, 154
General Electric Company (GEC), 66
General Motors, 57
General Survey Outline, 75
generally accepted accounting
    principles (GAAP), 109

Geneva, Switzerland, 27, 29, 178
geometry, 21, 33
Germany, 220, 233–4, 235, 240,
    247, 251
Gilbert, William Schwenck, 52
Gilby, Nicholas, 215
Gladstone, William, 45, 47, 50
Glasgow, Scotland, 45, 48
    City of Glasgow Bank, 51, 147
    Institute of Accountants and
        Actuaries, 47
    University of Glasgow, 136
Glass–Steagall Act (1933), 60
GlaxoSmithKline, 163, 167, 169
Glickauf, Joseph, 77–8
'Go-Go' years (1960s), 59, 62, 65,
    67
Goerdeler, Reinhard, ix, 235, 240
von Goethe, Johann Wolfgang, 235
Gol, 242–3
Goldman Sachs, 121, 134–5, 139,
    148, 157
Goldsmith, James, 66, 86
goodwill, 60–61
Goodwin, Fred, 136, 137, 139
Google, 164, 165, 178, 271
Gordhan, Pravin, 250
Gordon Riots (1780), 38
Gordon, Andrew, 218
Gosling, Richard, 202
GPT, 214–19
Gramegna, Pierre, 170
Great Crash and Depression
    (1929–39), 14, 57–8, 59–60,
    66, 73, 75, 80, 118
Great Northern Railway, 46
Great Western Railway, 46
Green, Philip, 260, 289
Greenspan, Alan, 122
Greenwich Capital Markets Inc., 136
Griffith-Jones, John, 146, 149, 150
Grigsby, John, 39, 40–41

Grondona, Julio, 225, 227
Grosvenor Street, Mayfair, ix–x, *x*, 277–8
Guardian, 170, 213
Gupta, Atul, 250

Haddrill, Stephen, 143, 209, 210
Halet, Raphaël, 171–7, 176, 181
Halet, Sophie, 172, 173
Halifax, 140
Hamersley, Michael, 161
Hamilton, Lewis, 7
Hamilton, Robert, 70
Hammond, Philip, 288
Hanson, Walter, 64
Harley, Robert, 39
Harris, Steven, 264
Hartnett, David, 166, 207
Harvard University, 57, 75, 99
Haskins & Sells, 56, 58
Haskins, Charles Waldo, 56
Haughey, Charles, 163
Haute Comité de la Place Financière, 171
Havelange, João, 220, 221
HBOS, x, 13, 140–41, 142–3, 149, 150, 257
Healey, Denis, 184
HealthSouth, 109
hedge funds, 113, 115
hedging, 99
Heineken, 246
Heintz, Guy, 175
Her Majesty's Revenue and Customs (HMRC), 179, 182
Hewitt, Patricia, 184
Hexham General Hospital, Northumbria, 191
HIH, 240
Hinchingbrooke hospital, Cambridgeshire, 193
Hinkley Point, Somerset, 204–6

Hippocratic oath, 276
Hodge, Margaret, 178
Hollinger, 154–5
Holocaust, 4
Holyland, William Hopkins, 49
Home Office, 201
Hong Kong, 240, 251–2
Hotel Baur au Lac, Zurich, 219, 224
House of Commons, 68
House of Lords, 68, 92, 93, 143, 146–7
Houston, Texas, 99–108
HS2, 197–9, 266, 289
HSBC, 166, 215, 229–30, 231, 256
Hudson, George, 44–5
humanism, 28
Hungary, 213
hypothetical future value, 100

IBM, 82, 272
Iceland, 127
ICI, 69
IKEA, 166
Illinois, United States, 54, 72–4
Imperial College, London, 197
Imperial Tobacco, 202
income tax, 46, 67, 153
Income Tax Act (1842), 46
India, 233, 238, 242, 245, 249
Industrial Revolution, 18, 42–7
Inferno (Dante), 33
inflation, 85
Inglis, John, 78–9
Institute of Chartered Accountants in England and Wales (ICAEW), 49, 52, 93, 210
integrated reporting, 18
interest rates, 85
Internal Revenue Service (IRS), 159, 160
International Accounting Congress (1938), 234

International Accounting Standards Board, 123–5, 126, 127, 147
International Consortium of Investigative Journalists, 169, 230, 247
International Financial Services Centre, 163
International Fiscal Association, 245
International Integrated Reporting Council, 18
International Monetary Fund (IMF), 273
International Sport & Leisure (ISL), 220–21, 222
Internet, 95
Introduction to Merchandise (Hamilton), 70
Iran, 230
Iraq, 225, 240
Ireland, 127, 143–4, 163–5
Isle of Man, 247–8
Issuers' and Investors' Summit on CDOs/Credit Derivatives (2006), 121
Istace, Vinciane, 173
Italy, 3, 16, 21–2, 24–36, 37, 239
ITT Corporation, 59, 61
Ivy League, 68

J. P. Morgan, 54–5, 139, 149
James Bond, 2
James O. McKinsey & Co., 75
Japan, 2, 82, 230–31, 234–5, 240–41
Jennings, Andrew, 220, 224
Jerome, Saint, 35
Jersey, 89, 94–5, 158
job costing, 43
Johnson Matthey Bank, 91, 128
Johnson, Lyndon Baines, 63
joint stock companies, 41
Joint Stock Companies Act 1844: 47

1856: 50
Jones, Lewis Davies, 54, 55, 56
Jowell, Tessa, 196
junk bonds, 85

Kanebo, 240
Kapital, Das (Marx), 3
Kattner, Markus, 225
Keating, Charles, 85–6, 91
Kellaway, Lucy, 275
Kershaw, Sue, 199
Kgosana, Moses, 250
Khodorkovsky, Mikhail, 237
King, Mervyn, 273
Kirby, Paul, 208
Klynveld Kraayenhof, 235
Klynveld, Piet, ix
KMG, 235
Knievel, Robert Craig 'Evel', 182
Koch Industries, 171
Kohl, Marius, 168, 174–7
KPMG, ix–x, 2, 10, 11, 48, 97, 116–19, 141–2, 149–50, 256–9, 264–7, 276, 288, 289, 290
and Barnier proposals, 255
and Bradford & Bingley, 141–2, 149
and Brexit, 203, 204
and British Aerospace/BAE Systems, 213
Canary Wharf base, 256
Chelsea Flower Show, 200
in China, 244, 245, 251–2
and Civil Service Live conference, 201
Claridges conference (2007), 122
and Co-operative Bank, 142, 149, 150
and Comroad, 240
and collateralized debt obligations (CDOs), 121
and Countrywide Financial

Corporation, 48, 118, 257
'Cutting Through Complexity',
    11–12
Data & Analytics (D&A), 272
and defence, 188, 189, 200, 202,
    216, 217, 265
establishment of (1987), 235
and European Central Bank, 10
and Federal National Mortgage
    Association ('Fannie Mae'),
    118–19, 257
and FIFA, 220–28
and Financial Crisis Inquiry
    Commission, 145
and Financial Reporting Council,
    144, 209
and General Electric, 5–6
governments, advice to, 186, 187,
    188, 189, 191, 192–3, 197–9,
    202–6, 249
and GPT, 216, 217
and HBOS, 141, 142–3, 149, 150,
    257
and Hinkley Point, 204–6
and Hollinger, 154–5
and Hong Kong protests (2014),
    251–2
and House of Lords committee
    (2010), 146
and HS2, 197–9
and HSBC, 229–30
and Imperial Tobacco, 202,
    266–7
in India, 249
integrated reporting, 18
key performance indicators, 12
and Lockheed Martin, 202, 265
and Miller Energy, 261
and Ministry of Defence, 188,
    189, 202, 216, 217, 265
and National Health Service
    (NHS), 192–3, 202, 266

and New Century Financial
    Corporation, 48, 116–18, 257
No. 20, Grosvenor Street,
    Mayfair, ix–x, x, 277–8
'One Firm' philosophy, 275
and 'patent box' tax breaks, 180
Performance Club 1999 trips,
    160
and Petrofac, 218
and private finance initiative
    (PFI), 186, 187, 188, 189, 191,
    249
and Privy Purse, 68
revolving door, 206, 207, 208
and Saudi British Joint Business
    Council, 218
Scott London Rolex scandal
    (2013), 15
and securitization, 121, 122
and Siemens, 240
in South Africa, 249–50
and subprime mortgages, 10, 48,
    116–19
and sustainable development, 200
and tax avoidance, 154–5, 157, 158,
    159–62, 180–81, 182, 186
thought leadership, 12
and thrifts, 87
and Tier One, 257
and Wachovia, 257
and Xerox, 109–10
Kreuger, Ivar, 57
Kubena, Mike, 237

Labour Party, 66, 94, 114, 178, 179,
    184–92, 194, 201, 209, 230
Lake Michigan, 73
Land, Nick, 144, 182
Lang, Ian, 95
Last Supper, The (Leonardo da
    Vinci), 33
Lateran Council, Third (1179), 24

Law Commission, 93
Lawson, Nigel, 146
Lay, Kenneth, 99–100, 104, 107, 108
Leary, Simon, 191
Lehman Brothers, 12, 13, 92, 119, 131–3, 138, 144, 145, 148–9
Leigh, Edward, 189
Lend-Lease programme, 60
Leonardo da Vinci, 33
Levin, Carl, 159, 161
Levitt, Arthur, 96–8, 104
Lewis, Leigh, 207
Lewis, Michael, 112, 118
Liber Abaci (Fibonacci), 21–2
Liberal party, 50, 52
Liechtenstein, 220
limited liability, 50, 52, 91–5, 114
Lincoln Savings and Loan, 85–7
Linklaters, 140
Little, Royal, 61
Liverpool, Merseyside, 49
LJM, 104–5
Lloyds Bank, 140
Lockheed Martin, 202, 212, 265
London, England
  Big Bang (1986), 156
  Canary Wharf, 256
  Chelsea Flower Show, 200
  Claridges, 122
  Gordon Riots (1780), 38
  Imperial College, 197
  'light touch' regulation, 114, 131, 209
  Medici Bank, 26, 30
  Olympic Games (2012), 196
  Price Waterhouse, 54
  Royal London Hospital, 190
  School of Economics, 197
  St Bartholomew's Hospital, London, 190
  Tate Modern, 16

Long Term Capital Management, 113
Louis XI, king of France, 31
low-balling, 79, 91
Lowe, Robert, 50
Luce, Edward, 17
Lucerne, Switzerland, 220
Luthiger, Fredy, 222, *223*, 227
Luxembourg, 165–77, 179, 180, 181, 182, 245, 267–71, 278, 290
LuxLeaks, 169–77, 179, 181, 245, 268, 269, 278
Lybrand, Ross Bros & Montgomery, 87
Lybrand, William, 56
Lynch, Loretta, 219, 223
Lyons, 31

MacGregor, John, 128
Mair, John, 42, 53
Management Consultancies Association, 190
Mandelson, Peter, 95, 207
Mapping the Market, 193
mark-to-market, 99–102, 113, 123, 124, 129–31
mark-to-model, 124–5, 126, 127, 131
mark-to-myth, 124, 131
Marlborough, Duke of, *see* Churchill, John
Martin, William, 122–3
Marwick, James, ix, 48–9, 56, 62, 119, 158, 217, 233, 277
Marx, Karl, 3
Masters Tournament, 104
Masters, Adrian, 191
matches, 57
Mauritius, 158
Maxwell, Robert, 66, 87–8, 91
May, George, 73, 78, 82, 277
May, Theresa, 203
McConnell, Jack, 207

McCreevy, Charles, 164
McDonald's, 170
McFall, John, 207
McKenna, Francine, 145, 274
McKinsey, 17, 74–7, 79, 81, 99, 108, 183, 191, 226, 263
McKinsey, James, 74–7
McLean, Bethany, 101
Measelle, Richard, 103
Medici family, 16, 26–32, 36
  Cosimo, 26, 27, 28, 29, 31
  Giovanni, 26
  Lorenzo, 28, 29, 30
Medvedev, Dmitry, 17
Melbourne, Victoria, 48
Mercer, Emma, 288
mergers and acquisitions, 11, 54, 59–69, 71, 87
Merrill Lynch, 121
Mesopotamia, 1
Messezentrum conference centre, Zurich, 228
Metcalf, Lee, 80
Metz, France, 172, 173, 176
Mexico, 229
Michael, Bill, 149–50, 290
Microsoft, 271
Milburn, Alan, 184, 191, 194, 207
Mill, John Stuart, 50
Miller Energy, 261
Ministry of Defence, UK, 188–90, 202, 212, 215–19, 265
Missal, Michael, 115, 116–17
Missouri, United States, 74
Mitchell, Andrew, 206, 208
Mitchell, Austin, 94, 230
Mitchell, Roger, 48, 56
Model T Ford, 71
Modern Times, 71
Monde, Le, 169
monetarism, 84
money laundering, 229–31

Montagu, Nicholas, 207
Monty Python, 15–16
Moore, Paul, 141
Morgan, Henry, 39
Morgan, John Pierpont, 54–5
Morgan Stanley, 119, 148
Morse, Amyas, 206
mortgage-backed securities (MBS), 120–21
Moselle, France, 171
Mossack Fonseca, 247
Mouget, Didier, 170, 171, 173
Mumbai, Maharashtra, 242
Munger, Charlie, 18, 135, 147
Myners, Paul, 146

Nally, Dennis, 5, 148
Nassau, Bahamas, 222
National Aeronautics and Space Administration (NASA), 76
National Audit Office, 187, 189, 206
National Crime Agency (NCA), 272
National Health Service (NHS), 183–4, 187, 190, 191–5, 266
National Westminster Bank (NatWest), 136
Nazi Germany (1933–45), 4, 234, 251
Neoplatonism, 28
Netherlands
  ABN Amro, 138
  Ballast Nedam, 218–19
  Klynveld Kraayenhof, 235
  Royal Ahold, 238–9
  Spanish (1556–1714), 36
  taxation, 163, 164–5
New Century Financial Corporation, 48, 115–18, 257
New Delhi, India, 245, 249
New Labour, 114, 184–92, 194, 209
New York, United States, 57
  beer business, 54

Britnell's 'Reform Revolution' speech (2011), 192–3
County Law Association, 153
Deloitte compensation case (2009), 239
FIFA indictment (2015), 219, 223
Harris' advisory services speech (2014), 264
Issuers' and Investors' Summit on CDOs/Credit Derivatives (2006), 121
Levitt's 'Numbers Game' speech (1998), 96, 98
Marwick & Mitchell, 48
Price Waterhouse, 54
Stock Exchange, 55, 115, 234
Wall Street, 54, 69, 96, 101, 120–21
New York Times, 118, 236
New Zealand, 256
Newton, Isaac, 22
Nicholson, Kevin, 178, 182
Nieuwe Instructie (Christoffels), 36
Nike, 163
No. 20, Grosvenor Street, Mayfair, ix–x, *x*, 277–8, 290
Noncomformism, 42
Norman, Jesse, 292
Norte del Valle Cartel, 229
Northern Rock, 125–9, 142–3, 148
Norway, 72
nuclear power, 204–6
'Numbers Game' speech (1998), 96, 98

O'Donnell, Augustine 'Gus', 207
O'Rourke, Feargal, 164, 165
off-balance-sheet financing, 101, 102, 104, 106
Office of Tax Simplification, 179
oil crisis (1973), 84
oil-for-food programme, 225, 240

Olympic Games (2012), 196
Olympus, 241
One Hundred Group, 254
OPIS (Offshore Portfolio Investment Strategy), 159, 162
Oppenheimer & Co., 112–13
Organization for Economic Co-operation and Development (OECD), 170, 181, 214
Osborne, George, 149, 182, 248
Oscars, 16
Overend & Gurney, 51, 126
Oxford University, 181, 184
Oxley, Michael, 114, 122

de Pacioli, Luca Bartolomeo, 32–6, *34*, 100, 124
Page, Stephen, 272
Pain, Jon, 208
Palin, Michael, 15–16
Palo Alto, Silicon Valley, 82
Panama Papers scandal (2016), 247
Panorama, 169, 220
Paradise Papers scandal (2017), 7, 247
Parmalat, 239, 243
Parrett, William, 148
partners, 8
Pearson, 169, 270
Pearson, Ian, 207
Peat, Marwick, Mitchell & Co., 48, 60, 63, 64, 79, 82, 233, 235
Peat, Michael, 68
Peat, William Barclay, ix, 48, 49, 68, 233, 277
Penn Central Transport Company, 64, 79
pension funds, 67
Pepsi, 166
Pergamon, 66
Perrin, Edouard, 168, 169, 171–2, 173, 174, 175

Persson, Mats, 208
Perugia University, 32
Pessoa, Fernando, 1
Peston, Robert, 197
Peterborough hospital,
    Cambridgeshire, 191
*Petits secrets des grandes enterprises,
    Les*, 169
Petrofac, 218
Pfizer, 163
Piot, Wim, 173, 181, 182
Pisa, Italy, 21
place value' system, 21
political donations, 98
Ponzi schemes, 89
'pooling-of-interest' accounting,
    61–2, 63, 67, 96
post-balance sheet events, 72
Powell, Ian, 128, 201–2
Poynter, Kieran, 148, 150
premiums, 45
Presbyterianism, 42
Price, Samuel Lowell, 49
Price Waterhouse & Co., 49, 53–6,
    57, 65, 67, 72, 73, 78–9, 82
  and conflicts of interest, 73, 277
  consultancy, 78–9, 81, 82
  Coopers & Lybrand, merger with
    (1998), 49, 95
  in Germany, 233
  and Great Crash (1929), 57
  in India, 233
  international co-ordinating
    company, 234
  and limited liability partnerships,
    94
  Palo Alto technology centre, 82
  and private finance initiative
    (PFI), 185
  in Russia, 236
  and tax avoidance, 164
  and tax code (1954), 153–4

  and United States Steel, 55, 62,
    233
PricewaterhouseCoopers (PwC), 2,
    5, 6, 49, 95, 97, 289, 290
  and American International
    Group, 134–5, 144, 145, 148
  and Bank of Tokyo-Mitsubishi,
    230–31
  and Barclays, 6
  Booz & Co. acquisition (2013),
    263–4
  and Brexit, 203
  and British Home Stores (BHS),
    260
  Building Public Trust Awards,
    256
  'Building Relationships, Creating
    Value', 12
  and Cattles plc., 142
  cyber-security, 272–3
  establishment of (1998), 49, 95
  and Financial Crisis Inquiry
    Commission, 145
  and Financial Reporting Council,
    142, 144, 209, 210
  global operations, 235–6
  and Goldman Sachs, 134–5, 148
  and Google, 271
  and GPT, 217, 218
  and Heineken, 246
  and Hong Kong protests (2014),
    251–2
  in India, 242
  integrated reporting, 18
  and Kanebo, 240
  and Labour Party, 201
  and National Health Service
    (NHS), 192, 194, 200
  and Northern Rock, 126, 127–9,
    142–3, 148
  and Olympic Games (2012), 196
  presentation (2017), 16

and private finance initiative
(PFI), 187, 188–91, 196, 249
profits, 5
revolving door, 207, 208
and RSM Tenon, 210, 261
in Russia, 236–8
and Saudi British Joint Business
Council, 218
and securitization, 121, 122, 129
and tax avoidance, 157, 165–79,
180, 182, 237, 246, 267–71, 278
thought leadership, 12
total tax contribution survey, 179
and Tyco, 109
in Ukraine, 238
and Vodafone, 165–6
Prince of Wales's charity, 181
principal/agent problem, 13
Prior, Nick, 190
Privatbank, 238
Private Eye, 169, 180, 215, 255
private finance initiative (PFI),
185–91, 196, 203, 249, 288
Privy Council, 94
Privy Purse, 68
production-line system, 71
productivity growth, 262–3
professional scepticism, 112, 130,
214, 224
professional services, 11, 72, 150,
183, 204–5, 251, 275, 279
Professional Standards Group,
105–7
Project Braveheart, 106
Project Nahanni, 102
Protestant work ethic, 3
Protestantism, 3, 42, 43
Prudential, 157
Public Accounts Committee, 281
Public Company Accounting
Oversight Board (PCAOB),
144–5, 242–3, 253, 261, 274

Puerto Rico, 163
Putin, Vladimir, 17, 237

Qatar, 228
Quakers, 42, 49

Railway Regulation Act (1844), 45
railways
United Kingdom, 44–7, 49, 115
United States, 51, 52, 53, 70, 73
Rake, Michael, 144, 149, 150, 162,
181, 257
Raptors, 105
Rayonier, 59
Reagan, Ronald, 80, 84, 154, 184
Reckoning, The (Soll), 27
Redpath, Leopold, 46
regulation, UK, 13, 127, 209–10,
213–14, 259
and Brexit, 273
deregulation (1980s), 95
and financial crisis (2007–8),
127–8, 137–45
Financial Conduct Authority, 140,
149, 281
Financial Reporting Council, 138,
142, 144, 149, 182, 209–10,
213–14, 259, 261
Financial Services Authority, 127,
128, 137, 138, 140
'light touch', 114, 131, 209–10
Railway Regulation Act (1844),
45
self-regulation, 88, 90
regulation, US, 91, 260
Bush administration (2001–
2009), 114, 145, 253
Celler–Kefauver Act *(1950), 59, 61*
competition on price, 79–80
deregulation (1980s), 84–5, 95, 112
derivatives, 122
and Enron, 99

and Lincoln Savings and Loan,
85–7
mark to market, 99
numbers-game era (1990s), 110
Public Company Accounting and
Oversight Board, 242–3, 253,
260
Roosevelt, Theodore
administration (1901–9), 56–7
Sarbanes–Oxley Act (2002), 114,
122
self-regulation, 61
Trump administration (2017–),
273, 274
and Westec collapse (1966), 63
see also Securities and Exchange
Commission
Renaissance, 3, 16, 22, 24–37
Renjen, Punit, 275
'Repo 105' technique, 131–3, 149
revolving door, 206–8, 272
Ripley, William Zebina, 57
Robson, Steve, 144, 207
Rockefeller, John Davison, 53, 71
Rolex, 15, 215
Rolls-Royce, 213
Roman numerals, 22
Rome, ancient, 24
Rome, Italy, 25, 27
Roosevelt, Franklin, 58
Roosevelt, Theodore, 56
de Roover, Raymond, 27
Rowland, Roland 'Tiny', 66
Royal African Company, 37
Royal Ahold, 238–9
Royal Bank of Scotland, 47, 90,
136–40, 142, 157, 241, 259
Royal London Hospital, 190
RSM Tenon, 210, 261
Russian Federation, 17, 236–8
Ryan, Tim, 134, 148

Saltwater Slavery (Smallwood), 37
Samek, Steve, 103
SANGCOM, 214–19
Sansepolcro, 32
Sarbanes, Paul, 114, 122
Sarbanes–Oxley Act (2002), 114,
122
Sassetti, Francesco, 16, 29, 30, 31,
41
Satyam, 242
Saudi Arabia, 212–19, 221
Saudi British Joint Business
Council, 218
Saunders, Stuart, 64
Save South Africa, 250
savings-and-loan mutuals, 84–7,
91, 99
Sberbank, 237
Scarlett, John, 207, 272
Schlich, William, 149
Schumpeter, Joseph, 3
scientific management, 71, 76
Scotland, ix, 42, 47–9, 70, 224
Scuola di Rialto, Venice, 32
Second World War (1939–45), 59,
60, 77, 234
Secret Intelligence Service, 207,
272
Securities Act (1933), 58
Securities and Exchange
Commission (SEC), 281
and consulting, 80, 104
and Enron, 99, 104, 108
and Hollinger, 154
Levitt's 'Numbers Game' speech
(1998), 96, 98, 104
and Lincoln Savings and Loan,
85, 86
and Penn Central Transport
Company, 64
and 'pooling-of-interest'
accounting, 61, 62

and Public Company Accounting
    Oversight Board (PCAOB), 144
PwC India fined (2011), 242
and Xerox, 109–10
securitization, 101–2, 116, 119–23,
    125, 129–31, 133–40, 148, 265
Seidler, Lee, 68–9, 79
self-regulation, 6, 61, 88
Serious Fraud Office, 213, 216, 217,
    218, 219
Sexton, Richard, 129, 268, 278
shadow banking system, 115
Shanghai, China, 17
Shaxson, Nicholas, 247, 291–2
Sheraton, 59
Sherlock, Neil, 208
short selling, 112, 115, 116
Siemens, 240
Sikka, Prem, 94
Silicon Valley, California, 82
Simec International Ltd, 214, 215
Sinaloa Cartel, 229
Sinclair, Upton, 14
Singapore, 163
Sino-Forest, 244
Skilling, Jeff, 99–100, 101, 105, 108
Skinner, Paul, 208
Slater, James, 65
slave trade, 4, 37
Smallwood, Stephanie, 37
Smallwood, Trevor, 158
Smartest Guys in the Room, The
    (McLean and Elkind), 101
Smith, Adam, 13, 292
Smith, Jacqui, 207
Snell, Charles, 40
Social Justice Commission, 184
Soll, Jacob, 27
Sombart, Werner, 3–4, 22
SOS (Short Option Strategy), 159, 162
South Africa, 213, 223–4, 249–50
South Sea Company, 39–41, 42, 44

Soviet Union (1922–91), 236
Spacek, Leonard, 62, 77–8
Spain, 36, 39, 241
special investment vehicles, 115
Spinwatch, 201
Sproul, David, 256, 258
St Bartholomew's Hospital,
    London, 190
St Louis, Missouri, 56
Standard & Poor's, 149
Standard Chartered Bank, 230, 231
Starbucks, 178
steam engine, 43
Stein, Jeffrey, 161
Stephenson, George, 44
Stevens, Mark, 82–3
Stevenson, James, 1st Baron
    Stevenson, 141
Stiglitz, Joseph, 114
stock market, 68, 69, 92, 96
    'Go-Go' years (1960s), 62, 65
    and Great Crash (1929), 57, 58
    and J. P. Morgan, 54–5
    and 'pooling-of-interest'
        accounting, 60–62, 96
    railways (UK), 45–7
Stone, Timothy, 188, 189, 190, 204
Strachan, David, 208
Strathclyde, Lord, see Galbraith,
    Thomas
stress testing, 10
subprime mortgages, x, 10, 36, 48,
    111–22, 126, 130, 133, 136, 142,
    274, 288
Suddeutsche Zeitung, 169, 247
Sullivan, Arthur, 52
Sun City, North West Province, 250
Sunbeam, 97
Sunday Times, 228
Sweden, 246
Switzerland, 163, 178, 219–28, 236,
    258

synergies, 60
Syvret, Stuart, 94

Tanzania, 213
Tanzi, Calisto, 239
Tate Modern, London, 16
tax, 46, 67, 81, 93–4, 153–82,
    229–30, 246–8
  Bermuda, 164
  British Virgin Islands, 246
  Cayman Islands, 104, 164, 246,
    247
  Ireland, 163–5, 168
  Isle of Man, 247–8
  Jersey, 89, 94–5, 158
  Luxembourg, 165–77, 267–71,
    278
  Mauritius, 158
  Netherlands, 163, 164–5
  Puerto Rico, 163
  Russia, 237
  Singapore, 163
  Switzerland, 163, 178
  United Kingdom, 7, 46, 67, 94,
    153, 155–9, 163–6, 177–82, 203
  United States, 67, 92, 153–5,
    159–63, 178, 236, 284
tax avoidance, 17, 84, 93–5, 153–82,
    229–30, 246–8
  Deloitte, 157, 158, 166, 203
  Ernst & Young, 7, 156–7, 162,
    180, 182, 246, 247
  KPMG, 154–5, 157, 158, 159–62,
    180–81, 182, 186, 229–30,
    248
  PricewaterhouseCoopers, 157,
    165–79, 180, 182, 237, 246,
    267–71, 278
tax havens, 154–5, 163–79, 203, 216,
    246–8
  Bahamas, 236
  Bermuda, 164, 203

British Virgin Islands, 213, 220,
    246
Cayman Islands, 104, 164, 214,
    239, 246, 247
Delaware, 92, 236, 284
Ireland, 163–5, 168
Isle of Man, 247–8
Jersey, 89, 94–5, 158
Liechtenstein, 220
Luxembourg, 165–77, 267–71,
    278
Mauritius, 158
Netherlands, 163, 164–5
Puerto Rico, 163
Singapore, 163
Switzerland, 163, 178, 230, 236
Tax Justice Network, 169
Taylor, Frederick Winslow, 71, 75
technocratism, 15
Teesside, England, 102
telegraph, 51
Telegraph, 154
Texas, United States, 91, 99–108
Textron, 61
Thatcher, Margaret, 84, 184
Thill, Marc, 174
'think straight, talk straight', 72
thrifts, 84–7, 91, 99
Tier One, 257
Times, The, 66, 137
Tokyo, Japan, 230–31, 234–5
'too big to fail', 40
'too critical to fail', 273
'too few to fail', 161
Tory party, 44
Tornado fighters, 212
Toshiba, 241
Touche Ross, 82, 89, 136
trade unions, 76
Treasure Islands (Shaxson), 247
Treasury, UK, 39, 68, 146, 179, 180,
    189, 201, 203

Tribunal d'Arrondissement, 174
Trinidad and Tobago, 221, 223, 224
Trump, Donald, 17, 161, 273, 274
Truth in Securities (1933), 58
Turley, James, 148–9
Turner, Jonathan Adair, Baron
　　Turner of Ecchinswell, 127
Tyco, 109, 264
Tyrie, Andrew, 197–8

UK Tax Planning Post-GAAR:
　　What's Left?, 248
UK Uncut, 166
Ukraine, 238
United Kingdom, 2, 6, 39–41,
　　42–52, 55–6, 65–9
　Bank of England, 38, 91, 126,
　　140, 273
　Banking Act (1879), 51
　Barlow Clowes collapse (1988),
　　89–90, 136, 209
　Blair ministries (1997–2007),
　　114, 157, 179, 184–92, 194,
　　209, 213
　Brexit, 195, 203–4, 273
　British Home Stores collapse
　　(2015–16), 260–61
　Bubble Act (1720), 44
　Cabinet Office, 200, 201
　Cameron ministries (2010–16),
　　149, 182, 192, 194, 195, 203
　chartered accountancy, 14, 16, 45,
　　47–8, 49, 53, 67
　City of Glasgow Bank collapse
　　(1878), 51, 147
　Companies Acts, 51, 52, 58, 66,
　　93
　credit crisis (1772), 43
　Davey committee (1894), 52
　Department for Business, 201
　Department for Exiting the EU,
　　204

　Department of Health, 188, 191,
　　192
　Financial Conduct Authority, 140,
　　149, 281
　financial crisis (2007–8), *see*
　　under financial crisis
　Financial Reporting Council, 138,
　　142, 144, 149, 182, 209–10,
　　213–14, 259, 261
　Financial Services Authority, 127,
　　128, 137, 138, 140
　First World War (1914–18), 71
　GCHQ (Government
　　Communications
　　Headquarters), 272
　Gordon Riots (1780), 38
　Her Majesty's Revenue and
　　Customs (HMRC), 179, 182
　HBOS bailout (2008), x, 140–41,
　　142–3, 149, 257
　Home Office, 201
　HS2, 197–9, 266
　Income Tax Act (1842), 46
　Industrial Revolution, 18, 42–7
　Institute of Chartered
　　Accountants in England and
　　Wales (ICAEW), 49, 52, 93,
　　210
　IAS39 rules, 123, 125, 127, 147
　Johnson Matthey collapse (1984),
　　91, 128
　Joint Stock Companies Acts
　　(1844, 1856), 47, 50
　'light touch' regulation, 114, 131,
　　209
　limited liability, 92–5
　May ministries (2016–), 203
　Maxwell publishing empire, 66,
　　87–8, 91
　mergers and acquisitions, 65–9
　Ministry of Defence, 188–90,
　　202, 212, 215–19

National Audit Office, 187, 189, 206

National Crime Agency (NCA), 272

National Health Service (NHS), 183–4, 187, 190, 191–5, 266

Northern Rock collapse (2007), 125–9, 142–3, 148

Overend & Gurney collapse (1866), 51, 126

Paradise Papers scandal (2017), 7

private finance initiative (PFI), 185–91, 196, 203, 249

Public Accounts Committee, 281

railways, 44–7, 49, 115

Railway Regulation Act (1844), 45

regulation, *see under* regulation

Royal Bank of Scotland bailout (2008), 47, 136–40, 142, 241

Saudi Arabia, relations with, 212–19

Secret Intelligence Service, 207, 272

Serious Fraud Office, 213, 216, 217, 218, 219

South Sea Company, 39–41, 42, 44

Tate, 16

taxation, 7, 46, 67, 94, 153, 155–9, 163–6, 177–82, 203, 247–8

Thatcher ministries (1979–90), 84, 184

Treasury, 39, 68, 146, 179, 180, 189, 201, 203

War of the Spanish Succession (1707–13), 38

Wilson ministry, first (1964–70), 66, 68

United Nations, 225, 245

United States, 2, 4, 52–8, 59–65, 66–9, 289

American Institute of Certified Public Accountants, 61

American International Group bailout (2008), 133–5, 144, 145, 148

antitrust laws, 59, 61, 75

Bear Stearns bailout (2008), 139, 145

Big Bang (1986), 156

Big Four, 2, 6, 9, 10

Bush administration (2001–2009), 98, 114, 145, 253

Celler–Kefauver Act (*1950*), 59, 61

certified public accountants, 53

Civil Rights Movement, 64

class-action lawsuit law (1966), 64

Congress, 56, 57, 58, 68, 73, 79–80, 98, 145

consultancy, 70–83

Department of Justice, 144, 161, 223

Eisenhower administration (1953–61), 76

Enron scandal (2001), *see under* Enron

Federal National Mortgage Association ('Fannie Mae'), 118–19, 145, 257

Federal Reserve, 122, 133

Federal Trade Commission, 79

FIFA indictment (2015), 219, 223

financial crisis (1873), 53

financial crisis (2007–8), *see under* financial crisis

Founding Fathers, 53

Gilded Age (c. 1870–1900), 48

Glass–Steagall Act (1933), 60

'Go-Go' years (1960s), 59, 62, 65

Great Crash and Depression (1929–39), 14, 57–8, 59–60, 66, 73, 75, 80, 118

Internal Revenue Code (1954), 154

Internal Revenue Service (IRS), 159, 160
International Accounting Standards, 123
Ivy League, 68
Johnson administration (1963–9), 63
Lehman Brothers collapse (2008), 12, 13, 92, 131–3, 138, 145, 148–9
limited liability partnerships, 91–2
Long Term Capital Management collapse (1998), 113
mergers and acquisitions, 59–62, 71
National Aeronautics and Space Administration (NASA), 76
Navy, 77
New Century Financial Corporation collapse (2007), 115–18, 257
Penn Central Transport Company collapse (1970), 64
presidential election (2000), 98
Public Company Accounting and Oversight Board (PCAOB), 144–5, 242–3, 253, 261, 274
railroads, 51, 52, 53, 70, 73
Reagan administration (1981–9), 80, 84, 154, 184
Roosevelt, Franklin administration (1933–45), 58
Roosevelt, Theodore administration (1901–9), 56–7
Sarbanes–Oxley Act (2002), 114, 122
savings-and-loan mutuals, 84–7, 91, 99
Securities Act (1933), 58
Securities and Exchange Commission (SEC), *see under* Securities and Exchange Commission

Sunbeam collapse (2001), 97
Tax Reform Act (1986), 154
taxation, 67, 153–5, 159–63, 178
Trump administration (2017–), 17, 161, 273, 274
Vietnam War (1955–75), 63
Wall Street, 54, 69, 96, 101, 120–21
Washington Mutual collapse (2008), 145
Watergate Scandal (1972–4), 212
Westec collapse (1966), 63
World Congress of Accountants (1904), 56
WorldCom scandal (2002), 6, 10, 109, 110, 130, 209, 264, 274
United States Steel Corporation, 55, 62, 233
universal automatic computer (UNIVAC), 77–8
University of Chicago, 75, 84
University of Pennsylvania, 77
Unleashing the Department Store (Bower), 75
usury, 24, 26
Utopia, Limited, 52

Valcke, Jérôme, 225
value-added tax (VAT), 7, 179, 247
Vandemeulebroeke, Marc, 172, 173
Varley, Steve, 16, 200, 256, 258
Vatican, 25
Veihmeyer, John, 250
Venice, Republic of (697–1797), 18, 21, 24, 26, 32–6
Victoria, queen of the United Kingdom, 47
Vietnam, 102
Vietnam War (1955–75), 63
Vincent, Janice, 86

Virgil, 33
Virley, Simon, 205, 206, 207
Vodafone, 165–6

W. B. Peat & Co., 48
Wachovia, 257
Walker, Steve, 234
Wall Street Journal, 61
Wall Street, New York, 54, 69, 96, 101, 120–21
Walpole, Robert, 40
Walsh, Peter, 88
Wanderley Olivetti, 243
War of the Spanish Succession (1701–14), 38
Warner, Jack, 221, 223–4, 227, 228
Warner, Norman, 208
Washington, George, 53
Washington Mutual, 145
Watergate Scandal (1972–4), 212
Waterhouse, Edwin, 49, 54, 217, 233
Watkins, Sherron, 107
Watson, Mark, 161
Watt, James, 42–3, 44
Weber, Max, 3
Wedgwood, Josiah, 43, 44, 70
Weinberger, Mark, 17
Westec, 63, 79
Westmacott, Peter, 208
Whinney, Smith & Whinney, 87

Whiting, John, 179
Wikileaks, 237
Wilson, Harold, 66, 68
window tax, 153
women, 15, 52, 86, 109
woollen industry, 26, 30
workers' pay, 76
World Congress of Accountants, 56
World Cup, 220, 221, 223, 225, 227
World Economic Forum, 17–18, 242
World Press Freedom Day, 174
WorldCom, 6, 10, 109, 110, 130, 209, 264, 274, 279

Xerox, 109–10

al-Yamamah, Saudi Arabia, 212
York & North Midland Railway, 45
Young, Arthur, 56
Yukos, 237

zaibatsu, 235
Zen-Ruffinen, Michel, 222, 226–8
zero coupon convertible bond (ZCCB), 167, 169
Zug, Switzerland, 220
Zuma, Jacob, 250
Zurich, Switzerland, 219, 224, 225, 227, 228